The treatment and taxation of foreign investment under international law

Melland Schill Studies in International Law
Series editor Professor Dominic McGoldrick

The Melland Schill name has a long-established reputation for high standards of scholarship. Each volume in the series addresses major public international law issues and current developments. Many of the Melland Schill volumes have become standard works of reference. Interdisciplinary and accessible, the contributions are vital reading for students, scholars and practitioners of public international law, international organisations, international relations, international politics, international economics and international development.

The treatment and taxation of foreign investment under international law

Towards international disciplines

Fiona Beveridge

Juris Publishing

MANCHESTER
UNIVERSITY PRESS

Published by Manchester University Press
Oxford Road, Manchester M13 9NR, UK
http://www.manchesteruniversitypress.co.uk

British Library Cataloguing-in-Publication Data
A catalogue record for this book is available from the British Library

ISBN 0 7190 4309 3 *hardback*

First published in the USA and Canada by
Juris Publishing, Inc. Executive Park,
One Odell Plaza, NY 10701

Library of Congress Cataloging-in-Publication Data applied for

ISBN 1 929446 08 X *hardback*

First published 2000

09 08 07 06 05 04 03 02 01 00 10 9 8 7 6 5 4 3 2 1

Typeset in 10/12pt Times
by Graphicraft Limited, Hong Kong
Printed in Great Britain
by Bookcraft (Bath) Ltd, Midsomer Norton

To my parents

Contents

Table of international treaties, legislation and other documents

International treaties and legal documents of international organisations

Energy Charter Treaty, *33 ILM* (1995) 360
Paris Convention for the Protection of Industrial Property, as revised July 14, 1967, *828 UNTS 305*
Montevideo Convention on Rights and Duties of States 1933, 165 *LNTS* 49
North American Free Trade Agreement, 1992, *32 ILM* (1993) 605
Washington Convention on Settlement of Investment Disputes Between States and Nationals of Other States, 1965 *4 ILM* (1965) 524
US–Canada Free Trade Agreement *27 ILM* (1988) 281

Council of Europe

Council of Europe/OECD Convention on Mutual Administrative Assistance in Tax Matters 1988, *ETS No. 99*

European Union

Third ACP-EEC Convention of 8/12/1984, Cmnd. 9511, *24 ILM* (1985) 571
Fourth ACP-EEC Convention of 15/12/1989, Cmnd. 1364, *UKTS 47* (1992)
Convention of 23 July on the Elimination of Double Taxation in Connection with the Adjustment of Profits of Associated Enterprises, *OJ 1990 L225/10*
Council Regulation (EC) No. 2271/96 protecting against the effects of the extra-territorial application of legislation adopted by a third country, *OJ 1996 L309/39*
Council Directive 93/22/EEC on investment services in the securities field *OJ 1993 L141/27*
Council Directive 77/799/EEC concerning mutual assistance by the competent authorities of the Member States in the field of direct and indirect taxation, *OJ 1997 L336/15*
Council Directive 90/435/EEC on the common system of taxation applicable in the case of parent companies and subsidiaries of different Member States, *OJ 1990 L225/6*

Council Directive 90/434/EEC on the common system of taxation applicable to mergers, division, transfers of assets and exchanges of shares concerning companies of different Member States, *OJ 1990 L225/1*

Council Regulation (EEC) No. 1408/71 on the application of social security schemes to employed persons and their families moving within the Community *OJ, English Spec. ED. 1971 (II), 416*

GATT/WTO

WTO *General Council Decision on Transparency*, 18 July 1996, WTO Doc. WT/L/162

Procedures for the Circulation and Destruction of WTO Documents of the 1996 Guidelines for Relations with NGOs, WTO Doc. WT/L/160.REVI

Agreement on Sanitary and Phytosanitary Measures, 1994 in GATT *The Results of the Uruguay Round of Multilateral Trade Negotiations: The Legal Texts* (GATT, 1994) 69

Agreement on Trade-Related Intellectual Property Rights, 1994 in GATT *The Results of the Uruguay Round of Multilateral Trade Negotiations: The Legal Texts* (GATT, 1994)

Agreement on Trade-Related Investment Measures, 1994 in GATT *The Results of the Uruguay Round of Multilateral Trade Negotiations: The Legal Texts* (GATT, 1994)

General Agreement on Tariffs and Trade, 1947

General Agreement on Tariffs and Trade, 1994 in GATT *The Results of the Uruguay Round of Multilateral Trade Negotiations: The Legal Texts* (GATT, 1994)

General Agreement on Trade in Services in GATT *The Results of the Uruguay Round of Multilateral Trade Negotiations: The Legal Texts* (GATT, 1994)

GATT – Ministerial Declaration on the Uruguay Round of Multilateral Trade Negotiations (1986) 20 September 1986, reproduced at 25 ILM (1986) 1623

Understanding on Rules and Procedures Governing the Settlement of Disputes, *GATT The Results of the Uraguay Round of Multilateral Trade Negotiations: The Legal Texts* (GATT, 1994) 404

Final Act Embodying the Results of the Uruguay Round of Multilateral Trade Negotiations, Annex 3 – Trade Policy Review Mechanism

OECD

OECD Directorate for Financial, Fiscal and Enterprise Affairs, *The Multilateral Agreement on Investment Negotiating Text*

OECD 'The Multilateral Agreement on Investment' Policy Brief No. 2–1997

Convention on the Organisation for Economic Co-operation and Development (OECD), Paris 1960 and Associated Protocols, *888 UNTS 179*, as amended.

Council Recommendations and Guidelines for Dealing with Harmful Tax Practices *OECD C(98)17* (OECD 1998)

Council Recommendation on the Granting and Design of Tax Sparing in Tax Conventions (OECD 1998)

OECD, DAC Orientations on Participatory Development and Good Governance, 1993, *OECD/GD(93)191*

Council of Europe/OECD Convention on Mutual Administrative Assistance in Tax Matters 1988, *ETS No. 99*

NGO/OECD Consultation on the MAI, Joint NGO Statement on the Multilateral Agreement on Investment (MAI), Paris 27 October 1997, available at http://www.corpwatch.org/trac/feature/planet/mai_ngo.html

Transfer Pricing Guidelines for Multinational Enterprises and Tax Administrations (OECD 1995)

Transfer Pricing Guidelines for Multinational Enterprises and Tax Administrations, Annex: Guidelines for Monitoring Procedures on the OECD Transfer Pricing Guidelines and the Involvement of the Business Community (OECD 1998)

Transfer Pricing Guidelines for Multinational Enterprises and Tax Administrations, Annex: Examples to Illustrate the Transfer Pricing Guidelines (OECD 1998)

Code on the Liberalization of Current Invisible Operations OECD/C(61)95

Code on the Liberalization of Capital Movements OECD/C(61)96

OECD Model Double Taxation Convention on Income and on Capital (OECD 1977)

OECD Declaration and Decisions on International Investment and Mulitnational Enterprises (OECD 1976, as revised)

OECD Guidelines on Multinational Enterprises (OECD 1976, and as revised June 2000)

Third Revised Decision of the Council on National Treatment (OECD 1992)

OECD Draft Convention on the Protection of Foreign Property of 1962 *1–2 ILM* 241 (1962–63)

OPEC

OPEC, General Agreement on Participation, December 1972, in OPEC *Selected Documents of the International Oil Industry* (1972) 107

United Nations

GA Res. 3281 (XXIX) of 12 December 1974, Charter of Economic Rights and Duties of States, *UN Doc. A/Res/3281 (XXIX), 15/1/1975*

GA Res. 3201 (S-VI) of 9 May 1974 on the Establishment of a New International Economic Order, *UN Doc. A/Res/3201(S-VI), 1/5/1974*

GA Res. 2625 (XXV) of 24 October 1970, Declaration on Principles of International Law Concerning Friendly Relations and Cooperation Among States in Accordance with the Charter of the United Nations, *UN Doc. A/Res/2625 (XXV), 24/10/70*

GA Res. 2123 (XX) of 21 December 1965, Declaration on the Inadmissibility of Intervention in the Domestic Affairs of States and the Protection of their Independence and Sovereignty, *UN Doc. A/Res/2123 (XX), 21/12/65*

GA Res. 1803 (XVII) of 14 December 1962 on Permanent Sovereignty Over Natural Resources, *UN Doc. A/Res/1803 (XVII), 19/12/1962*

Draft UN Code of Conduct on Transnational Corporations *22 ILM* (1983) 177

Table of treaties, legislation and documents

National laws

Canada

Foreign Extraterritorial Measures Act, C F-29, 1996, *36 ILM* (1997) 111

Mexico

Act to Protect Trade and Investment from Foreign Norms that Contravene International Law of 23 October 1996, *36 ILM* (1997) 133

United Kingdom

Shipping Contracts and Commercial Documents Act, 1964, C. 87 of 1964
Protection of Trading Interests Act, 1980, C. 11 of 1980
Income and Corporation Taxes Act, 1988

United States

US Cuban Liberty and Democratic Solidarity (Libertad) Act of 1996, Public Law 104-114-Mar. 12, 1996, reproduced at *35 ILM 357* (1996) (Helms–Burton Act)

Table of cases

European Court of Justice

Alpine Investments BV v. *Minister van Financien* Case C-384/93 [1995] ECR I-1141
Asscher v. *Staatsecretaris van Financien* Case C-107/94 [1996] ECR I-3089
Avoir Fiscal (Commission v. *France)* Case 270/83 [1986] ECR 401
Bachmann v. *Belgian State* Case C-204/90 [1992] ECR I-249
Biehl v. *Administration des Contributions de Luxembourg* Case C-175/88 [1991] ECR I-1779
Cinetheque v. *Federation Nationale de Cinemas Francais* Cases 60, 61/84 [1985] ECR 2605
Co. Frutta (Cooperative) Srl v. *Amministrazione delle Finanze dello Stato* Case 193/85 [1987] ECR 2085
Commission v. *Belgium* Case C-300/90 [1992] ECR I-305
Commission v. *Belgium* Case 2/90 [1992] ECR I-4431
Commission v. *Denmark* Case 302/86 [1988] ECR 4607
Commission v. *France* Case 270/83 [1986] ECR 401
Commission v. *Germany* Case 205/84 [1986] ECR 3755
Commission v. *Italy* Case 24/68 [1969] ECR 193
Commission v. *Luxembourg* Case C-151/94 [1995] I-STC 1047
Finanzamt Köln-Altstadt v. *Roland Schumacker* Case C-279/93 [1995] ECR I-225
Futura Participations SA and Singer v. *Administration des Contributions* Case C-205/95 [1997] ECR I-2471
Gaston Schul v. *Inspecteur der Invoerrechten en Accijnzen* Case 15/81[1982] ECR 1409
ICI v. *Commission (Dyestuffs)* Case 48/69 [1972] ECR 619
Keck and Mithouard Joined Cases C-267 and C-268/91 [1993] ECR I-6097
Lutticke v. *Hauptzollamptm Saarlouis* Case 57/65 [1966] ECR 205
P.H. Asscher v. *Staatssecretaris van Financien* Case C-107/94 [1996] ECR I-3089
R v. *HM Treasury, ex parte Daily Mail* Case 81/87 [1988] ECR 5483
R v. *Inland Revenue Commissioners, ex parte Commerzbank AG* Case C-330/91 [1993] ECR I-4017
R v. *Secretary of State for Transport, ex parte Factortame Ltd and Others (Factortame III)* Case C-48/93 [1996] ECR I-1029

REWE-Zentral AG v. *Bundesmonopolverwaltung fur Braantwein (Cassis de Dijon)* Case 120/78 [1979] ECR 649

Reyners v. *Belgium* Case 2/74 [1974] ECR 631

Rush Portuguese v. *Office National d'Immigration* Case C-113/89 [1990] ECR I-1417

Stoke-on-Trent and Norwich City Councils v. *B & Q* Case C-169/91 [1992] ECR I-6457

Torfaen Borough Council v. *B & Q plc* Case 145/88 [1989] ECR 765

Van Binsbergen v. *Bestuur van de Bedrifjsvereniging Metaalnijverheid* Case 33/74 [1974] ECR 1299

Van Gend en Loos v. *Nederalndse Administratie der Belastingen* Case 26/62 [1963] ECR 1

Werner v. *Finanzampt Aachen Innenstadt* Case C-112/91 [1993] ECR I-429

Wielockx G H E J v. *Inspecteur der Directe Belastingen* Case C-80/94 [1995] ELR I-2493

WTO, Opinion 1/94 (1994) ECR I-5267

GATT/WTO

Canada – Administration of the Foreign Investment Review Act (FIRA Case), adopted on 7 February 1984, *BISD Supp. 30* 140

EC – Measures Concerning Meat and Meat Products (Beef Hormones Case) Report of the Appellate Body, WT/DS26/AB/R, WT/DS48/AB/R

EEC – Regulation on Imports of Parts and Components, adopted 16 May 1990, *BISD Supp. 37* 132

United States – Customs User Fee, adopted 2 February 1988, *BISD Supp. 35* 243

United States – Measures Affecting Alcoholic and Malt Beverages, adopted 19 June 1992, *BISD Supp. 39* 206

United States – Tax Legislation, BISD Supp. 23 82

United States – Prohibition on Imports of Tuna (Tuna I), *30 ILM* (1992) 1598

United States – Prohibition on Imports of Tuna (Tuna II), *33 ILM* (1994) 839

United States – Import Prohibition of Certain Shrimp and Shrimp Products (Sea Turtles Case), WT/DS58/AB/R

United States – Measure Affecting Government Procurement, Complaint by the European Communities, WT/DS88/1

United States – Measure Affecting Government Procurement, Complaint by Japan, WT/DS95/1

United States – Tax Treatment for Foreign Sales Corporations (FSC Case), WT/DS108/1

International courts and arbitral bodies

American Independent Oil Co. v. *Government of Kuwait 21 ILM* (1982) 976

Anglo-Iranian Oil Co. Case (Preliminary Objection) (UK v. Iran) (1955) *ICJ Rep.* 93

Barcelona Traction, Light and Power Co. Case (Second Phase) (Belgium v. Spain) (1970) *ICJ Rep.* 3

BP Exploration Co. (Libya) Ltd v. *Libyan Arab Republic 53 ILR* (1974) 297

Elettronica Sicula (the *ELSI Case*) (US v. Italy) (1989) *ICJ Rep.* 15
Interhandel Case (Switzerland v. *US)* (1959) *ICJ Rep.* 6
Lena Goldfields Arbitration (1925) *5 ILR* 1
Libyan Arab American Oil Co. v. *Libyan Arab Republic 62 ILR* (1977) 140
Lithgow and Others [1986] ECHR 2/1984/74/112-18, *8 EHRR* (1986) 373
Nicaragua v. *US (Merits), Judgement*, (1986) *ICJ Rep.* 14
Revere Copper and Brass Inc. v. *Overseas Private Investment Corporation 56 ILR* (1978) 258
Sapphire International Petroleum Ltd v. *National Iranian Oil Co. 35 ILR* (1963) 136
Saudi Arabia v. *Arabian American Oil Company 27 ILR* (1958) 117
Serbian and Brazilian Loans Cases (1929) *PCIJ Rep.* Ser. A. Nos. 20, 21
Starrett Housing Corporation v. *Islamic Republic of Iran*, Award No. ITL 32–24–1 of 19 December 1983, *4 Iran-US CTR* 122
Texaco Overseas Petroleum Company and California Asiatic Oil Company v. *Libyan Arab Republic 53 ILR* (1977) 389
The Lotus Case (1927) *PCIJ Reps.* Ser. A. No. 10
The Nottebohm Case (1955) *ICJ Rep.* 4
The Wimbledon Case (1923) *PCIJ Reps.* Ser. A. No. 1
Advisory Opinion on the Legality of the Threat or Use of Nuclear Weapons, (1996) *ICJ Rep.* 1
US Diplomatic and Consular Staff in Tehran Case (US v. *Iran)*, (1980) *ICJ Rep.* 3

US courts

Barclays Bank plc v. *Franchise Tax Board, an Agency of the State of California* [1994] 129 L. Ed. 2d 244
Complete Audio Transit Inc. v. *Brady* [1977] 430 US 274, 51 L. Ed. 2d 326, 97 S. Ct. 1076
Container Corp. of America v. *Franchise Tax Board* [1983] 463 US 159, 77 L. Ed. 2d 545, 103 S. Ct. 2933
International Shoe Co. v. *Washington* [1954] 326 US 310
Mannington Mills Inc. v. *Congoleum Corporation* [1979] 595 F. 2d 1287
Shaffer v. *Heitner* [1977] 433 US 186
Siderman de Blake v. *Republic of Argentina* [1992] 965 F. 2d 699
Timberlane Lumber Company v. *Bank of America* [1976] 549 F. 2d 597
US v. *Aluminum Company of America and Others* 44 F. Supp. 97; 148 F. 2d 416
US v. *Watchmakers of Switzerland Information Center Inc.* [1955] 133 F. Supp. 40; [1955] 134 F. Supp. 710
Wardair Canada, Inc. v. *Florida Dept. of Revenue* 477 US 1; 91 L. Ed. 2d 1

UK courts

Anisminic v. *Foreign Compensation Commission* [1969] 2 AC 147
R v. *Secretary of State for Foreign and Commonwealth Affairs, ex parte Pirbhai* (1985) 129 SJ 756

Series editor's preface

This book is an important critique of foreign investment and taxation under international law. Each of these areas is complex in its own right but an understanding of their inter-relationship is crucial. The treatment ranges widely from classical issues of sovereignty, the establishment of international standards and the application of international principles of jurisdiction through to the dynamics of taxation and foreign investment within free trade paradigms of the European Union, the North American Free Trade Agreement and the World Trade Organisation. Close attention is given to the political and legal ideologies at issue and the tensions within and between them. The book concludes by looking forward to how international disciplines on foreign investment can be developed in the light of environmental, social and other concerns, questions of forum and the prospects for a future multilateral agreement on investment.

Acknowledgements

My interest in this area originates in my postgraduate studies at the University of Nottingham under the supervision of Professor David Harris between 1983 and 1985, and I remain deeply grateful to Professor Harris for the guidance and assistance which I received then.

The research into trade-related investment measures which forms part of this study was carried out with the assistance of a Small Grant from the Nuffield Foundation (SOC/100/1157) for research into 'Trade-related Investment Measures (TRIMs) and corporate responsibility: the laws and policies of developing countries' and I am grateful to the Foundation for their assistance. I also record with thanks the efforts of Mr David Booton, who was employed as a researcher on that project.

Earlier drafts were read and commented upon by Professor Dominic McGoldrick, University of Liverpool, and Professor Asif Qureshi, University of Manchester. I am immensely grateful for their assistance. I remain wholly responsible, of course, for the views expressed in this work and for the errors and shortcomings which remain.

Thanks are due also to colleagues past and present at the Faculty of Law, University of Liverpool, who have offered support in a variety of ways. In particular, I would like to thank Marie Ball, Steve Cooper and Hadassah Max, who have provided invaluable assistance with the production of the text.

Finally, I would like to record an enormous debt of gratitude to Simon, Katriona and Alex for their forbearance and support.

Abbreviations

ACP	African, Caribbean and Pacific States (parties to the Lome Convention)
AJIL	*American Journal of International Law*
AMU	Arab Maghreb Union
ANZCERTA	Australia–New Zealand Closer Economic Regulations Trade Agreement
ASIL Proceedings	*Proceedings of the American Society of International Law*
BISD	*Basic Instruments and Selected Documents* (of GATT)
BITs	Bilateral Investment Treaties
BPIL	British Practice in International Law
BYIL	*British Yearbook of International Law*
CARICOM	Caribbean Economic Community
CFCs	Controlled Foreign Corporations
CMLR	*Common Market Law Review*
Cornell JIL	*Cornell Journal of International Law*
DSB	WTO Dispute Settlement Body
DSU	WTO Understanding on Dispute Settlement
EC	European Community
ECGA	UK Export Credit Guarantee Agency
ECHR	European Court of Human Rights
ECJ	European Court of Justice
ECOWAS	Economic Community of West African States
EEC	European Economic Community
EHRR	*European Human Rights Reports*
EIPR	*European Intellectual Property Review*
EL Rev.	*European Law Review*
ETS	European Treaty Series
EU	European Union
FCN	Friendship, Commerce and Navigation treaties
FDI	Foreign Direct Investment
FIRA	Foreign Investment Review Act
FSC	Foreign Sales Corporation

Abbreviations

GA	General Assembly (of the UN)
GAOR	*General Assembly Official Records*
GATS	General Agreement on Trade in Services
GATT	General Agreement on Tariffs and Trade
GSP	generalised system of preferences
GYIL	*German Yearbook of International Law*
HRQ	*Human Rights Quarterly*
ICC	International Chamber of Commerce
ICJ	International Court of Justice
ICJ Rep.	*International Court of Justice, Reports of Judgements, Advisory Opinions and Orders*
ICLQ	*International and Comparative Law Quarterly*
ICSID	International Centre for the Settlement of Investment Disputes
ICSID-FILJ	*International Centre for the Settlement of Investment Disputes – Foreign Investment Law Journal*
ILM	*International Legal Materials*
ILR	*International Law Reports*
IMF	International Monetary Fund
IPPAs	Investment Promotion and Protection Agreements
JIEL	*Journal of International Economic Law*
JWT or *JWTL*	*Journal of World Trade* (formerly *Journal of World Trade Law*)
LNTS	*League of Nations Treaty Series*
MAI	Multilateral Agreement on Investment
Mercosur	Common Market of the Southern Core
MFN	most-favoured nation
MIGA	World Bank Multilateral Investment Guarantee Agency
MNE	multinational enterprise
NAFTA	North American Free Trade Agreement
NGOs	non-governmental organisations
NIEO	new international economic order
NMEs	new market economies
NYIL	*Netherlands Yearbook of International Law*
NYUL Rev.	*New York University Law Review*
OAU	Organisation of African Unity
OECD	Organisation for Economic Co-operation and Development
OPEC	Organisation of Petroleum Exporting Countries
OPIC	US Overseas Private Investment Corporation
OJ	*Official Journal* (of the European Community)
OSCE	Organisation for Security and Co-operation in Europe
PCIJ	Permanent Court of International Justice
PCIJ Rep.	*Permanent Court of International Justice, Judgments, Orders and Opinions*
SPS	Sanitary and Phytosanitary Agreement
TNCs	transnational corporations
TPRM	Trade Policy Review Mechanism
TRIMs	Trade-Related Investment Measures (Agreement on)
TRIPs	Trade-Related Aspects of Intellectual Property Rights (Agreement on)

UN	United Nations
UNCITRAL	UN Commission on International Trade Law
UNCTAD	UN Conference on Trade and Development
UNCTC	UN Commission on Transnational Corporations
UNTS	*UN Treaty Series*
USSR	Union of Soviet Socialist Republics
VaJIL	*Virginia Journal of International Law*
YBILC	*Yearbook of the International Law Commission*
WTO	World Trade Organisation

Introduction

This book examines some of the challenges which globalisation throws up for the international community from a legal perspective. Its focus is on two aspects of the treatment of foreign investment by states: the general rules concerning access, operation and expropriation of foreign investment and the *lex specialis* of international taxation. The central concerns of the book are the ideological content of the international law rules in these areas, the changes in that ideological content over time and the implications of this for the international community and for the discipline of international law. Particular attention is paid to the implications for developing states which have in the past resisted the international law rules relating to the expropriation of foreign investment and sought instead the development of a new international economic order including *inter alia* the establishment of binding rules addressing the behaviour of transnational corporations (TNCs). In the field of taxation, attention has focused on the imperative to establish a level playing field for firms with foreign investors, particularly by addressing double taxation problems, and on the need to develop rules and co-operation mechanisms to limit anti-social behaviour by TNCs, such as tax evasion and transfer pricing.

In each of these areas, the negotiation of better rules has been undertaken within the confines of well-established concepts and general principles of international law such as state sovereignty, economic self-determination, sovereign equality, *pacta sunt servanda* and the principle of peaceful settlement of disputes. But the precise content ascribed to these general principles is not fixed and at any time reflects the particular ideological concerns of the actors involved. Thus, the meaning and implications of these principles are pliable and evolve, reflecting and contributing to evolutions in political and economic ideology. Similarly, such evolutions both reflect and support the development of new laws, legal concepts and legal techniques.

In this study traditional legal approaches are first outlined, then a range of recent developments examined. An attempt is made to trace the development of new legal concepts and techniques in different contexts and locations: in bilateral relations, in multilateral conventions and negotiations and in regional economic integration systems. In relation to both foreign investment and taxation, a central question is whether states can agree to subsume their individual sovereign personae and interests within a supranational legal order so as to move closer to an optimal solution. A supranational order may take many forms – it may be merely normative, establishing common rules based on some perceived common or community interest, or it may have structural elements – the establishment of supervisory or reporting systems or the endowment of a rule-making capacity or the establishment of binding dispute resolution processes. The forms which such legal orders assume reflect the extent to which states have been prepared to move beyond the Hobbesian model of international relations. But the form also contributes to a steady evolution of the content and meaning of the basic concepts and principles of international law and in so doing, contributes to the evolution of the ideological content of international law.

Recent developments in international economic law, including but not exclusively the World Trade Organisation (WTO) Agreements, reflect the ascendancy in political and economic spheres of a free trade orthodoxy. In turn, they play their own part in embedding and reinforcing that orthodoxy in international economic relations. However, the negotiating framework established in accordance with the principles of state sovereignty, economic self-determination, sovereign equality and *pacta sund servanda* serves to ensure that many other interests and ideologies are also reflected in the WTO Agreements and in other recent developments; aspects of these agreements reflect economic nationalism, political independence, preferential trading arrangements, different and more favourable treatment and the doctrine of non-intervention. The wide scope of the Uruguay Round and the linking of the separate agreements in the WTO 'package' serve to illustrate how the battle between old and new ideological strands can be played out simultaneously in different ways in different locations and with different results; it also serves to highlight how ideology drives the transfer and leakage of legal concepts and principles from one field to another.

The treatment of foreign investment is addressed only peripherally in the WTO Agreements, while taxation is scarcely touched upon. However, recent developments show that the WTO Agreements have served to embed certain concepts and techniques in international law which have important consequences for future efforts to address foreign investment. However, the WTO Agreements do not represent a monopoly on such developments and there are other developments, in particular within regional economic integration areas, which have also had important consequences for the way in which foreign investment issues are approached. Each of these developments is considered from the standpoint of developing as well as developed countries. This reflects a belief that developing countries do not stand to benefit in the same manner, if at all, from the ascending free trade orthodoxy and a recognition that the ideological shift involved in embracing some recent proposals is both different and of a greater magnitude for many developing states. Of course, many developing states have signed up to the WTO Agreements and have embraced the free trade orthodoxy in other areas. But recent and future developments in relation to the treatment and taxation of foreign investment will still constitute in some areas an assault on long-held ideological constructs hitherto shielded from or accommodated within other free trade developments.

A final theme which emerges concerns the actors in the international law arena. It is increasingly the case that states do not have a monopoly on law-making in the international community and this is evident in relation to the treatment and taxation of foreign investment and elsewhere. It is therefore pertinent to consider the role of other actors in shaping the negotiating processes and the outcomes of such processes, and the wider contribution this makes to the discipline of international law.

Outline

Chapters 1 and 2 outline the traditional international law concerning the treatment of foreign investment and review the efforts of states unilaterally, bilaterally and multilaterally to develop and secure standards for the treatment of foreign investment, prior to the conclusion of the WTO Agreement. Chapters 3 and 4 then repeat this exercise in relation to the taxation of foreign investment. In each case, the enquiry focuses on the framework of classical international law and the imprint which this has made on the legal regime which has evolved and on subsequent developments. In Chapter 5 some of the major weaknesses of the traditional approaches are considered. Chapter 6 examines the emergence of new patterns of institutions and law-making, of laws concerning the treatment and taxation of foreign investment and of dispute resolution processes in two regional economic integration areas, the European Union (EU) and the North American Free Trade Agreement (NAFTA). These, it is submitted, are important in two distinct ways: first, because of the influence which the concepts and laws developed within these contexts has had beyond that context and, second, because the creation of such areas has in itself acted as a driving force for the adoption of free trade principles on a wider scale.

Chapter 7 considers a number of recent developments in relation to the treatment of foreign investment which, it is argued, have been of great significance in determining the future approach to regulation of the treatment of foreign investment. First, the *Foreign Investment Review Act* (*FIRA*) *case*, is considered. This case concerned a General Agreement on Tariffs and Trade (GATT) dispute between the United States and Canada over Canada's restrictive approach to the admission of foreign investment, which established for the first time that such policies could fall foul of GATT, where they were trade restricting. Then two of the WTO Uruguay Round agreements, the General Agreement on Trade in Services (GATS) and the Agreement on Trade-Related Investment Measures (TRIMs), are examined. Finally, the Organisation for Economic Co-operation and Development's (OECD) efforts in the late 1990s to negotiate a Multilateral Agreement on Investment (MAI) are subjected to scrutiny and the reasons for the failure of this effort examined. The failure of the MAI negotiations bears many lessons for the future: the MAI may prove to be as influential as a non-agreement as it might have been as an agreement on future developments in relation to foreign investment specifically and international economic law more generally.

The issues arising from the MAI are taken up again in Chapter 8, where consideration is given to the possible conclusion and operation of an MAI under the auspices of the WTO. The suitability of the WTO as a forum for such a development is considered. And with the demise of the OECD's MAI negotiations and the severe disruption of the WTO Ministerial Conference in Seattle in mind, some of the wider issues of governance facing the WTO are considered.

Some of these issues – transparency, accountability and democracy in international law-making, due respect for the principle of sovereign equality and the right to economic self-determination – are of general concern in international law, as is the issue of regulation of multinational enterprises. Recent developments in relation to foreign investment demonstrate that, despite the widespread adherence to a new free trade orthodoxy, this area remains highly contentious within the international community.

1

Foreign investment and international law

Introduction

The subject of foreign investment is well trodden in both the practice and literature of international law. Activity can be broadly divided into two areas, standard-setting and dispute resolution, though there is a considerable degree of interpenetration between these fields. Underpinning each area is a common problem: the question of how private interests can be promoted and protected through a regime of public law founded on the principle of state sovereignty. This chapter examines the specific issues which flow from the operation of the principle of state sovereignty in the field of foreign investment examined, highlighting the range of such techniques and the areas of international law which have historically been of significance in relation to the treatment of foreign investment.

1.1 Foreign investment and international law

There are two distinct facets of state sovereignty in the law and practice of states relating to foreign investment. On the one hand, it is generally accepted as a principle of international law that states may regulate their national economies as they choose, and that in so doing they have wide discretion to regulate the activities of foreign investors. Thus, foreign investors are generally subject to the directly relevant company and taxation laws of the host state, as well as a plethora of regulations relating to employment, environmental protection, marketing and selling and competition. In the absence of positive restraints, the element of discretion enjoyed by states is very wide indeed. Thus, governments could determine which sectors of the economy they would permit foreign investors to operate in, what financial limits (minimum or maximum) they might place on such investments, what restrictions, if any, they would place on the import or export of materials, on the allocation of work permits, on remittal of profits, on the forms in which enterprises should be established and on taxes and other levies to be paid.

On the other hand, and flowing from the concomitant principle of sovereign equality, states are also taken to be subject to certain obligations towards other states to respect foreign nationals, including foreign investors operating within their state. Historically, the discretion of states in relation to foreign investment has been perceived as restricted to three main areas. First, and most pervasively, certain restrictions were seen to flow from the particular way in which the apparently permissive doctrine of sovereignty itself was constructed, and these must be contextualised and examined before the issue of sovereignty in North–South economic relations can be properly understood. Second and more recently, a non-discrimination rule has been formulated which has become part of customary international law. However, this rule too must be contextualised before its role in the regulation of foreign investment can be understood, and again it is important to examine the particular implications of the rule in North–South relations. Third, the international law regarding expropriation must be examined. Expropriation is one extreme on a continuum of acts of regulation/interference with foreign investment; however, it is the area which has been singled out historically as being of concern to international law. Thus, there is a great deal of state practice, treaty activity and expressed opinion on this one phenomenon. While recently concern has shifted to other regulatory issues, expropriation is the issue which has done most to shape the debate between capital-exporting and capital-importing states about the treatment of foreign investment, and attitudes formed around this issue undoubtedly also come to bear on wider debates about the regulation of foreign investment. As well as seeking to explain why expropriation, more than any other area, has been the subject of such attention, it can also be asked what consequences have spilled over into other areas from the historic focus on this issue.

1.1.1 *State sovereignty*

International law is founded on a doctrine of state sovereignty, itself based on a concept of state sovereignty held by the international community. However, that concept is not fixed and static, but pliable, capable of remoulding to accommodate the changing perceptions of the international community. International law, as a discipline distinct from international relations, can be seen at times to reflect, to resist and to contribute to this process of remoulding. Developments in international economic relations and in the ways these relations have been understood over the last fifty years have served to remould the concept of state sovereignty. An important question, therefore, is whether any such remoulding is reflected in contemporary international law.

In relation to foreign investment the challenge has come from conflicts between the developed (capital-exporting) states and the developing (capital-importing) states. State sovereignty in economic relations was perceived historically as a political sovereignty, a statement of equality of *political capacity*, though not of political strength or of social or economic equality. Sovereign states were enfranchised in a formal sense, though their votes weighed very little in the scales of international power. Enfranchised, however, they were endowed in the liberal tradition with both the capacity to make binding commitments and the responsibility to maintain them. Thus, the principle of *pacta sunt servanda*, that agreements freely made must be respected, played an important part in the discourse around the treatment of foreign investment. Two important sets of claims relating to the treatment of foreign investment rested on this principle. The first was that even newly independent states were bound by the agreements entered into by the previous sovereign (the colonial power, usually) in relation to their territory.[1] Thus, concession agreements for the extraction of oil or other natural resources, for example, were said to be binding, notwithstanding the obvious injustice of those agreements in many instances, and notwithstanding that some concession agreements, if honoured, would significantly infringe on the discretion of the state to regulate economic activity within its territory.[2] The second was that (some) agreements between a newly independent sovereign state and a private foreign investor should be upheld under international law, notwithstanding that private actors were not traditionally recognised as subjects of international law.[3]

[1] This was in keeping with the classical rules on succession of states.

[2] There are many examples. The D'Arcy concession granted in 1901 covered the whole of the Persian Empire (Iran) and was for 60 years, extended in 1933 to 92 years. The original concession granted by Kuwait to the Kuwait Oil Company in 1934 was for 75 years, later extended to 92 years. No provision was made for review of any element of these agreements. The financial benefits to the state were extremely modest by modern standards and the state had no control over matters such as production levels. For a fuller discussion, see F. C. Boyd 'Expropriation of Alien Property in International Law: A Study of Recent State Practice Concerning British Nationals' M.Phil. thesis, University of Nottingham, 1988 (unpublished), Chapter Three. See generally H. Cattan *The Evolution of Oil Concessions* 1967; F. Rouhani *A History of OPEC* 1971, Part I; G. W. Stocking *Middle East Oil* 1970, 1971 edn, Part I.

[3] On the 'internationalisation' of foreign investment agreements cf. the three Libyan oil concession arbitrations: the *Texaco Case* (*Texaco Overseas Petroleum Company and California Asiatic Oil Company* v. *Libyan Arab Republic* (1977) *53 ILR* 389); the *BP Case* (*BP Exploration Co. (Libya) Ltd* v. *Libyan Arab Republic* (1974) *53 ILR* 297); and the *Liamco Case* (*Libyan Arab American Oil Co.* v. *Libyan Arab Republic* (1977) *62 ILR* 140); also the *Aminoil Case* (*American Independent Oil Co.* v. *Government of Kuwait* (1982) *21 ILM (1982)* 976). For discussion see, e.g. A. El Kosheri 'The Law Governing a New Generation of Petroleum Contracts' *1 ICSID Rev.* (1986) 259; C. Greenwood 'State Contracts in International Law – The Libyan Oil Arbitrations' *53 BYIL* (1982) 27; E. Paasivirta 'Internationalisation

Against this liberal *political capacity* model of state sovereignty were pitted the claims of newly independent states seeking to take effective control over their national economies. It became a commonplace observation that political independence would be pointless unless it was accompanied by matching economic independence. Thus, the concept of *economic sovereignty* took root, and found its expression in the widespread economic reforms embarked on by states. This was not a phenomenon confined to developing states. The post-war period in Europe was also characterised by the increasing levels of state control, in particular in heavy industry and the utilities, though there are wide variations in the ways in which this desire to regulate the economy in the wider interests of the state was manifested. It was at this time commonly accepted that an important role of government was to regulate private interests in the public good and to play a major role as a direct provider of public services or in facilitating their provision.

The conceptualisation of the new-found regulatory powers of states as an aspect of sovereignty meant that other notions previously linked to political sovereignty could now be utilised in the moulding of this economic dimension of sovereignty. Equality of capacity, presumed in the political sense, could not be presumed so easily, especially where most power appeared to have been removed by the prior conclusion of a concession agreement. Economic sovereignty, like political sovereignty, was in theory inalienable and some existing arrangements were difficult to reconcile with this theory. And since economic sovereignty might entail the subjugation of private interests to the public good, it was ipsomatic that foreign investment fell to be regulated under the laws of the host state, and for the greater good of the state. Of course, strictly speaking, none of this was new. But in terms of the discourse of state sovereignty, with the emphasis firmly on the rights of the sovereign in the economic sphere rather than on the principle of *pacta sunt servanda*, acquired rights diminished in importance while respect for national goals, economic policy and laws rose in importance.

The emphasis placed on the economic dimension of sovereignty found expression in international law and international institutions in a variety of ways. Resolutions of the United Nations (UN) General Assembly, spanning from 1952 to 1975, reflected the growing emphasis on this area.[4] However, it is clear that this level of activity did not reflect any growing consensus. On

and Stabilisation of Contracts *Versus* State Sovereignty' *60 BYIL* (1989) 315; M. Sornarajah *The International Law on Foreign Investment* 1994, Chapter Eight.

Though the awards of these *ad hoc* tribunals can be, and have been, severely criticised, it should be noted that the basic elements of this approach – an acceptance of the jurisdiction of the tribunal and a permissive choice of law clause – have served to institutionalise this approach to dispute settlement in ICSID and other more recent developments.

[4] N. Schrijver *Sovereignty Over National Resources: Balancing Rights Over Duties* 1997, Chapters One and Two. See, e.g. GA Res. 1803 (XVII) of 14 December 1962

the contrary, the emphasis on the economic dimension of sovereignty led to conflict and uncertainty over exactly what sovereignty might entail, and how previously accepted rules might now operate. The conflict and uncertainty are repeatedly on view in the areas of expropriation and standard-setting discussed below.

Over the same period, successive evolutions in economic theories of development and underdevelopment brought further challenges to international law. Classical theories of economic growth postulated development as a succession of stages through which countries must pass. Development would follow if internal obstacles to growth were removed and if less developed states could trade freely with developed states to stimulate the transfer of capital, skills and technology and to permit specialisation.[5] This matched neatly the liberal approach to international law with its unspoken presumption that all states stood to gain equally from the doctrine of sovereign equality and the consent-based approach to international law-making. However, evolutions in theories of development gave credibility to claims to *different and more favourable* treatment for developing states. Writers such as Bennouna harnessed the notion of *duality of norms* to the claims of less developed states. This is the notion that norms which offer formal equality of treatment can operate in circumstances of inequality to deliver inequality; hence it legitimised differential treatment of unequals.[6] Hence it came to be accepted that international economic law might embrace different standards of treatment for different countries.[7]

More recent evolutions in state theory take the issues one step further by focusing on the economic duties of government rather than their rights, so

---

on Permanent Sovereignty Over Natural Resources, *UN Doc. A/Res/1803 (XVII), 19/12/1962*; GA Res. 3201 (S-VI) of 9 May 1974 on the Establishment of a New International Economic Order, *UN Doc. A/Res/3201(S-VI), 1/5/1974*; GA Res. 3281 (XXIX) of 12 December 1974, Charter of Economic Rights and Duties of States, *UN Doc. A/Res/3281 (XXIX), 15/1/1975.*

[5] For an account of successive evolutions in development theories see, for example, M. P. Todaro *Economic Development in the Third World* 7th edn, 2000; M. Williams *International Economic Organisations and the Third World* 1994, Introduction.

[6] The concept was later criticised by writers such as Benchick and Bedjaoui as permitting specific and limited exceptions to formal equality but doing nothing to tackle structural inequality and the international division of labour. See further M. Flory 'A North–South Legal Dialogue: The International Law of Development' and M. Bedjaoui 'Some Unorthodox Reflections on the "Right to Development"', both in F. Snyder and P. Slinn (eds) *International Law of Development: Comparative Perspectives* 1987 at pp. 11 and 87, respectively.

[7] The best examples of this are undoubtedly the adoption in the GATT Tokyo Round of the Enabling Clause, permitting (though not requiring) developed states to set favourable terms for trade with developing countries, and the subsequent development of the generalised system of preferences. For an account, see J. Jackson *The World Trading System: Law and Policy of International Economic Relations* 2nd edn, 1997; R. E. Hudec *Developing Countries in the GATT Legal System* 1987.

that future remouldings of the concept of state sovereignty may reflect in part the emerging concept of 'good governance'.[8]

1.1.2 *A general requirement of non-discrimination*

Discrimination is the norm in international economic relations. The principle of sovereignty allows a state to determine its own economic and social system, and there may be many legitimate reasons for a state to wish to discriminate against foreign investment, which in itself can pose a range of threats, temporarily or on a more long-term basis, to a state's economy, and which, by virtue of its connection to another state, also has political significance. Baade notes[9] '(d)iscrimination can be dictated by a number of reasons: preferences based on consideration of foreign policy, military alliances, and the like; ethnic or cultural preferences or aversions; retaliation; or, . . . , decolonization in fact as well as in law'. It is clear that, while in some cases these concerns can legitimately be the subject of discriminatory treatment vis-à-vis indigenous enterprises,[10] there may be some instances where less favourable discriminatory treatment of foreign investment does fall foul of some rule of customary international law. Customary international law does, however, contain a prohibition on racial discrimination and this norm has been found to be a rule of *jus cogens*.[11]

However, acts directed against the nationals of other Member States, which may constitute *indirect* or even *direct* racial discrimination, may in certain circumstances be justified and are not uncommon. The legality of such acts can only be determined after further investigation into the nature and purpose of the act and the discrimination. Various examples exist of states which have sought to reduce foreign influences to protect their culture.[12]

[8] OECD, DAC Orientations on Participatory Development and Good Governance, 1993, *OECD/GD(93)191*; UN Secretary-General *Development and International Economic Co-operation – An Agenda for Development* Report of the Secretary-General, *UN Doc. A/48/935 1994*; D. McGoldrick 'From the New International Economic Order to the Agenda for Development' in J. F. McEldowney (ed.) *National and International Perspectives on Law and Privatisation* 1999, p. 190.

[9] H. W. Baade 'Permanent Sovereignty Over Natural Wealth and Resources' in R. S. Miller and R. A. Stanger (eds) *Essays on Expropriation* 1967, p. 3 at p. 24.

[10] There is, for instance, no requirement that foreign investors suffer no greater taxation than indigenous investors, and it is commonplace that screening processes may exist in relation to foreign investment where none exists for indigenous investment.

[11] See for example the *Barcelona Traction Case*, where the ICJ found the prohibition on racial discrimination to be a rule of *jus cogens*: *Barcelona Traction, Light and Power Co. Case (Second Phase) ICJ Reports* (1970) 3 at 32. See also *Siderman de Blake* v. *Republic of Argentina* [1992] 965 F. 2d 699.

[12] Both Iran in the aftermath of the Islamic revolution in 1979 and Malaysia in recent years have sought to regulate 'un-Islamic' influences. Canada and France provide two examples of states which have sought to defend their cultural industries from Americanisation.

Furthermore, programmes of positive discrimination may be justified in certain circumstances. Thus, it is insufficient to speak of a general principle of non-discrimination on the grounds of race, without further investigating whether the acts complained of are justified in the circumstances; 'whether a particular differentiation of aliens and nationals has a reasonable basis in the common interest of the larger community must . . . depend not only upon the value primarily at stake in the differentiation but also upon many particular, and varying, features of the context in which the differentiation is made'.[13]

Unlawful racial discrimination is discrimination which is arbitrary and unjustified:

> [j]ust as certain types of discriminatory status have been rejected in municipal legal systems on the ground of public policy, so the international community has condemned discrimination as contrary to international policy . . . those kinds of status which predicate unreasonable and arbitrary inequalities are prohibited, while categories which give special protection to particular groups in order to enable them to attain real and genuine equality are permitted.[14]

Discrimination against foreign investment can be broadly divided into two groups: discrimination viz. nationals of the host state and discrimination between different groups of non-nationals. Discrimination of the first sort is commonplace, as noted earlier, and it is difficult in the absence of separately agreed standards of treatment to argue that such differences in treatment are unlawful; there is no rule of customary international law providing that *national treatment* must be accorded to foreign investors.[15] To state the contrary would be to deny the principle of state sovereignty to such a degree as to render it nugatory. On the other hand, if discrimination against foreign investment appears to be motivated purely by arbitrary racial discrimination and lacks any objective justification in domestic public policy, then it would seem to be contrary to the prohibition on race discrimination.

Discrimination between investors must be approached by a similar method. There is no requirement of customary international law which requires treatment of foreign investment in accordance with the *most-favoured nation* (MFN) principle of international trade.[16] Indeed, many states practise

[13] M. S. McDougal, H. D. Lasswell and L. Chen *Human Rights and World Public Order* 1980 at p. 738. See also B. H. Weston 'The Charter of Economic Rights and Duties of States and the Deprivation of Foreign-Owned Wealth' *75 AJIL* (1981) 437 at p. 445.

[14] W. McKean *Equality and Non-discrimination Under International Law* 1983. For further discussion see I. Brownlie *Principles of Public International Law* 5th edn, 1998 at pp. 602–5.

[15] The *national treatment* standard of international trade requires that foreign nationals are treated at least as well as nationals in the same circumstances.

[16] This would require treatment at least as favourable as that enjoyed by the national of any other state, in effect equality between non-nationals.

discrimination between nationals of other states systematically through the granting of trading preferences.[17] However, if discrimination between foreign investors appears to be motivated purely by arbitrary racial discrimination and without justification, it will be contrary to the prohibition on race discrimination.

Two examples in state practice serve to illustrate this argument. Under the Nigerian indigenisation programme commenced in 1972,[18] foreign investors were required to divest themselves of holdings in certain sectors of the economy. Exception was made, however, for people of African descent resident in an Organisation of African Unity (OAU) country which operated reciprocal arrangements (that is, which permitted Nigerian participation in the relevant sectors of its economy). This exception appears to have been made to reduce the risk of retaliation against Nigerians with businesses or investments in other states, these being concentrated in neighbouring states. Some economic and/or political grounds could probably be made out to satisfy the demands of international public policy in this case.[19] The second example concerns the expulsion from Uganda in 1972 of thousands of people of non-African origin, a measure which was directed against and affected in particular Asian residents. As well as suffering expulsion, these individuals suffered the loss of their property, private and/or commercial, an action which amounted *de facto* to expropriation. This action was almost certainly in breach of the prohibition on racial discrimination.[20]

A further factor to bear in mind is that international tribunals in practice will usually accord to states a fairly wide margin of appreciation over decisions in areas of public policy, such as national economic well-being, political necessity or national security. Only the most blatant acts of discrimination

[17] Two major examples drawn from international trade law amply exemplify this: discrimination between foreign nationals is inherent in the establishment under WTO rules of *free trade areas*, where tariffs and quantitative restrictions on trade are abolished between members, placing them in a much more favourable position than non-members, and also in the operation of the *generalised system of preferences* (GSP), by which more favourable terms of trade are offered to (some) less developed countries, sometimes only once certain conditions have been satisfied by those states. While free trade areas are founded on a notion of reciprocity, the GSP rests on the notion of *different and more favourable treatment* and is criticised because there is no objective control over its granting. See further J. Jackson *The World Trading System, supra* note 7 and R. E. Hudec *Developing Countries*, *supra* note 7.

[18] F. C. Beveridge 'Taking Control of Foreign Investment: A Case Study of Nigeria' *40 ICLQ* (1991) 302 and references cited therein; A. O. Sanda *The Challenge of Nigeria's Indigenisation* 1982.

[19] See also the case of Indonesian nationalisations of Dutch assets discussed by Domke: M. Domke 'Indonesian Nationalisation Measures Before Domestic Courts' *54 AJIL* (1960) 305 at pp. 315–16.

[20] See, e.g. Boyd *Expropriation*, *supra* note 2 at pp. 97–8 and 319–20.

would be likely to come under scrutiny, assuming that a tribunal was able to exercise jurisdiction in any case.

In conclusion, the generally wide discretion enjoyed by states in the treatment of foreign investment is fettered in principle by the customary international law prohibition on racial discrimination. However, the scope for justifying discrimination is very wide in practice, meaning that most instances of indirect discrimination and many instances of nationality-based discrimination will not be contrary to the international norm. Only the most blatant acts of racial discrimination against foreign investment could be regarded as unlawful under customary international law.

1.1.3 *The significance of expropriation*

The second area in which it can be said that the principle of state sovereignty has determined the role of international law in relation to foreign investment is in the field of expropriation. Though definitions vary, expropriation is used to mean the taking of property, usually, though not necessarily, into public ownership, and international law has been brought to bear on the subject only where the property of foreign nationals is involved. In such cases there are said to be rules of customary international law laying down certain minimum standards of treatment to be observed. As will be seen below, these rules have engendered a great deal of controversy, principally between capital-exporting and capital-importing states and this controversy has in turn given rise to a succession of efforts to place foreign investment on a more secure legal footing.

The sites of controversy have varied over the years, depending on a variety of factors ranging from the geographic location of expropriatory conduct to the availability of dispute resolution mechanisms and the political balance in arenas such as the UN General Assembly. For instance, during the inter-war years and during the 1950s much of the focus was on Latin America, by then largely decolonised and nationalistic in outlook. The US, as a principal investor in this region, was heavily embroiled in both real and academic conflict and the debate was encapsulated in the early work of the International Law Commission on the establishment of rules regarding the responsibility of states[21] and in the debates over the validity of the Calvo Clause[22] and the Hickenlooper Amendment.[23]

[21] See further F. V. Garcia-Amador, L. B. Sohn and R. R. Baxter *Recent Codification of the Law of State Responsibility for Injuries to Aliens* 1974; R. B. Lillich (ed.) *International Law of State Responsibility for Injuries to Aliens* 1983.

[22] This was a legal device by which states sought to remove investors, with their consent, from the protection of their home states. Its validity was never accepted by the US and others at whose investors it was aimed.

[23] See C. Lipson *Standing Guard. Protecting Foreign Capital in the Nineteenth and Twentieth Centuries* 1985.

From the 1950s to the 1970s, the stability of concession agreements in the natural resource sector was the subject of much controversy as, in the Middle East and elsewhere, concessions dating from colonial times were challenged.[24] Action taken in relation to the property aspects of concession agreements were accompanied by efforts to bring about improvements in the terms of trade. The Organisation of Petroleum Exporting Countries (OPEC) price rises of the early 1970s went hand in hand with the pursual by OPEC of a participation policy whereby, by negotiation or nationalisation, OPEC members acquired progressively a shareholding in their own oil industries.[25]

And in the newly independent states of Africa and Asia economic nationalism held sway from the 1960s through to the early 1980s (which brought the debt crisis), raising wider questions of economic sovereignty. Here the focus was largely on the right of governments to shape their national economies in accordance with their own political preferences, and choices were on the agenda as a multiplicity of new states in Africa and Asia made their demands for economic self-determination and adopted policies founded in economic nationalism. A wide variety of techniques of varying (and increasing) levels of sophistication, ranging from the Marxist self-reliance policies of Tanzania,[26] through policies of nationalisation of 'key' industries, to the indigenisation policies of Ghana,[27] Nigeria[28] and others. This latter phase was also reflected in the debates of the General Assembly (GA), in which calls for a 'new international economic order' (NIEO) were made (see further below). The unresolved controversies associated with this period are clearly evidenced in the proceedings of the Iran–US Claims Tribunal.[29]

[24] See generally L. Allen *OPEC Oil* 1979; Anon. 'From Concession to Participation: Restructuring the Middle East Oil Industry' *48 NYUL Rev.* (1973) p. 774; Boyd *Expropriation, supra* note 2, Chapter Three; H. Cattan *The Evolution of Oil Concessions* 1967; F. Rouhani *A History of OPEC* 1971, Part 1; G. W. Stocking *Middle East Oil* 1970, Part 1.

[25] OPEC, General Agreement on Participation, December 1972, in OPEC *Selected Documents of the International Oil Industry* 1972, p. 107. This Agreement, known as the Riyadh Agreement, provided that governments should acquire immediately a 25 per cent equity participation stake, rising to 51 per cent by January 1981.

[26] A. W. Bradley 'Legal Aspects of the Nationalisations in Tanzania' *3 East African Law Journal* (1967) 149; C. Dias 'Tanzanian Nationalisations: 1967–70' *4 Cornell JIL* (1970) 59.

[27] See, e.g. D. J. C. Forsyth and R. F. Solomon 'Restrictions on Foreign Ownership of Manufacturing Industry in a Less Developed Country: The Case of Ghana' *12 Journal of Developing Areas* (1978) 281; G. MacDonald 'Recent Legislation in Nigeria and Ghana Affecting Foreign Private Direct Investment' *6 Int. Lawyer* (1972) 548.

[28] MacDonald, *ibid.*; Beveridge 'Taking Control', *supra* note 18; T. J. Biersteker *Multinationals, the State, and Control of the Nigerian Economy* 1987; O. A. Osunbor 'Nigeria's Investment Laws and the State's Control of Multinationals' *3 ICSID-FILJ* (1988) 38.

[29] See further Sornarajah *Foreign Investment, supra* note 3 at pp. 384–96 and references cited therein.

But, despite attracting until relatively recently the overwhelming weight of attention both in practice and in academic writings, expropriation was and increasingly is of relative insignificance in economic terms. Can this claim be justified? Any attempt to analyse the existing literature presents many challenges. First, though there are numerous writings on individual instances or programmes of expropriation, there are few global or even regional surveys and even fewer which attempt to be comprehensive. Instances of expropriation affecting US investors have been well documented over the years in government reports,[30] but this is the exception rather than the rule. An earlier survey by this author detailed instances affecting United Kingdom (UK) investors from 1965 to 1986 inclusive. In 1972, the OECD published a report which attempted to analyse the link between expropriatory action and foreign investment flows.[31] Between 1973 and 1983, the UN Commission on Transnational Corporations (UNCTC) published a series of reports which examined expropriatory action as part of a wider examination of the role of foreign investment in development.[32] A number of risk analysis studies on expropriation have also been carried out by economists such as Truitt,[33] Burton and Inoue,[34] Kobrin[35] and Fagre and Wells.[36] In addition, it should be noted that governmental investment guarantee agencies (such as the US Overseas Private Investment Corporation (OPIC), the UK Export Credit Guarantee Agency (ECGA)[37] and the World Bank Multilateral Investment Guarantee Agency (MIGA)), along with private

[30] US Department of State, Bureau of Intelligence and Research *Nationalisation, Expropriation and Other Takings of Foreign Property Since 1960* November 1971; *Disputes Involving US Foreign Direct Investment: July 1, 1971 through July 31, 1973* February 1974; *Disputes Involving US Foreign Direct Investment: Aug 1, 1973–Jan 31, 1975* March 1975; *Disputes Involving US Foreign Direct Investment: Feb 1, 1975 –Feb 28, 1977* September 1977; *Disputes Involving US Foreign Direct Investment: Mar 1, 1977–Feb 29, 1980* August 1980; *Disputes Involving US Foreign Direct Investment: Mar 1, 1980–Sept 30, 1982* February 1983.

[31] OECD Development Centre *The Relation of Expropriatory Action By Developing Countries to Foreign Private Investment Flows* 1972 OECD.

[32] UN Commission on Transnational Corporations *Multinational Corporations in World Development* 1973 UN Doc. E/C. 10/38, 1973; *Transnational Corporations in World Development: A Re-examination* 1978 UN Doc. E/C. 10/38, 1978; *Transnational Corporations in World Development. Third Survey* 1983, UN Doc. ST/CTC/46, 1983.

[33] J. F. Truitt *Expropriation of Private Foreign Investment* 1974.

[34] F. N. Burton and H. Inoue 'Expropriations of Foreign-Owned Firms in Developing Countries: A Cross-National Analysis' *18 JWTL* (1984) p. 396.

[35] S. J. Kobrin 'Enterprise and Forced Divestment in LDCs', *International Organisation* (1980) 65.

[36] N. E. Fagre and L. T. Wells Jr 'Bargaining Power of Multinational and Host Governments' *13 Journal of International Business Studies* (1982) 9.

[37] Formerly the Export Credit Guarantee Department of the Department of Trade and Industry, now an Executive Agency, responsible to the Minister for Trade and Industry.

insurers in the field, are constantly in the business of quantifying such risks on a commercial basis.[38]

A number of studies deal with expropriation risks; however, the wide variations in data collection techniques make it difficult to analyse how significant a risk expropriation actually constitutes.[39] As a preliminary matter two 'measures' must be distinguished. First, attempts to measure objectively the real threat posed by expropriation to investments (reflected, for instance, in the variations in rates for insurance premiums for investments in different industrial sectors or geographic locations). Second, the perceived risk of expropriation by investors and home states, which may affect on the one hand investment flows, and on the other governmental policies and activities in this field.

It is clear from the studies carried out that it is important to keep the rather small risk of expropriation in perspective; expropriation is only one of a number of risks borne by foreign investors, and it is of limited commercial significance. Other risks such as those relating to currency transmission, inflation and fluctuations in world markets are undoubtedly of greater significance for many investors. Looking only as risks directly associated with host country policies, companies are more immediately concerned about their day-to-day operating conditions – the existence of competitive conditions, stability of local markets and security of property – than with more remote political risks.

Even if perceived risk rather than real risk is examined, it seems clear that expropriation, while it may have been a factor of some importance in deterring potential investors,[40] was only one of many factors which influenced investment decisions. The evidence in all but a few situations is inconclusive. Moreover, it is at least plausible that fear of expropriation was historically fuelled rather than reduced by the efforts of developed nations to press the case for security for investments and to secure legal guarantees from host states (e.g. in Bilateral Investment Treaties (BITs)). With the benefit of hindsight, a significant contrast can be made between the evidence regarding the relationship between foreign investment flows and the existence of paper guarantees against uncompensated expropriation and the emerging evidence on the relationship between investment flows and privatisation policies. While it may be argued that the perceptions of risk justify the attention which

[38] For further information about the operations of these agencies see, e.g. OECD *The Export Credit Financing System in OECD Member and Non-Member Countries* 1995; IMF *Officially Supported Export Credits – Development and Prospects, World Economic and Financial Surveys* 1995.

[39] For an excellent overview of the issue, see D. F. Vagts 'Foreign Investment Risk Reconsidered: The View From the 1980s' 2 *ICSID Rev.–FILJ* (1987) 1.

[40] The demonstrable willingness of at least some investors in some countries at certain periods to pay substantial investment guarantee premiums attests to this, though expropriatory risks were not the only risks covered.

governments have paid to this issue, there is a danger that there is in operation a vicious circle whereby governments, by focusing unduly on an extreme and commercially (relatively) insignificant risk, have vested it with significance.

Why then has expropriation assumed such importance in international law? The traditional treatment of expropriation in international law as a branch of the topic of treatment of 'aliens' or foreign nationals is of significance. While the concept of state sovereignty assured the host state of a great deal of freedom in choosing who to admit to or expel from its territory, the concomitant notion of sovereign equality underpinned the notion that an injury suffered by a national of another state was an injury to that state itself. This in turn rests on a view of the investor, like the eighteenth-century traveller, as a representative or *emissary* of the home state.[41] Though this notion emerged in a wholly different era, and retains its philosophical roots in that period, it was later imbued with a different significance in post-colonial situations, and now sits uneasily with the modern commercial realities of international capital mobility, multinational corporations, joint ventures and institutional investors. Nevertheless, it has served for over two centuries of international law as a conduit through which concerns regarding the treatment of foreign investors abroad could be channelled, and is the tool by which those concerns can be placed in opposition to the economic freedoms flowing from the claim of economic sovereignty. Indeed, and this is where its significance lies, it is the only tool of customary international law by which a home state can seek to impose legal restraint on the economic sovereignty of the host state. Thus, it served as the legal conduit for efforts by capital-exporting (developed) states to protect their investments, particularly in capital-importing (developing) states.

In the wider context of economic and political relations between these two groups of states, it was never of crucial importance whether on paper capital-importing states were committed to the Hull formula or some lesser level of compensation in the (unlikely) event of expropriation. In practice, few capital-exporting states wished their foreign policy to be dictated by expropriation disputes, and the vast majority of expropriation cases were settled on some compromise basis. But capital-exporting states could have their say in relation to expropriation where the principle of state sovereignty dictated that they had no legal say over matters such as taxation, entry restrictions, import and export restrictions, and difficulties posed by local regulations (e.g. in matters such as employment). Hence, the field of expropriation has assumed a symbolic importance in excess of its economic importance. The lack of guarantees of a minimum standard of treatment became a stick to shake at weaker countries who were desperate to attract foreign investment to boost the local economy but who, often for reasons unconnected

[41] Vattel, for instance, saw an injury to a citizen as an injury to the state itself: *Le Droit des gens* Book 11, Chapter vi at 71.

with the treatment of foreign investment, were unable to reassure would-be investors as to the stability of their economic policy. It was the only stick available under customary international law and hence became the battleground over which arguments regarding the value of foreign investment and its regulation and control were fought.

Of course further incentives were deployed to enhance the effectiveness (or perhaps to disguise the ineffectiveness) of this stick. In 1962, the US enacted the Hickenlooper Amendment,[42] which required the suppression of bilateral aid to states which had expropriated or discriminated against US investors, though it was only used once (against Ceylon in 1963) before ceasing to be mandatory in 1973.[43] In the 1980s, the conclusion of BITs, entailing the acceptance of certain standards of investment protection guarantee, became a precondition for the availability of investment insurance in some home states[44] and the conclusion of Lome III in 1984[45] saw the introduction of a link between the treatment of foreign investment by developing states and the wide range of benefits to which Lome III regulated access.[46] But in the rhetoric of states and in state practice expropriation remained the focus of attention. As will be seen in Chapter 7, it was not until the second half of the 1980s that this changed, to be replaced by concerns regarding market access and the day-to-day treatment of investors.

1.1.4 *Expropriation – the legal issues*[47]

The protection by the home state of foreign investors abroad in the face of expropriation began with the exercise of the right of diplomatic protection.

[42] See K. J. Vandevelde 'Reassessing the Hickenlooper Amendment' *29 VaJIL* (1988) 115.

[43] C. Lipson *Standing Guard, supra* note 23, Chapter Six; B. O. Brookens 'Diplomatic Protection of Foreign Economic Interests. The Changing Structure of International Law in the New International Economic Order' *20 Journal of Inter-American Studies and World Affairs* (1978) 37 at pp. 47–52. See also the Helms–Burton legislation, discussed in Chapter 5, below.

[44] The existence of a BIT was a precondition, e.g. under the US Investment Guaranty Programme and under the Dutch programme and was helpful in gaining approval in, e.g. the Belgian and German programmes. Sweden originally tried to impose further conditionality, relating for example to labour standards, through treaty, but this was abandoned in the face of opposition from Swedish companies: R. Stilwell 'Encouraging Investment in LDC's: The US Investment Guaranty Programme' *8 Brooklyn Journal of International Law* (1982) 365; J. Voss 'The Protection and Promotion of European Private Investment in Developing Countries' *31 ICLQ* (1982) 686.

[45] Third ACP-EEC Convention of 8/12/1984, Cmnd. 9511, *24 ILM* (1985) 571.

[46] See further F. C. Beveridge 'Privatisation and Deregulation – Changing Agendas in the International Law of Private Investment' in J. McEldowney (ed.) *National and International Perspectives on Law and Privatisation* 1999, p. 168 at p. 176. See further Chapter 2, below.

[47] See A. A. Akinsanya *The Expropriation of Multinational Property in the Third World* 1980; S. K. B. Asante 'International Law and Foreign Investment: A

The resultant diplomatic correspondence and pursuance of international claims[48] were where the exchange of views regarding the norms in instances of expropriation first developed.

Home states, whose investors had suffered expropriation, would exhort the taking state to restore the property or at least to provide compensation and would state their case that the compensation should reach an adequate level. The Hull formula of 'prompt, adequate and effective' compensation became the standard demanded by Western states, though in practice settlements rarely reached this level.[49]

The diplomatic efforts of individual states was supplemented by a number of arbitral awards. These can be divided into two main groups: the awards of 'mixed claims tribunals' established following a bilateral agreement to settle a number of outstanding claims existing between two states, and the awards of *ad hoc* tribunals established to hear a particular dispute, often in accordance with a dispute resolution provision of a primary commodity exploitation concession or an investment agreement.[50] In addition to the pronouncements of these tribunals, domestic tribunals or claims commissions were at times established after the conclusion of a lump-sum settlement between two states, and these domestic tribunals also looked to international law as the applicable law in some circumstances, though they also applied their own rules of assessment and procedure. National courts have also been called upon from time to time to pronounce on the validity of expropriation cases, or on the adequacy of compensation, for instance in cases dealing with ownership of the assets in question.

Many efforts have been made to analyse the extent to which these sources support the existence of customary international law standards. It is clear, however, that the awards of tribunals were at best unpredictable and ambiguous as to the required standards.[51] Certainly by the latter half of the 1950s, there was very little comfort to be drawn by capital-exporting states or investors from the precedents then existing. In addition, effective dispute

Reappraisal' *37 ICLQ* (1988) 588; R. Higgins 'The Taking of Property by the State: Recent Developments in International Law' *176 Recueil des Cours* (1982–83) 259; S. Jain 'Nationalisation of Foreign Property: A Study of North-South Dialogue' 1983; Sornarajah *Foreign Investment, supra* note 3; W. D. Verway and N. J. Schrijver 'The Taking of Foreign Property Under International Law: A New Legal Perspective?' *15 NYIL* (1984) 3.

[48] See further Section 1.3 below.

[49] Ibid.

[50] See further S. J. Toope *International Mixed Arbitration* 1990.

[51] For a recent and very full review, see Sornarajah *Foreign Investment, supra* note 3, especially Chapter Nine. Sornarajah's discussion is notable for the scepticism displayed towards the many writers (and at times, arbitrators) who have used the awards of tribunals selectively to support a particular viewpoint, while ignoring conflicting interpretations or evidence, or the particular facts of the case.

settlement provisions remained the exception rather than the rule. Efforts over the last thirty to forty years have thus turned to strategies which seek to establish greater legal certainty and predictability into this area of conflict. However, before turning to examine these efforts, the position and attitudes of developing states should also be examined.

Resistance to the standards peddled by Western states can first be noted in Latin America.[52] While most Latin American jurists accepted that there was an international obligation towards foreign nationals,[53] many rejected the notion of an international minimum standard and argued instead for a national treatment standard, i.e. that foreign nationals should be treated no worse than nationals.[54] A further development in the resistance of the international standard was the development of the Calvo Clause,[55] whereby an investor would be required to sign an agreement with the host state waiving the right to diplomatic protection and the protection of international law in the event of interference by the host government, and thus accepting in advance that any dispute would fall to be settled under the domestic law and before the domestic tribunals of the host state.[56]

Resistance to the international minimum standard was particularly marked in the wake of decolonisation, as the newly independent states of Africa and Asia turned their minds to the management of their economies and to economic planning. Successive ripples of expropriatory action were observed as governments sought to take control over strategic industries and utilities.[57] As noted above,[58] developing states began to assert their case for a new economic deal in the international arena, particularly in the UN Conference on Trade and Development (UNCTAD) and the GA.[59] The principle of state sovereignty came under renewed inspection with developing states asserting that political independence would be pointless unless it was accompanied by

[52] Though Sornarajah notes that the conflict in views can be traced back to Vitoria and Vattel: Sornarajah *Foreign Investment*, *supra* note 3 at p. 123.

[53] The notable exception was Guha Roy 'Is the Law of State Responsibility Part of Customary International Law?' *55 AJIL* (1959) 552.

[54] See further Garcia-Amador *YBILC* (1956) Vol. II (1957) Vol. II.

[55] Named after the Mexican jurist who first introduced it.

[56] For discussion, see K. Lipstein 'The Place of the Calvo Clause in International Law' *22 BYIL* (1945) 130; D. Shea *The Calvo Clause: A Problem of Inter-American and International Law and Diplomacy* 1955.

[57] For accounts of actions affecting UK investors see Boyd *Expropriation*, *supra* note 2, Chapter Two; for accounts of actions affecting US investors, see the US Department of State surveys cited *supra* note 30. See also Akinsanya *The Expropriation of Multinational Property*, *supra* note 47.

[58] *Supra* Section 1.1.1.

[59] Activity in the General Assembly reached a high point in 1974 with the adoption of a Declaration and a Programme of Action on the creation of a New International Economic Order: GA Res. 3201 (S-VI) of 9 May 1974 Declaration on the Establishment of a New International Economic Order.

some economic independence. And evolutions in theories of development gave credibility to claims to *different and more favourable* treatment for developing states.[60]

In relation to expropriation, resistance to the international standard favoured by the West was articulated with increasing frequency. Particularly at issue were the following:

1 whether there was a 'right to expropriate' and, if so, in what circumstances this right would be regarded as having been fettered by the acceptance of other obligations;
2 whether there is any meaningful 'public purpose' requirement in international law;
3 whether and in what circumstances there would be a duty to compensate following expropriation and the basis on which compensation was to be assessed; and
4 the role which international as opposed to domestic law should play in determining these issues.

1.2 International law and expropriation

1.2.1 *The right to expropriate*

The right to expropriate foreign investment in the territory of a state is well established in customary international law and is implicit in the concept of an inalienable economic sovereignty. It is unclear, however, whether states may bind themselves by treaty not to expropriate.[61] By one view, this runs contrary to the notion of inalienable economic sovereignty:

> Contemporary international law recognises the right of every State to nationalise foreign-owned property, even if a predecessor State or a previous government engaged itself, by treaty or by a contract, not to do so . . . The description of the sovereignty as permanent signifies that the territorial State can never lose its legal capacity to change the destination or the method of exploitation of those resources.[62]

Brownlie argues however, that there is insufficient evidence to support this view. In *The Wimbledon Case*,[63] the Permanent Court of International Justice (PCIJ) described the power to conclude treaties as an attribute of

[60] *Supra* Section 1.1.1.
[61] For example, in a Treaty, such as a BIT. BITs do not usually contain such an obligation; typically they merely make provision for compensation.
[62] Jiménez de Aréchaga 'General Course in Public International Law' *159 Recueil des Cours 1978-I* (1979) 1 at pp. 297–8.
[63] *PCIJ Reps*. Ser. A. No. 1, p. 25 (1923).

rather than a fetter to sovereignty. Brownlie argues, 'To give permanent sovereignty the role of forbidding, after the fashion of *jus cogens*, the making of valid treaties relating to investment and economic development in general, is to place a very strong fetter upon the sovereignty of States in economic matters'.[64]

In practice, this is not an issue, since general investment protection agreements, including BITs, NAFTA, the Energy Charter Treaty and the MAI Draft all stop short of such a requirement, focusing instead on the public purpose and compensation requirements, the applicability of a MFN standard and, in some cases, of a national treatment standard.

A closely related question is whether a host state may enter into a specific agreement with an investor under which they bind themselves not to expropriate the investment. Normally any agreement between a private party and a government would be regarded as a matter of domestic law, not within the realm of international law at all.[65] However, in a number of cases, tribunals have found contracts to be governed, at least in part, by international law. In the *Lena Goldfields Arbitration*,[66] the Tribunal found a concession contract between the Soviet government and a foreign company to be governed in part by 'general principles of law', and this was repeated in the *Aramco Arbitration*[67] and the *Sapphire Case*.[68] The same conclusion was reached in each of the three Libyan Oil arbitrations, the *Texaco Case*,[69] the *BP Case*[70] and the *Liamco Case*,[71] and in the *Aminoil Case*.[72] In each case, the conclusion that the contract had in some way been 'internationalised', that is made subject, at least in part, to public international law, was closely linked to questions regarding the proper interpretation of the choice of law clause and of the 'stabilisation' clause. The findings of the arbitrators can therefore be seen as having as much to do with addressing the problem of finding appropriate means of dispute resolution (avoiding a *non liquet*), as about determining

[64] I. Browlie 'Legal Aspects of Natural Resources in International Law (Some Aspects) *162 Hague Recueil* (1979-I) 245 at p. 310.

[65] In the *Anglo-Iranian Oil Co. Case (Preliminary Objection)* (*UK* v. *Iran*), ICJ, the ICJ rejected the UK's argument that the contract between the Government of Iran and the Anglo-Iranian Oil Company was of a dual character: 'It is nothing more than a concessionary contract between a Government and a foreign corporation' (1955) *ICJ Rep*. 93 at p. 112; see also the *Serbian and Brazilian Loans Cases* (1929) *PCIJ Reps*. Ser. A. Nos 20, 21, e.g. no. 20 at p. 42.

[66] [1925] *5 ILR* 1.

[67] *Saudi Arabia* v. *Arabian American Oil Company* (1958) *27 ILR* p. 117 at pp. 167–72.

[68] *Sapphire International Petroleum Ltd* v. *National Iranian Oil Co*. (1963) *35 ILR* p. 136 at pp. 172–6.

[69] *Supra* note 3 at p. 389.

[70] *Supra* note 3 at p. 329.

[71] *Supra* note 3 at p. 194.

[72] *Supra* note 3 at p. 976.

the obligations of the parties. Nevertheless, they have been taken by some writers as supporting the view that states can fetter their right to expropriate by entering into an agreement not to do so.

One further justification for 'internationalisation' offered by certain of the arbitrators in question is that the agreements concerned are 'economic development agreements', apparently of a different character to other investment agreements or arrangements:

> such a solution seems particularly suitable for giving the guarantees of protection which are indispensable for foreign companies, since these companies undergo very considerable risks in bringing financial and technical aid to countries in the process of development. It is in the interest of both parties to such agreements that any disputes between them should be settled according to the general principles universally recognised and should not be subject to the particular rules of national laws.[73]

Sornarajah is particularly trenchant in his criticisms of writers who have supported this variant of the 'internationalisation' thesis:

> The idea that foreign investment is motivated by altruistic motives of developing the economy of the host state is such an absurdity that it can hardly be the basis of any rule that deserves even a casual consideration. Transnational corporations which make overseas investments are not charitable institutions doling out largesse but are companies in search of profits . . . [T]he argument . . . only shows the paucity of justifications possessed by international lawyers, all of whom, of course, will claim a high degree of rectitude, scholarship and impartiality, in formulating theories to advance the cause of foreign investors belonging to their state.[74]

Whether or not internationalisation is deemed to have occurred, it is not in any case clear what impact the existence of an agreement not to nationalise might have on the damages to be paid where expropriation does occur.

The views of two of the arbitrators can be contrasted. Professor Dupuy, the Sole Arbitrator in the *Texaco Case*, reasoned that where such a contract existed nationalisation was unlawful and *restitutio in integrum* was required, '[I]n respect of the international law of contracts, a nationalisation cannot prevail over an internationalised contract, containing stabilisation clauses, entered into between a State and a foreign private company'.[75] Dr Mahmassani, the Sole Arbitrator in the *Liamco Case* reasoned, on the contrary, that a state could fetter its right to nationalise by contract, but

[73] *Sapphire Case, supra* note 68 at pp. 175–6; see also the *Texaco Case, supra* note 3 and *Revere Copper and Brass Inc.* v. *Overseas Private Investment Corporation* (1978) *56 ILR* 258.

[74] Sornarajah *Foreign Investment, supra* note 3 at p. 342.

[75] *Texaco Case, supra* note 3 at para. 73.

that the existence of such a contract could not prohibit the state from nationalising the investment. It would, however, increase the requirement of compensation.[76] More recent arbitrations have done little to clarify this issue and writers are deeply divided about it.[77]

In conclusion, it can be seen that the right to nationalise is firmly established and is an attribute of sovereignty. The developing attention given to the economic dimension of sovereignty has resulted in deep divisions in opinion about the extent to which states can fetter the right to expropriate foreign property. Arguments about the 'internationalisation' of contracts are indeed arguments about the nature of economic sovereignty itself.

1.2.2 *The 'public purpose' requirement*

In their commentary on the Harvard Draft Convention, Sohn and Baxter state:

> In view of the fact that there is no precedent – although considerable doctrine – in favour of the restitution of property which has not been taken for a 'public purpose', it is only with some hesitation that reference has been made to the concept in this Convention. Because the verbal formula has so often been employed, it was considered unwise to omit it at this point, empty though it may be of any operative legal content.[78]

This hesitation finds many echoes elsewhere, notably in the American Restatement on Foreign Relations Law[79] and in Oppenheim.[80] Sornarajah notes that it is included in BITs, but comments, 'This may be due to the compulsion to follow a time-tested formula rather than to any conviction that the requirement continues to have any force'.[81]

These doubts stem from the fact that there is little evidence of takings being found to be illegal for want of a 'public purpose', rather than for breach of some distinct rule of customary international law. Arbitral tribunals will not usually question the motive of the taking state and will in any case accord states a wide margin of appreciation in such matters. Weston notes that no international decision has turned on the public purpose requirement

[76] *Liamco Case*, *supra* note 3 at pp. 189–93, 196–200.

[77] *Revere Copper and Brass Inc. Case*, *supra* note 73.

[78] L. B. Sohn and R. R. Baxter 'The Harvard Draft Convention On the International Responsibility Of States For Injuries To Aliens' *55 AJIL* (1961) 545 at pp. 555–6.

[79] American Law Institute *Restatement of the Foreign Relations Law of the United States* 3rd edn, 1987, para. 712.

[80] R. Y. Jennings and A. D. Watts (eds) *Oppenheim's International Law Vol. 1* 9th edn, 1992 (hereinafter *Oppenheim*), para. 407.

[81] Sornarajah *Foreign Investment*, *supra* note 3 at p. 316.

alone[82] and Tschanz states '[w]hen a state clearly purports to act in the public interest, a transnational tribunal may refrain from reviewing the adequacy of the alleged public purpose'.[83] However, there are exceptions. When Libya nationalised all the Libyan operations of BP (in which the UK government had a 49 per cent holding), it was done in retaliation for the alleged failure of the UK government to prevent Iranian occupation of certain islands in the Persian Gulf which, it was claimed, the UK was under a duty to protect.[84] The UK protested that the taking was unlawful because there was no public purpose and because compensation had not been paid, and that a taking which was arbitrary, discriminatory or motivated by 'considerations of a political nature unrelated to the internal well-being of the taking state' was contrary to international law and therefore invalid.[85] The Sole Arbitrator Judge Lagergran found that the taking was in breach of international law, being made 'for purely extraneous political reasons and . . . arbitrary and discriminatory in character'.[86] This case is often compared to the *Liamco Case*, also involving an oil company in Libya, and arising around the same time. In that case, the Sole Arbitrator Dr Mahmassani stated that there was no public purpose requirement, 'Motives are indifferent to international law, each state being free to judge for itself what it considers useful or necessary for the public good'.[87] However, the direct political motive present in the *BP Case* was not present here; the nationalisation of *Liamco* was part of a rolling programme of enforced participation arrangements in which the Libyan government adopted a 'nationalise first, negotiate later' policy to secure state participation in the country's oil industry. Though there was an element of discrimination in the policy in that the

[82] B. H. Weston 'The Charter of Economic Rights and Duties of States and the Deprivation of Foreign-Owned Wealth' *75 AJIL* (1981) 437 at pp. 439–40.

[83] P. Tschanz 'The Contributions of the Aminoil Award to the Law of State Contracts' *18 International Lawyer* (1984) 245 at p. 272. In the *Lithgow Case*, the ECHR held that they were bound to respect the judgement of the legislature unless it was 'Manifestly without reasonable foundation': '[a] decision to enact nationalisation legislation will commonly involve consideration of various issues on which opinions within a democratic society may reasonably differ widely. Because of their direct knowledge of their society and its needs and resources, the national authorities are in principle better placed than the international judge to appreciate what measures are appropriate . . . consequently the margin of appreciation available to them should be a wide one': ECHR Case of *Lithgow and Others* [1986], Case 2/1984/74/112–18, *8 EHRR* (1986) 373. The case concerned the right to property under the First Protocol to the ECHR.

[84] *The Times* (London, 8 December 1971).

[85] Note of protest from the UK government to the Government of Libya, reproduced in *BP Exploration Co. (Libya) Ltd* v. *Libyan Arab Republic* (1974) *53 ILR* 297 at p. 319.

[86] *BP* v. *Libya*, *ibid.*, at p. 329.

[87] *Libyan Arab American Oil Co.* v. *Libyan Arab Republic* (1977) *62 ILR* 140 at p. 194.

foreign companies were tackled in waves, rather than all at once, the case was rather different to the *BP Case* above.[88]

Mahmassani did appear to recognise that the element of discrimination implicit in the policy might render the taking unlawful.[89] This approach corresponds with that advanced by Brownlie, who suggests that 'categories of illegality . . . can only depend on particular rules of international law'.[90] By this view there is no distinct public purpose requirement, only recognition that the right to expropriate is tempered by the other rules of customary international law. Practice suggests that the continued reiteration of this rule in international agreements serves little purpose.

1.2.3 *The duty to compensate and the basis for the assessment of compensation*

'Compensation for nationalisation of foreign investment is a topic steeped in controversy.'[91] As discussed above, expropriation was really the only area in the treatment of foreign investment where international law had any substantial remit. Within this field, it was the topic of compensation which provided the *microforum* for the playing out of wider controversies regarding the regulation of foreign investment. Two explanations can be offered for this.

First, the question of remedies, requiring agreement on the heads of damage and on the method of quantification, perhaps serves to focus sharply the conflicting views regarding expropriation, whereas the need to arrive at statements of broad principle in fora such as the GA produces a tendency to obscure conflict. This could be said to be true particularly of the word 'appropriate', used as the measure of compensation *inter alia* in the Resolution on Permanent Sovereignty Over Natural Resources, as well as in many BITs. One can only pity the arbitrator faced with such a weasel word and the task of awarding damages between two widely opposed parties, since it is the arbitrator who must translate the doctrine of permanent sovereignty into heads of damage, and the concept of acquired rights into a valuation method.

Second, by undertaking the act of expropriation the host state has empowered itself in relation to that single issue (though it may face more broadly based recriminations). Playing the card of territorial sovereignty, taking the property, gives the expropriating (developing) state a voice louder than it otherwise possesses and allows it to impose its view of compensation

[88] The Libyan Arab Oil company was one of six companies which refused to accede to the nationalisation in 1973 of a 51 per cent share and the negotiation of a participation agreement, and was subsequently wholly nationalised in 1974. See further B. Shwadran *Middle East Oil Crises Since 1973* 1986; Boyd *Expropriation*, *supra* note 2, Chapter Three, Section 4.2.

[89] *Liamco* v. *Libya*, *supra* note 87 at p. 194.

[90] I. Brownlie *Principles of Public International Law* 5th edn, 1998 p. 547.

[91] Sornarajah *Foreign Investment*, *supra* note 3 at p. 357.

on to the other party. Possession is nine tenths of the law, though the taking of possession in this fashion may lead to a different set of problems.[92]

The major issue giving rise to conflict in relation to compensation is the actual standard of compensation itself, though it should be noted at the outset that this debate is of greater ideological significance than legal significance, since the competing standards themselves have 'no single, locally determined, fixed meaning'.[93]

The US and the UK usually adhered in diplomatic correspondence, in the pursuit of claims and in international debate, to the Hull formula of 'prompt, adequate and effective' compensation.[94] An explanation of this formula is offered in the Harvard Draft Convention on the International Responsibility of States for Injuries to Aliens;[95] 'prompt' refers to the timing of payment in relation to the taking, adequacy to the valuation of the property (and the inclusion of an element of interest on any payment) and effectiveness to the transferability of payments of compensation into other currencies.[96]

The phraseology, however, is not reproduced in any major GA Resolutions and, while it appears in some BITs, equally an alternative formulation such as 'adequate', 'fair' or 'just' appears in many others.

The GA Declaration on Permanent Sovereignty Over Natural Resources[97] uses the phrase 'appropriate' and though the US representative maintained throughout the committee debates and after the vote that this meant 'prompt, adequate and effective', other states, such as the Union of Soviet Socialist Republics (USSR), clearly rejected the latter formulation.[98] 'Appropriate'

[92] One possible consequence is that the dispossessed investor will take steps to recover property to which he believes he has title once it leaves the jurisdiction of the host state: see, e.g. I. Shihata 'Destination Embargo of Arab Oil: Its Legality Under International Law' *68 AJIL* (1974) 591; M. Sornarajah *The Pursuit of Nationalised Property* 1986; C. Staker 'Public International Law and the *Lex Situs* Rule in Property Conflicts and Foreign Expropriations' *58 BYIL* (1987) 151. Another is that the home state of the investor may take acts of retorsion or reprisal, and may seek support from other states in such action: see, e.g. D. W. Bowett 'Economic Coercion and Reprisals by States' *13 VaJIL* (1972) 4; the Hickenlooper Amendment, text at note 23 *supra*; and the Helms–Burton legislation, Chapter 5 below.

[93] C. Gray *Judicial Remedies in International Law* 1987, p. 19.

[94] The term was first used by US Secretary of State Hull in a note to the Mexican government in 1940: *3 Hackworth* 662.

[95] L. B. Sohn and R. R. Baxter 'The Harvard Draft Convention on the International Responsibility of States for Injuries to Aliens' *55 AJIL* (1961) 545. See also Oppenheim, para. 407.

[96] In some fairly recent instruments, the phrase is expounded at some length, though it is not always seen as appropriate to do see. See for instance NAFTA Arts. 1109 and 1110 and the MAI Text, Chapter IV, Article 2: Expropriation and Compensation and Commentary thereon, discussed further in Chapter 7 below.

[97] *Supra* note 4.

[98] K. N. Gess 'Permanent Sovereignty Over Natural Resources' *13 ICLQ* (1964) 398.

is also used in the Charter of Economic Rights and Duties of States[99] and treaty practice varies widely.[100] Following an exhaustive review of the sources of international law on this matter Sornarajah concludes '[o]ne had to be a committed advocate to a cause that is furthered by the claim to full compensation to believe that it does represent the norm of international law'.[101]

Subsumed within this debate are questions regarding particular issues such as loss of future profits (*lucrum cessans*) and legitimate expectations, which relate back to the issue of the right to nationalise and the accompanying concept of economic sovereignty. The claim to lost future profits is rooted in a doctrine of acquired rights and includes a claimed right of investors, once established, to remain in operation in the territory of the host state indefinitely. But, as some writers have noted, this diminishes the significance of any distinction between 'legitimate' and 'illegitimate' takings[102] and is difficult to reconcile with the concept of permanent sovereignty. Such claims seem to permit consideration only of the investor's concerns – legitimate expectations, market value, loss of future profits – and to exclude the legitimate concerns of the state – past profits, depletion of resources, the duration of the investment, the particular needs and/or circumstances of the host state.[103] Nevertheless, the practice of tribunals is divided. In the *Aminoil Case* the arbitrators referred in their award to the going concern value of 'the enterprise itself considered as an organic totality . . . the value of which is greater than that of its component parts, and which must also take account of the legitimate expectations of the owners'.[104] In the *Liamco Case*, by contrast, the arbitrator found that the principle of compensation for loss of profits was too controversial in international law to be regarded as an established rule.

1.2.4 *The role of international, as opposed to domestic, law*

There is also some controversy concerning the proper role of international as opposed to domestic law in determining compensation for expropriation.

[99] *Supra* note 4, Art. 2(2)(c).

[100] For a thorough review see Sornarajah, *Foreign Investment*, *supra* note 3 at pp. 361–3.

[101] *Ibid.*, p. 401.

[102] D. W. Bowett 'State Contracts with Aliens: Contemporary Developments on Compensation for Termination or Breach' *59 BYIL* (1988) 49 at p. 63; Jiménez de Aréchaga 'General Course in Public International Law', *supra* note 62 at pp. 286–7. For a discussion of the various meanings of 'acquired rights' see Higgins 'The Taking of Property', *supra* note 47 at pp. 286–7.

[103] Sornarajah *Foreign Investment*, *supra* note 3 at p. 408; Verway and Schrijver 'Taking', *supra* note 47.

[104] *Aminoil Case*, *supra* note 3 at p. 976.

The GA Declaration on Permanent Sovereignty Over Natural Resources,[105] for instance, states that in the event of expropriation compensation is to be paid 'in accordance with the rules in force in the State taking such measures . . . and in accordance with international law'. The Charter of Economic Rights and Duties of States, by contrast, provides that 'where the question of compensation gives rise to a controversy, it shall be settled under the domestic law of the nationalising State and by its tribunals, unless it is freely and mutually agreed on by all States concerned that other peaceful means be sought on the basis of the sovereign equality of States and in accordance with the principle of free choice of means'.[106] Writers are divided as to the significance of the omission of any reference to international law in this later resolution, which was not adopted by consensus.[107]

The relationship between international and domestic law in relation to expropriation is further complicated by the operation of the local remedies rule, by which investors would normally, in the absence of any agreed alternative method of dispute resolution, be required to exhaust remedies available in the courts and tribunals of the host state.[108] An additional element to be taken into consideration in evaluating the respective roles of international and domestic law is the operation of a 'margin of appreciation'.[109]

The uncertainty cast by these issues over the treatment of foreign investment in the event of expropriation has been described as 'inimical to economic development' since it fails to give the investors the security they need if they are to invest in developing countries.[110] As noted above, it seems that while this uncertainty is unacceptable to the lawyer's point of

[105] GA Res. 1803 (XVII) of 14 December 1962 on Permanent Sovereignty Over Natural Resources, *supra* note 4.

[106] GA Res. 3281 (XXIX) of 12 December 1974, Charter of Economic Rights and Duties of States, *supra* note 4, Art. 2(2)(c).

[107] Contrast the views of F. V. Garcia-Amador 'The Proposed New International Economic Order: A New Approach to the Law Governing Nationalisation and Compensation' *12 Lawyer of the Americas* (1980) 1 at 24–9; Brownlie *Principles*, *supra* note 90 at p. 545; Jiminez de Arachaga 'General Course in Public International Law', *supra* note 62 at pp. 303–4. There was a substantial body of opposition from capital-exporting states to Art. 2(2)(c).

[108] See, e.g. the *Interhandel Case* (*Switzerland* v. *US*) (1959) *ICJ Rep.* 6 at p. 27.

[109] This has not often been addressed directly in expropriation cases, but see the case of *Lithgow and Others* (1986), ECHR 2/1984/74/112–18, *8 EHRR* (1986) 373. See generally, J. Morrison 'Margin of Appreciation in European Human Rights Law' *6 Human Rights Journal* (1973) 263; D. J. Harris, M. O'Boyle and C. Warbrick *Law of the European Convention on Human Rights* 1995 at pp. 12–15; T. O'Donnell 'The Margin of Appreciation Doctrine: Standards in the Jurisprudence of the ECHR' *4(4) HRQ* (1982) 474.

[110] *Oppenheim* 407.

view,[111] the damage inflicted on international investment flows may well be overstated.[112]

In many circumstances, the uncertainty surrounding the applicable standard of compensation and other rules on expropriation has been eclipsed by the conclusion of BITs between the host and home states. These and other relevant matters concerning standard-setting in the field of foreign investment are considered in Chapter 2 below.

1.3 Dispute resolution

Most investment disputes are settled privately between investors and host states, with the home state of the investor playing only a background watching or supportive role. It is only occasionally that the home state becomes formally involved in an expropriation dispute; this involvement can range from protest to formal espousal to retorsion or reprisal.

1.3.1 *Protest, espousal and settlement*

The diplomacy of the home state begins, as noted above, with constant vigilance and supportive representations, possibly flanked with further policies such as a policy to try to conclude BITs or of being a party to the International Centre for the Settlement of Investment Disputes (ICSID). In the event of expropriation, or the threat of expropriation, the home state will typically step up these efforts and representations may take the form of protest; 'Lodging of protest is a definite disapproval of the policies of the government of the receiving state for its failure to do its duty under international law'.[113] In many cases, matters will proceed no further. The protest will serve to support the expropriated investor in subsequent negotiations over compensation, and compensation will be agreed on some compromise basis. However, diplomatic protection as a method of protection of foreign investment can be problematic for both (home and host) states and for the investor. Home states will often be wary of involving themselves more deeply for fear of reducing the possibility for compromise[114] or of politicising the dispute beyond its importance to the home state,[115] and may even

[111] Certainty or predictability may be said to be one of the basic 'values' of the law to which a legal system is normally expected to aspire.

[112] See above at Section 1.1.3.

[113] B. Sen *A Diplomat's Handbook of International Law and Practice* 1965 at p. 339.

[114] The home state will not wish to be too closely identified with a compromise which cannot be reconciled with its stated view of the applicable rules.

[115] The dispute is typically only one of many issues between the two states, and will often be of minor importance overall to the state Parties. In some cases, however,

in some cases be wary of aligning themselves with particular investors.[116] Host states may resent the involvement of any other state in what they see as being a domestic issue of economic regulation. For expropriated investors, there is no guarantee that their interests will coincide with those of the home state. In particular, they may wish to renegotiate the working relationship in the country, rather than accept compensation and leave. Alternatively, they may not feel that the home government is doing enough to protect their interests, which the home government must balance against its other interests in the host state (e.g. those of investors who remain there, or of traders).[117]

In some cases matters proceed further. Espousal is the formal process by which a state presents an international claim. It involves an assertion that a breach of an international obligation has occurred, and a request for redress (the normal form of which would be damages). Espousal has two major consequences, one legal and one political. Legally espousal involves the presentation by the state of its *own* claim, rather than its support of the claim of the investor. Thus, while on the diplomatic front it may appear as the next option on a continuum of measures, it is, from the perspective of international law, a qualitatively different act: the commencement of a legal action. Once commenced, this action must be either seen through to a satisfactory conclusion or abandoned. Although private negotiations may continue between the host state and the investor after espousal (and indeed may be encouraged), it is now the home state which must determine when a satisfactory solution has been reached. This may lead to the total subjugation of the interests or wishes of the investor to those of the host state.[118] On an international political level, the act of espousal does serve to politicise the dispute, certainly adding pressure to the host state to reach a settlement acceptable to the home state. Yet it may make settlement more remote by focusing attention on the (controversial) international law standard; where a state has formally espoused a claim, it may be more difficult subsequently for that state to distance itself from a compromise acceptable to the investor as the best likely to be forthcoming, but falling far below the standard heralded by the government. Muchlinski comments:

---

the state may choose to politicise the issue deliberately, as part of a wider political agenda; see, e.g. the Helms–Burton dispute, discussed in Chapter 5.

[116] BP's interests in Nigeria were expropriated in 1979, in retaliation for the complicity of the company and the UK government in breaches of an OPEC oil embargo against Rhodesia. Though this move was interpreted as timed to maximise pressure on the UK government at the imminent conference of Commonwealth Heads of Government, the protests of the UK were probably somewhat muted in the face of these breaches.

[117] See, e.g. *R* v. *Secretary of State for Foreign and Commonwealth Affairs, ex parte Pirbhai* (1985) 129 SJ 756.

[118] *Ibid.*

(Diplomatic protection) amounts to a rather limited and anachronistic method for the resolution of investment disputes. Invoking the protection of the national (i.e. the home) state of the MNE in its dealings with the host state is reminiscent of 'gunboat diplomacy'. Moreover, it may make little business sense, particularly where the corporation and the host state intend to continue their economic relationship.[119]

1.3.2 *Lump-sum settlements,* ad hoc *arbitrations and dispute settlement clauses*

Lump-sum settlements have been used in instances where large numbers of claims, perhaps on both sides, have been unresolved. Typically, the payments received in such instances have been for only a fraction of the total of the cases agreed to be settled by the payment, so that it can be concluded that this type of settlement is particularly suited to the instance where there is little prospect of achieving a settlement of the magnitude required to meet the claims in full, and/or the outstanding claims themselves are of less interest or importance to the claimant state than the need to settle them. Following the conclusion of a lump-sum settlement, the claimant state will usually establish some sort of domestic administrative body or tribunal to assess individual claims and distribute the moneys received between claimants,[120] serving to further distance the government from the actual settlements received by claimants.

Another device serving similar ends is the mixed claims tribunal, where a tribunal is established to deal with agreed classes of claim, making awards either against the respective governments or against a fund set aside for the purpose.[121] Like the lump-sum settlement, the creation of such a body allows the claimant government to close the cases and at the same time to distance itself from the payments actually made. Once the tribunal is established, diplomatic relations can return to a normal footing, all else being equal, even while the tribunal does its work. And the element of compromise measured against the proclaimed international standard is heavily masked.

Both the lump-sum settlement and the establishment of a mixed claims tribunal have the merit that they achieve settlement of the disputes and distance the claimant state to an extent from the size of the award. However, they can only really achieve the latter where large numbers of claims are involved, e.g. following a large-scale nationalisation or outbreak of civil unrest or revolutionary change of government, where they are particularly suitable. Moreover, they still involve the two governments in the negotiation

[119] Muchlinski *Multinational Enterprises and the Law* 1995 at p. 536.

[120] The Foreign Compensation Commission sometimes performs this role in the UK; at other times a specialist team is established within the Foreign Office itself. In the US, the Foreign Compensation Claims Commission performs the same function.

[121] This was the case with the Iran–US Claims Tribunal.

of the agreement, which may then become the opportunity for fraught exchanges regarding the applicable principles of law or the obligations of the parties. These may be precisely the questions on which there is disagreement. While these methods are still utilised at times, substantial diplomatic efforts have been directed towards creating more regular mechanisms suited to one-off investment disputes and providing a depoliticised forum for negotiation and settlement. Thus, attention has turned to arbitration, to the bolstering of arbitral institutions and to the establishment of arbitral clauses in foreign investment relationships.

Ad hoc arbitrations are common in practice but substantial problems may attend the negotiation of an arbitration agreement once a dispute has already arisen. Muchlinski identifies the following as possible problems: the inequality of bargaining power between the parties, the difficulties of reaching agreement on the nature of the dispute or applicable law, the difficulties in selecting mutually acceptable arbitrators, the potential for delay and problems of enforcement of awards.[122] Thus, an agreement in advance to arbitrate, with at least a default provision regarding matters such as the appointment of arbitrators, the applicable law, etc., offers many advantages. Such an agreement may be contained in a multilateral or bilateral treaty to which both host and home state are parties, or it may be included in an investment agreement between the actual investor and the host state. In either case, the aim will be to provide a reliable and mutually acceptable avenue for dispute settlement which 'delocalises' the dispute without politicising it by involving the home state directly in its resolution.

One important development in this context has been the BIT programmes discussed above. For instance, it is acknowledged that one of the objectives of the US BIT programme is to provide depoliticised routes for the settlement of investment disputes. Articles V–VII of the US Model BIT provides for both inter-state and Investor–State settlement mechanisms, the former by negotiation or adjudication, the latter by recourse to ICSID (see Section 1.3.3). Similar provisions can be found in some, though not all, UK BITs.[123]

1.3.3 *Arbitration of foreign investment disputes*

A further innovation was the establishment of the ICSID,[124] an institutionalised arbitration and conciliation facility which is dedicated to investment

[122] Muchlinski *Multinational Enterprises*, *supra* note 119 at p. 538.

[123] E. Denza and S. Brooks, 'Investment Protection Treaties: United Kingdom Experience' *36 ICLQ* (1987) 908 at p. 911.

[124] Established under the Washington Convention on Settlement of Investment Disputes Between States and Nationals of Other States 1965 *4 ILM* (1965) 524; 575 UNTS 159. The Convention came into force in 1966 and currently has 131 parties. A further 16 states have signed but not ratified the Convention (as at 1 October 1999).

disputes and which operates under the auspices of the World Bank. This provides an arbitration facility where both the host state of an investor, and the state of which the investor is a national, are parties to the Washington Convention and both host state and investor have agreed in writing to ICSID arbitration. While the need for consent ensures that the host state retains control over the dispute, this consent cannot later be withdrawn, giving the investor an element of certainty. And while the parties still have control over the applicable law, this facility serves for the investor to delocalise the dispute by bringing it under the formidable auspices of the World Bank. While the concept of 'internationalisation' of investment contracts may be objectionable,[125] the facility offered by ICSID recognises the demand by foreign investors that the contract not be entirely subject to local law, and the willingness of host states to accede to this demand; 'By acceding to the Washington Convention the host state accepts that its sovereign power to regulate disputes with foreign investors is to be subjected to review in accordance with the international procedures set out under the Convention and the Rules promulgated under its authority'.[126]

It is a moot point whether any of the dispute settlement techniques outlined have contributed, or will contribute, anything towards the provision of a more secure climate for foreign investment. Cynics might well comment that institutionalised arbitration will simply replace *ad hoc* arbitration for those disputes where there is a will to work towards settlement. The previous sections demonstrated that divisions on the rights of states in relation to foreign investment and on the rules applicable in the event of expropriation are far from settled. If a substantial shift from the current economic orthodoxy were to occur in the future, it is unlikely that the existence of such institutions would do much to stem any tide of expropriatory action, or to contain the subsequent political reaction. While ICSID might continue to provide a depoliticised forum for the settlement of disputes, it would scarcely satisfy the demands of capital-exporting states. However, as will be seen in Chapter 7, dispute settlement remains an important issue in international law discourse on foreign investment.

[125] Sornarajah *Foreign Investment*, *supra* note 3 at p. 338 *et infra*.
[126] Muchlinski *Multinational Enterprises*, *supra* note 119 at p. 542.

2

Setting standards for the treatment of foreign investment

Introduction

Much of the history of international law relating to foreign investment concerns the efforts of developed states to set and encapsulate in binding legal norms minimum standards of treatment for foreign investment, and the efforts of developed states to resist the imposition of these standards, at least in part. As was seen in Section 1.1, customary international law remained uncertain and failed to provide legal security for foreign investors. Moreover, customary international law maintained an almost exclusive focus on expropriation, only one extreme on the continuum of state regulation. Economic nationalism had led to a questioning of the benefits of foreign investment, and to efforts by states to regulate the entry and operation of foreign investment, as well as to expropriation in a small percentage of cases. As attention turned to other parts of the lifecycle of foreign investments, so the efforts of states were refocused. The discourse of international law on foreign investment reflected these changes.

In this section early efforts to set standards for the treatment and protection of foreign investment are outlined; in particular the phenomenon of BITs and the Code Movements are examined. Later, in Chapter 7, more recent developments including the conclusion of GATS and TRIMs, and the negotiation of the draft MAI will be examined.

2.1 Bilateral Investment Treaties (BITs)

Until the 1960s, efforts to secure improvements in the treatment and protection of foreign investment proceeded almost exclusively on a bilateral basis,[1]

[1] Muchlinski records that two private draft codes were published in the 1950s, later leading to the first OECD Draft Convention on the Protection of Foreign

through states exercising the right of diplomatic protection over nationals abroad. Though, as noted above, only expropriation was seen to fall within the scope of customary international law, the diplomatic efforts of capital-exporting states always embraced a wider range of concerns, ranging from ease of entry into the country, freedom to remit profits back to the home state, the conclusion of appropriate taxation arrangements to avoid excessive double taxation and security of nationals living and working abroad.

While the area of taxation has traditionally been dealt with *sui generis*,[2] perhaps because it is regarded as technically complex, some of the remaining concerns were addressed together in bilateral treaties. Historically, two groups of treaties can be identified: the broad-based Friendship, Commerce and Navigation (FCN) treaties, as favoured by the US until the 1980s and the more investment-focused Investment Promotion and Protection Agreements (IPPAs) or BITs, which became commonplace in the 1970s and 1980s.[3] These treaties typically address a range of issues. They usually provide for at least MFN standard of treatment for investments of the state parties on a reciprocal basis, recognition and respect for foreign investment agreements and referral of any investment disputes to arbitration. Often this arbitration will be under the auspices of the ICSID, though *ad hoc* arbitration is also commonly provided for.

In concluding a BIT, a state generally guarantees to foreign investment fair and equitable treatment under its laws and regulations, full protection and security and treatment no less favourable than that required under international law. As Vandevelde notes, 'full protection and security' is generally understood not to mean that the investor is protected absolutely, but that the host state will take reasonable measures to protect it.[4] Invariably, BITs also address the subject of expropriation explicitly. Typically the right of the host state to expropriate for a public purpose and with payment of compensation is recognised, though, as noted above,

Property of 1962 *1–2 ILM* 241 (1962–3); P. T. Muchlinski *Multinational Enterprises and the Law* 1995 at p. 574; see also A. Denza and S. Brooks 'Investment Protection Treaties: United Kingdom Experience' *36 ICLQ* (1987) 908 at p. 910.

[2] See Chapters 3 and 4 below.

[3] Vandevelde notes that the first BIT was concluded by Germany (with Pakistan) in 1959 and that, between 1959 and 1968, seventy-four BITs were concluded worldwide. There are now more than 1,800 such agreements: K. J. Vandevelde 'The Political Economy of a Bilateral Investment Treaty' *92 AJIL* (1998) 627; United Nations Centre on Transnational Corporations *Bilateral Investment Treaties in the Mid-1990s* 1998; UNCTAD *World Investment Report 1999: Foreign Direct Investment and the Challenge of Development* 1999.

[4] Vandevelde 'Political Economy', *supra* note 3, at p. 631. What is reasonable will depend on the circumstances and on the standard of fault required under international law rules on state responsibility. See for instance the *Hostages Case: US Diplomatic and Consular Staff in Tehran Case* (*US* v. *Iran*) ICJ Reps. 1980 3.

there are considerable variations in the formulation of the compensation standard.[5]

The conclusion of BITs or IPPAs has become a major element of international trade policy for many developed states. The UK embarked on a policy of encouraging the negotiotion and conclusion of such agreements in its bilateral relations in 1963 and to date has concluded ninety-three.[6] Other European countries have also been active in securing such agreements. In 1977, the US adopted a policy of seeking the conclusion of BITs,[7] though it has concluded only twenty-three to date.[8] In addition, a substantial number of agreements have been concluded by developing states *inter se.* The objectives of developed states in concluding these agreements were to protect existing investments and to eclipse as far as possible the existing uncertainty over the rules to be applied in the event of expropriation.[9]

Writers are divided as to the effect that this now extensive network has had in establishing standards of treatment. Where an investment is covered by a BIT, the applicable law will be clearer, though there may still be significant room for differences in interpretation of the terms of such an agreement. In addition, a government, in concluding a BIT, signals its acceptance of the standards therein and commits future governments to the legal obligations which arise from the BIT. The inclusion of provisions on dispute settlement provides an additional element of reassurance and security. Thus, in relation to specific investments, the existence of a BIT serves both a legal and an economic purpose, providing a specific legal framework for the investment and building investor confidence: 'the states which are parties to such treaties . . . have created a solid legal framework for the protection of investments . . . This framework has reduced or circumvented many of the uncertainties found in customary international law'.[10]

It is less clear, however, whether the multiplicity of such agreements has played any role in clarifying or developing the rules of customary international law on matters such as expropriation and compensation. The first problem concerns the weight which should be attached to the treaty practice of states, in particular, whether it can be said to constitute the 'state practice' and *opinio juris* required to establish the existence of a rule of

[5] *Supra*, Section 1.1.3.

[6] As at January 2000. Eighty-four of these were then in force: www.dti.gov.uk/ots/ippa/index.html.

[7] K. J. Vandevelde 'The BIT Programme – A Fifteen Year Appraisal' *1992 ASIL Proceedings* 532.

[8] http://www.state.gov/www/issues/economic/7treaty.html.

[9] S. K. B. Asante 'The Concept of the Good Corporate Citizen in International Business' *4 ICSID-FILJ* (1989) 1 at p. 2; Vandevelde 'The BIT Programme', *supra* note 7 at p. 534.

[10] G. Gallins 'Bilateral Investment Protection Treaties' *2 Journal of Energy and Natural Resource Law* (1984) 77.

custom. In the *Barcelona Traction Case*,[11] the International Court of Justice (ICJ) had to consider a similar question, whether the practice of states of concluding lump-sum agreements in respect of acts of expropriation had contributed to the development of any rule of customary international law regarding expropriation and compensation. The conclusion of the ICJ was that it did not, but this aspect of the judgment was heavily criticised by Lillich.[12] Mann queries whether a state which had, for instance, accepted the Hull formula of 'prompt, adequate and effective' compensation for expropriation in one or more treaties could plausibly argue that the standard required by customary international law was lower.[13] Though states can, as a general rule, accept more onerous obligations under treaties than those to which they would otherwise be bound under customary international law, Mann argues that where the treaties replicate a rule which has some claim to standing as a rule of custom, the practice of the states who are parties to such treaties is significant: 'The paramount duty of States imposed by international law is to observe and act in accordance with the requirements of good faith. From this point of view it follows that, where these treaties express a duty which customary international law imposes or is widely believed to impose, they give very strong support to the existence of such a duty and preclude the contracting state from denying its existence'.[14]

But as Villiger notes, '[s]tates may be ratifying such treaties precisely because they believe that no customary rules exist'.[15] Thus, before any significance can be attached to the practice of states in concluding BITs, an assessment has to be made as to whether the state's act can be interpreted as satisfying separately both the state practice and the *opinio juris* elements of customary international law.[16]

A second question which arises in analysing the impact of BITs is whether their content is sufficiently consistent to justify the conclusion that they do in fact support the existence of any rule of custom. Denza and Brooks[17]

[11] *Barcelona Traction, Light and Power Co. Case (Belgium* v. *Spain)* ICJ Rep. 1970 p. 3.

[12] R. Lillich 'The Rigidity of Barcelona' Editorial Comment *65 AJIL* (1971) 522. See also S. D. Metzgar 'Nationality of Corporate Investment under Investment Guaranty Schemes – The Relevance of Barcelona Traction' *65 AJIL* (1971) 532.

[13] F. A. Mann 'Note on British Treaties for the Promotion and Protection of Investments' *52 BYIL* (1981) 241 at pp. 249–50.

[14] *Ibid.*

[15] M. E. Villiger *Customary International Law and Treaties* 2nd edn, 1997; R. R. Baxter 'Treaties and Custom' *129 Hague Recueil* (1970–71) 75.

[16] *Nicaragua* v. *US* (*Merits*), *ICJ Rep.* (1986). See also W. D. Verway and N. Schrijver 'The Taking of Foreign Property under International Law' *15 NYIL* (1984) 3.

[17] *Supra* note 1. See also J. W. Salacuse 'BIT by BIT' (1996) *Int. Lawyer* 655.

suggest that BITs have made some contribution in this respect. But others, including Sornarajah[18] and Muchlinski[19] deny this.

2.2 The Code Movements

As Sornarajah notes, the various attempts to regulate foreign investment can be divided into two categories: the attempts (principally) by developed countries to limit and otherwise regulate the scope of host state action vis-à-vis foreign investment, thus producing a more secure and advantageous investment climate, and attempts by developing countries to regulate the activities and power of Multinational Enterprises (MNEs).[20] No synthesis has emerged between the concerns and approaches of the two groups.

2.2.1 *The regulation of host state conduct*

As was noted above, it remains moot whether the multiplicity of BITs has produced or contributed to any more general customary international law obligations regarding the treatment of foreign investment. But even if it has done so, such obligations would seem to arise only in the context of expropriation. Provisions of BITs on entry restrictions and non-expropriation concerns regarding the treatment of investors, such as MFN and/or national treatment obligations and performance requirements, cannot be regarded as having given rise to customary international law obligations. Such matters have, however, been addressed to a limited extent by the OECD in its work on liberalisation of capital movements, principally addressed in the two Codes on Liberalization of Invisibles and of Capital Movements,[21] and in the National Treatment Instrument.[22] Essentially, the Invisibles Code covers trade and investment in services, while the Capital Movements Code covers direct investment. The National Treatment Instrument covers the treatment

[18] M. Sornarajah 'State Responsibility and Bilateral Investment Treaties' *20 JWTL* (1986) 79.

[19] Muchlinski *Multinational Enterprises, supra* note 1 at p. 639.

[20] M. Sornarajah, *The International Law on Foreign Investment* 1994, Chapter 5.

[21] Code on the Liberalization of Current Invisible Operations *OECD/C(61)95*; Code on the Liberalization of Capital Movements *OECD/C(61)96*. Cf Muchlinski *Multinational Enterprises, supra* note 1 at pp. 248–50.

[22] OECD Guidelines on Multinational Enterprises and the Third Revised Decision of the Council on National Treatment: OECD *The OECD Declaration and Decisions on International Investment and Multinational Enterprises* 1992. For a full discussion of the National Treatment Instrument, see Muchlinski *Multinational Enterprises, supra* note 1 at pp. 583–7. Though the Guidelines themselves are merely recommendatory rather than binding, the work of the OECD Committee on International Investment and Multinational Enterprises on the National Treatment standard is regarded as the most authoritative to date: Muchlinski, *ibid.*, p. 584.

of existing investments owned or controlled by non-residents; 'Together, the various OECD Codes provide an integrated set of principles by which the progressive liberalization of investment and establishment can be furthered among the OECD Member States. They establish the OECD Member's general policy on investment, a policy which gives an indication of the kinds of regulatory principles that these states are seeking to apply to the global economy as a whole'.[23]

The Codes provide for liberalisation of trade and investment on a reciprocal basis in the areas to which they apply. Since 1984 the Capital Movements Code has included a 'right of establishment' – an obligation on Member States not to use regulations or practices which raise special barriers or limitations for non-residents as compared to residents and which 'have the intent or the effect of preventing or significantly impeding inward direct investment by non-residents'.[24]

Sectoral coverage is not total and is anticipated to expand over time. The obligations are also subject to country-specific exceptions and to exceptions based on considerations of public order, public health, morals or safety, national security or the fulfillment of international peace and security obligations.

These OECD Codes are binding on Members and are subject to amendment from time to time by decisions of the OECD Council. In addition, compliance with the Codes is monitored by the Committee on Capital Movements and Invisible Transactions. An important part of the Committee's work concerns the scrutiny of Member States' reservations and derogations which are subject to a process of notification and examination.[25] The benefits of liberalisation can be withdrawn from states which do not comply with these procedures.[26]

These OECD initiatives have played an important role in setting the agenda of developed states in relation to foreign investment. An important element is the inclusion of a national treatment obligation, which by its nature encourages scrutiny and monitoring of host state policies, by other states and by, in this case, a committee of an international organisation. It therefore constitutes a major departure from the 'exclusive sovereignty' notion that the treatment of foreign investment falling short of expropriation is the concern solely of the host state.

This pattern is echoed elsewhere.[27] The World Bank Group, in connection with its advocacy of free trade policies, developed its own *Guidelines on*

[23] Muchlinski, *ibid.*, p. 250.

[24] Code on the Liberalization of Capital Movements, *ibid.*, Annex A.

[25] Codes Arts 12 and 13.

[26] Codes Art. 8.

[27] See F. Beveridge 'Privatisation and Deregulation – Changing Agendas in the International Law of Private Investment' in J. F. McEldowney (ed.) *National and International Perspectives on Law and Privatisation* 1999, p. 168 at pp. 175–9.

the Treatment of Foreign Direct Investment,[28] which are used as a benchmark in its negotiations with borrower and/or debtor countries. The Guidelines promote liberalisation of investment regimes generally, but accept that limitations may be imposed by states in relation to national security concerns. They also recognise that restrictions on foreign investment may be justified on economic grounds, by exigencies in the national interest or for reasons of public policy, public health or environmental protection. Transparency, however, is demanded and the Guidelines also encourage states not to maintain overly complicated or burdensome approval or admission procedures. High levels of protection for established investors are also promoted: the Guidelines demand fair and equitable treatment, national and MFN treatment and the maintenance of favourable operating conditions generally.

Improving access for foreign investment and providing greater security for existing investors, along the lines established in the Guidelines, will often appear as a constituent element of the conditionality packages which accompany World Bank development loans or International Monetary Fund (IMF) financial assistance. Indeed programmes of reform designed to open up the economies of developing countries through liberalisation of investment regimes and through complementary initiatives, such as privatisation programmes, are specifically the focus of Structural and Sectoral Adjustment lending by the Bank.[29] Thus, the Bank, like the OECD, will take a close interest in the laws and policies of developing countries which affect the operations of foreign investors, and in any reforms undertaken in these areas.

Similarly, the EU in its dealings with third states placed the liberalisation of investment regimes increasingly high on its agenda. This had particularly noteworthy consequences in two areas: the Lome Agreements and relations with the new market economies (NMEs) in Central and Eastern Europe.

The Lome Agreements are an important vehicle for development assistance from the EU to the African, Caribbean and Pacific (ACP) group of states and for trade relations between the two groups of states. Though their content has evolved through successive negotiations, they provide, broadly speaking, a structured and institutionalised framework within which trade in goods, trade in services, development assistance and cultural and social matters are addressed.[30] Foreign investment was first addressed in the Lome

[28] World Bank Group *Guidelines on the Treatment of Foreign Direct Investment* 1992, reproduced in *31 ILM* (1992) 1366.

[29] See M. K. Addo 'The Role of International Financial Institutions in Privatisation and the Need for Constitutional Reform' in McEldowney (ed.) *Privatisation*, *supra* note 27, p. 145; P. Mosley and J. Toye 'The Design of Structural Adjustment Programmes' *6 Development Policy Review* (1988) 395.

[30] See further M. K. Addo 'A Critical Analysis of the Perennial International Economic Law Problems of the EEC–ACP Relationship' *33 GYIL* (1990) 37; C. Cosgrove and P. H. Laurent 'The Unique Relationship: The European Community

context in Lome III.[31] Under Article 240, the Contracting Parties agreed to accord 'fair and equitable' treatment to investors who 'comply with the objectives and priorities of their development co-operation'. The Parties expressed their support for the policy of concluding IPPAs and agreed to conduct a study on a joint insurance and guarantee scheme to complement existing national provision, though nothing resulted from this proposal.[32] These provisions amounted to little of substance, but created a formal link between the issue of the treatment of foreign investment and that of access by members of the ACP group of states to European Community (EC) markets for goods and services.[33] Lome IV[34] provided for a more concrete set of obligations. Under Article 258, states were obliged to take measures to create and maintain a 'predictable and secure' investment climate and to encourage investors who 'comply with the objectives and priorities of ACP–EEC development co-operation'. Article 261 encourages the extension of existing and future IPPAs to other Contracting Parties on an MFN basis, provided that reciprocity is maintained. Investment was to be encouraged which complied with the objectives of Lome IV (whereas Lome III made reference to the host state's own development goals). Thus, between the group of states involved, some eighty-five states in total, the existing web of bilateral treaties was overlaid with a further set of obligations, in which there was explicit linkage between access to benefits (principally access for ACP states to EU markets for their products) and treatment of foreign investment (principally flowing from EU states to ACP states).[35]

The development of strong economic and political relations with the emergent NMEs of Central and Eastern Europe has been a high priority for the EU since the political revolutions of the late 1980s and early 1990s in those regions.[36] The development of these relations has occurred within a wider framework encompassing the Organisation for Security and Co-operation in Europe (OSCE), the UN's Economic Commission for Europe and international and European financial institutions including the World

---

and the ACP' in J. Redmond (ed.) *The External Relations of the European Community: The International Response to 1992* 1992; K. R. Simmonds 'The Fourth Lome Convention' *28 CMLR* (1991) 521.

[31] Third ACP–EEC Convention (Lome III) of 8/12/1984, Cmnd. 9511, *24 ILM* (1985) 571: Title IV.

[32] Simmonds 'The Fourth Lome Convention', *supra* note 30.

[33] This argument was previously made in Beveridge, 'Privatisation and Deregulation', *supra* note 27 at p. 176.

[34] Fourth ACP–EEC Convention (Lome IV), UKTS 47 (1992).

[35] See further Section 2.3, below.

[36] See further M. Maresceau (ed.) *The Political and Legal Framework of Trade Relations Between the European Community and Eastern Europe* 1989; M. Maresceau and E. Montaguti 'The Relations Between the European Union and Central and Eastern Europe: A Legal Appraisal' *32 CMLR* (1995) 1327.

Bank Group and the European Bank for Reconstruction and Development.[37] The market policies advocated and actively promoted by these bodies and the accompanying strictures on governance contain many strands relevant to foreign investment, such as the establishment of rule of law, the protection of private property, the privatisation of state-owned enterprises, the dismantling of monopolies and the introduction of competition, including in the sphere of public procurement, the development of markets and the fostering of investments. The foreign investment codes adopted by NMEs typically reflect the view that an open-door policy and legal security for foreign investment will contribute to the economic transformation which those states seek.[38] Moreover, much of the technical assistance and financial support available to assist transformation was dependent on the adoption of such policies. Again, it was clearly signalled that the domestic policies of states towards foreign investment were a matter of international concern and would affect their ability to make their way as economic actors in the world.

2.2.2 *The regulation of MNEs*

The regulation of MNEs has been felt to be an issue of international concern, particularly by developing countries, since the 1970s and a number of attempts have been made to develop a legal regime in which standards of behaviour for these enterprises could be established and enforced. In this respect should be noted the OECD Guidelines 1976[39] and the Draft UN Code of Conduct on Transnational Corporations.[40]

[37] See D. McGoldrick 'From the New International Economic Order to the Agenda for Development' in McEldowney (ed.) *Privatisation*, *supra* note 27, at p. 190.

[38] See, e.g Muchlinski *Multinational Enterprises*, *supra* note 1, at pp. 187–8, 192–4 and references therein; I. Pogany 'Privatisation and Regulatory Change in Hungary' in M. Moran and T. Prosser (eds) *Privatisation and Regulatory Change in Europe* 1994 at p. 111; I. Pogany 'The Regulation of Foreign Investment in Hungary' *4 ICSID–FILJ* (1989) 39; I. Pogany 'Recent Developments in the Law Relating to Foreign Investment in Hungary' *6 ICSID–FILJ* (1991) 114.

[39] See OECD, Declaration and Decisions on International Investments and Multinational Enterprises (1976).

[40] *22 ILM* (1983) 177. Asante lists the following measures dealing with discreet areas of concern: Tripartite Declaration of Principles Concerning Multinational Enterprises and Social Policy (1977); Multilaterally Agreed Equitable Principles and Rules for the Control of Restrictive Business Practices, UNCTAD/TD/RBP/Conf. 10/REV.1 (1980); the UNCTAD Code of Conduct on Transfer of Technology TD/CODE TOT/47, 20 June 1985; International Code of Marketing of Breast Milk Substitutes, adopted by the World Health Organisation and the UN Children's Fund, Res. WHA 27.43 (1981); International Guidelines for Consumer Protection, GA Res. 39.248, UN GAOR Supp. No. 51 (A/39/51) at 179 (1985): Asante 'The Good Corporate Citizen', *supra* note 9 at p. 3.

Asante notes that 'the Code movement is predicated on the fundamental premise that the protection of TNCs and foreign investors must be matched by decent conduct on their part'[41] and in 1985 identified the pertinent issues as follows:[42]

1 the excessive influence of MNEs in economic sectors regarded as being key to the attainment of development objectives;
2 undesirable practices (such as transfer pricing);
3 the adverse impact of remittances on foreign exchange balances;
4 the effect on local industries;
5 unequal agreements;
6 insensitivity to host state development objectives; and
7 corruptive practices (including practices leading to environmental damage, adverse health implications, etc.).

Developing states have also been anxious to ensure that appropriate transfer of technology and development of indigenous capacity has occurred.[43]

Thus, the stated objective of the UN Draft Code of Conduct on Transnational Corporations is 'to maximize the contributions of TNCs to economic development and growth and to minimize the negative effects of the activities of these corporations'.[44]

Substantial progress was made in developing 'standards' for multinational behaviour in many of the areas listed above, but commentators have greeted the emerging texts with varying degrees of enthusiasm. Asante sees the emergence of a measure of consensus as 'highly significant';[45] '[t]he prospective good corporate citizen now has a reference point as to decent conduct'.[46] Others have been less enthusiastic.[47] Sceptics can point to the negotiating history of the UN Draft Code of Conduct for support. Two major issues revealed a basic clash in policy outlook between developed states and developing states. One was the legal status of the Code. Developed states, though accepting that there were legitimate matters of concern, did not want to create a binding international regime and hence rejected the

[41] *Ibid.*

[42] Asante S. K. B. Remarks in Panel Discussion 'Should Investment in the Third World be Internationally Protected? What Role for the United Nations?' *ASIL Proceedings* (1985) 378 at p. 390.

[43] See Muchlinski *Multinational Enterprises*, *supra* note 1, Chapter Twelve and references cited therein.

[44] Preamble, Draft UN Code of Conduct on Transnational Corporations, UN Doc. E/1990/94, 12 June 1990, quoted in N. Schrijver *Sovereignty Over Natural Resources. Balancing Rights Over Duties* 1997, at p. 182.

[45] Asante 'The Good Corporate Citizen', *supra* note 9 at p. 5.

[46] *Ibid.*

[47] See generally N. Horn (ed.) *Legal Problems of Codes of Conduct for Multinational Enterprises* 1980; K. Hossain (ed.) *Legal Aspects of a New International Economic Order* 1980.

idea of incorporating the agreed principles into a Convention. Instead, the view of the OECD states was that broad equitable guidelines should be agreed in a non-binding forum, such as the GA, leaving it up to individual states to develop effective controls at the national (domestic law) level. Developing countries were keen to adopt a binding international code of conduct.[48]

The second issue was that of linkage between questions regarding the behaviour of multinational corporations and questions regarding their treatment by host governments in particular, which developed states insisted had to be incorporated into discussions on a Code of Conduct:

> the formulation of standards to regulate the behaviour of TNCs accomplishes the original objective of the vast majority of the U.N. community. The expansion of the scope of the Code to encompass restraints on host governments as to the treatment of TNCs was a subsequent concession to OECD countries which strenuously pressed for an instrument that would provide minimum protection for TNCs as well as prescribe guidelines for their conduct.[49]

In any case, subsequent events suggested that any appearance of an emerging synthesis of the concerns of the OECD states and those of the developing states was illusory. The World Bank *Guidelines on the Treatment of Direct Foreign Investment*[50] published in 1992:

> provide a framework for *bona fide* investments only and do not deal with sensitive issues such as disclosure of information, restrictive business practices, the avoidance of corrupt practices and non-interference in domestic affairs. Thus, they do not formulate rules of good behaviour on the part of foreign investors nor do they address the policies of their home states with respect to these and other issues. They only formulate rules of behaviour for host States and mainly from the perspective of the interests of foreign investors with a view to promoting foreign investment.[51]

Similarly, in the context of the GATT Uruguay Round, it was not perceived as necessary to address questions of corporate behaviour alongside questions of the treatment of foreign investors.[52]

2.3 New directions

Other developments complemented these standard-setting initiatives. Most developed countries offered some form of political risk insurance to outward investments in selected countries at favourable terms to those available on

[48] See the unresolved debate over the location and status of the OECD Guidelines in the Draft MAI, Section 7.4 below.

[49] Asante 'The Good Corporate Citizen', *supra* note 9 at p. 5.

[50] *Supra* note 25.

[51] Schrijver *Sovereignty Over Natural Resources*, *supra* note 44 at p. 184.

[52] See the discussion on TRIMs in Section 7.3.1 below.

the open market, though the OECD took steps to ensure that these evolved into commercial operations, eliminating any element of state subsidy.

As noted above, the EC also adopted a policy of promoting the conclusion of BITs as part of a package of provisions in the Lome Agreements with the ACP states.[53] The link thus created between investment protection and collateral benefits can be seen (with the benefit of hindsight, perhaps) as a development which helped to set the foreign investment debate on a new course. Moreover, it can be noted that the acceptability of foreign investment is determined under this agreement by reference to the objectives of the Lome Agreement itself, rather than by reference to the development goals of the host state. Although the objectives of Lome IV include respect for state sovereignty (Article 2) and the right of each state to determine its own political, social, cultural and economic policy options (Article 3), the objectives of the Treaty laid out in Chapter One of the Agreement do embrace a particular view of 'appropriate development'[54] and it is perhaps surprising that no general affirmation of the principle of state sovereignty is found within the titles on investment promotion or protection.

Meanwhile, the 'free trade' paradigm was being asserted on many different fronts[55] – through the policies of the World Bank Group,[56] within the EU[57] and other regional trading blocs[58] and through the domestic laws and policies of many states.[59]

Developments within the EU are perhaps particularly worthy of note. The opening up of the markets of the Member States to 'internal' competition, in effect market access and 'national treatment' guarantees for foreign

[53] See Section 2.1, above.

[54] Chapter One embraces a concept of 'people-centred' development (Art. 5(1)), affirms the importance of respect for human rights (Art. 5(2)), promotes 'self-reliant' development (Art. 6(1)), respect for the environment (Art. 6(2)) and embraces the principle of different and more favourable treatment for least-developed states (Art. 8).

[55] See further T. W. Waelde 'International Investment under the 1994 Energy Charter Treaty' *29(5) JWT* (1995) 5 at pp. 12–19.

[56] See the World Bank Group, *supra* note 28. The lending policies of the World Bank Group imposed conditions concerning market access, reduction of foreign investment controls and privatisation requirements on many developing countries in the 1980s and 1990s. An important aspect of these policies was that it involved these external agencies in regular scrutiny of the domestic policies of borrower countries, including laws and policies which affected foreign investors. See further Addo 'Privatisation', *supra* note 29.

[57] EC rules on capital movements, on public procurement, on state aids and on the free movement of goods, the provision of services and on the movement of workers have all helped to mould in law the 'free trade' paradigm of economists, producing, at least in some measure, a 'right to trade'. The most important aspect of this, from an international perspective, has been the focus on the rights and freedoms of traders (for which read multinationals) and the restriction of the power of Member States (for which read sovereign states) to regulate domestic markets: see further Section 6.1.1.

[58] Such as NAFTA, see Section 6.1.2, below.

[59] See Muchlinski *Multinational Enterprises*, *supra* note 1, Chapter Six.

investors based within the EU, did not pass unnoticed in other developed states, especially in the US. Though the general concept of 'free trade' areas is tolerated under GATT,[60] a number of major rows have developed over the 'privileged' position of EU-based enterprises, as compared to third-country-based enterprises, under EC law.

These developments, it is submitted, had significant 'spillovers' into the debate on the treatment of foreign investment. The favourable access conditions guaranteed within the EU stood in sharp contrast to the lack of access guarantees available generally in this area, helping to shift the focus of attention from the traditional locus of expropriation and compensation to this issue. In other free trade areas, such as NAFTA, attention was shifting similarly towards a focus on access for foreign investment, increasingly regarded as a corollory to free trade.

In addition, the reliance within the EU on the 'non-discrimination' principle meant that between the Member States at least, the MFN principle gave way to the more penetrative 'national treatment' principle. Powerful third states, such as the US and Japan, were unlikely to stand by for long while their own foreign investors were excluded from the opportunities thus opened up to European companies within the EU.

Of great significance was the formation of UNCTAD and the work carried out by this body, which reflected a wider range of concerns than had previously been addressed. The political alignment of less developed states under the Group of 77 umbrella also served to emphasise the North–South divide over the issue of foreign investment, and influenced debates within the UN General Assembly.[61]

These developments, along with the efforts at standard-setting outlined in the preceding section, form the backdrop against which recent developments have taken place. They give insight into both the range of substantive issues to be addressed if an effective regime for foreign investment is to be sought, and the structural problems inherent in the international legal system within which future developments must take place. These concerns will arise again in Chapter 7, where three relatively recent developments with important implications for the treatment of foreign investment in the future will be examined. These are the General Agreement on Trade in Services (GATS), the Agreement on Trade-Related Investment Measures (TRIMS) and the Draft Multilateral Agreement on Investment (MAI).

[60] Art. XXIV; see M. Hilf, F. G. Jacobs and E. U. Petersmann (eds) *The European Community and GATT* 1986; A. H. Qureshi *The World Trade Organisation: Implementing International Trade Norms* 1996, Chapter 10; S. Woolcock 'The European acquis and the multilateral trade rules: are they compatible?' 31 *J. Common Market Studies* (1993) 539. See further 6.1, below.

[61] See, e.g. Schrijver's account of negotiations over the NIEO Declaration and Action Programme in Schrijver *Sovereignty Over Natural Resources*, *supra* note 44 at pp. 96–100.

3

Taxation and international law: jurisdictional aspects

Introduction

The taxation of multinational business interests is of immense economic significance for states, and spawns industries of its own, as tax advisers and accountants constantly seek ways to minimise the liabilities of their clients and states constantly seek to capture more exactly in their legal provisions the tax base and hence the tax which they determine is due to them. It is a trite observation that states would reap enormous economic benefits from greater co-ordination of their tax policies and tighter co-operation disciplines, but international efforts to address these issues are characterised by weak provisions, weak enforcement disciplines and the lack of any strong body or international organisation to take matters forward. Where policy co-ordination has been achieved, it has rested firmly on classical international law understandings of sovereignty and jurisdiction, and the activities of states in the tax field appear to reaffirm rather than upset in any way these notions. In this chapter, an outline will be given of the traditional bases of state jurisdiction and of the limitations on tax jurisdiction stemming from principles of customary international law.

Following this in Chapter 4, the main legal concepts and practices employed by states in delimiting their tax jurisdiction from that of others with overlapping interests will be examined. Finally, the general impact of the trade disciplines of the WTO on tax matters will be examined.

3.1 State jurisdiction

Jurisdiction connotes the power of the state to prescribe and enforce its laws and is traditionally described by reference to a set of connections, expressed as legal principles, which justify the exercise of such power in relation to particular 'facts'. Thus, territoriality, nationality, passive personality, protection of the state, universality and extra-territoriality are all recognised bases of jurisdiction in international legal discourse[1] and debate centres on their applicability or acceptability in particular circumstances. Typically, lawyers will attempt to identify the bases on which jurisdiction over certain actors or transactions might be claimed by various states seen as having some connection with or interest in the parties or events in question, and an attempt is made to prioritise these potential claims. The distinction drawn between prescriptive and enforcement jurisdiction is an important tool in this task.

Yet it is also widely recognised that the 'principles' referred to, while they may be useful descriptors, are 'more a matter of convenience than of substance'.[2] While they provide useful shorthand to describe the justifications offered by states for seeking to exercise jurisdiction in various situations, they are not prescriptive; that is, they do not in themselves indicate the jurisdictional outcome, or possible outcomes, of situations which arise.

However, to continue to conceptualise the exercise of jurisdiction in the ways in which these principles invite us to do so may also affect our perceptions of the underlying actors and relationships. The jurisdictions and competences of a state are part of what defines its sovereignty and part of what defines the relationship between the state and its 'subjects' or 'citizens'. In a study of international law and taxation, it is pertinent to ask whether the practice of states is accurately reflected and whether policy issues can best be addressed through these existing principles and concepts.

3.1.1 *Territoriality*

The principle of territorial jurisdiction reflects the view of the state as an essentially territorial creature and denotes the primacy of the power of the state within its territory. The state is viewed as having an extensive discretion to submit conduct taking place within its territory to its laws, and to prevent the exercise of power by another state within its boundaries. This latter aspect is reflected in the principle of non-intervention, recognised as a fundamental principle of international law. Because of the centrality of territory in international legal discourse, the territoriality principle of jurisdiction has been relied on heavily by states to justify their conduct and as a result has been extended to encompass a variety of situations where the conduct over which jurisdiction has been sought did not actually occur, or did not occur in its entirety, on the territory of the state claiming jurisdiction. One such example is found in the notion of objective territoriality, used in

[1] See, e.g. M. Akehurst 'Jurisdiction in International Law' *46 BYIL* (1972–73) 145; D. Bowett 'Jurisdiction: Changing Patterns of Authority Over Activities and Resources' *53 BYIL* (1982) 1; F. A. Mann, 'The Doctrine of Jurisdiction in International Law' *III Recueil des cours* (1964–I) i; R. Y. Jennings and A. D. Watts *Oppenheim's International Law Vol. 1* 9th edn, 1992 (hereinafter *Oppenheim*) 456 *et infra.*

[2] *Oppenheim* 457.

relation to conduct taking place outside the territory, which brings about a result within the territory of a state over which it claims jurisdiction. Brownlie cites the examples of a shot fired across a frontier, causing homicide in the territory of the state and of a conspiracy where the illicit conduct is planned to take place within the territory of the state.[3]

Another example of the importance placed on this principle is its use in relation to crimes taking place on board ships and aircraft, where for the purposes of asserting criminal jurisdiction alleged offences are deemed to have taken place in the territory of the state of registration. A 'constructive' presence may also be relied on as the basis of jurisdiction and may be founded on ties[4] such as the ownership of property within a jurisdiction, the conduct of business there or the location of a subsidiary company there. Territory can therefore be seen to have assumed great importance in the area of jurisdiction. Arguably, though, this concept has been shaped by an outmoded view of the state and is ripe for reassessment.

The above mode of analysis takes as its starting point a notion which is far from self-evident – the primacy of territorial state jurisdiction. Too often statements regarding jurisdiction depend on an assertion that there is an intimate connection between a state and territory, such that the state should be automatically recognised as having an exclusive right to determine the treatment and fate of the individuals, business enterprises and activities falling within the territory; a right to govern.[5] However, while it cannot be denied that control of territory is a basic requirement of statehood,[6] it does not follow that a state must be recognised as having absolute and exclusive

[3] I. Brownlie *Principles of Public International Law* 5th edn, 1998 301.

[4] The existence of a 'genuine connection' is often regarded as the true basis of jurisdiction. See, e.g. Mann 'Jurisdiction', *supra* note 1 at pp. 43–51; Brownlie *Principles*, *supra* note 3 at pp. 306–7. The US Supreme Court has developed a test of 'minimum contacts': see further, *International Shoe Co.* v. *Washington* (1954) 326 US 310; *Shaffer* v. *Heitner* (1977) 433 US 186. These cases are discussed further *infra*.

[5] This is not to suggest that territoriality is the only recognised basis of jurisdiction or that it can never give way to some other claim to jurisdiction, but merely that our concepts of jurisdiction depend on the acceptance of a sovereign possessing certain exclusive rights in relation to territory. The point is that this should be demonstrated, not taken for granted, in any analysis of jurisdiction.

[6] *Montevideo Convention on Rights and Duties of States* 1933, *165 LNTS* 49, Article 1; see also J. Crawford *The Creation of States in International Law* 1979. The requirements remain today, though they have probably been supplemented. The UK government has stated: 'The criteria which normally apply for the recognition of a state are that it should have, and seem likely to have, a clearly defined territory with a population, a Government who are able of themselves to exercise effective control of that territory and independence in their external relations. There are, however, exceptional cases when other factors, including relevant U.N. resolutions, may have to be taken into account.' *Hansard* HC55, col. 225 (Written Answer, 29/02/1984). The impact of the principle of self-determination on the creation of states may be one such factor: 'the principle of self-determination . . . as an autonomous legal

control over all that occurs or happens within its territory. Such a claim, it is submitted, is not self-evident and misrepresents the relationship between territory and sovereignty.

That territory is a prerequisite for statehood cannot be denied. In addition, it is still the case today that states are the most important actors on the international stage, though it should not be overlooked in an examination of jurisdictional principles that certain international organisations also have jurisdiction over certain matters, although they are not territorial entities in any sense.[7] There is, however, a tendency to move from the proposition that territory is a prerequisite for statehood to a proposition that the state has an all-encompassing, absolute jurisdictional power to determine and enforce its laws within set physical boundaries; exclusive control over territory is regarded as a consequence as well as a prerequisite of statehood. It is argued here that such an approach is wrong, that it places too much emphasis on the importance of territory and that this is neither accurate nor helpful in constructing a picture of the bases on which jurisdiction is exercised by states in the modern world.

The overemphasis of territoriality complained of here arises from reliance on an outmoded concept of state sovereignty, one which conceptualises the state as the abstract, legal reflection of a *de facto* power situation. In relation to this 'state as power-bloc', the sovereign is in *de facto* control of territory and from this personality and right follow. However, in modern times an element of legitimacy has been added to most concepts of state. The modern state is generally accepted to be founded on notions of community and consent and sovereignty as arising from the consent of the community. From this consent flows the right to govern throughout the community, but within constitutional limits established by reference to that consent, albeit that these limits may be entirely notional or, perhaps, mythical.

This constitutionalist view of the state, found in prevailing political philosophy, is reflected in domestic law and politics and in this sense informs the practice of states. This in turn has repercussions in the international arena; hence, though not explicitly recognised in the discourse of international law, a constitutionalist view of the state does play a significant role in international law. The sovereignty, or *right*, of the modern state is founded on two independent attributes: legitimacy (the moral aspect of sovereignty) and power (the physical aspect of sovereignty). Jurisdiction is the recognition or representation in international law of this sovereignty. It is a reflection of the operation of sovereign power and of the acceptance within the international community of that exercise of power. Thus, it is defined by

---

principle . . . must clearly affect and modify the law governing territorial sovereignty', *Oppenheim* 715.

[7] The clearest example is probably the Security Council: others would include the General Assembly and the International Criminal Tribunal for the Former Yugoslavia.

reference to legitimacy rather than by reference to power, of which it is merely descriptive.

Under this constitutionalist view of the state, territory remains essential as a precondition for recognition of the state, and remains one of the most striking attributes of the state.[8] It is also true to note that no other state can exercise physical control over persons or things while they remain within the territory of another state, without the consent of that state, though they can exercise jurisdiction in other ways; enforcement jurisdiction is territorial if it means only that. However, the territorial principle, as it relates especially to prescriptive jurisdiction, is of little help in defining the outermost reaches of state power. While the territorial connection, the existence of situations or occurrence of events within the territory of a state, may be the decisive factor *de facto* in a majority of assertions of jurisdiction, territorial connection does not assume any *de jure* primacy under this model of the state.

An examination of the existing practices of states in relation to jurisdiction will demonstrate that the traditional emphasis on territoriality is not justified. This enquiry might be approached from two distinct angles: first, by looking at the matter as a question of competing rights between equal sovereign states (the horizontal aspect); and, second, by examining the nature of the relationship between the state claiming such a right and the individual, company or transaction over which the right is claimed (the vertical aspect).

The horizontal aspect

Accepting for the moment the premise that jurisdiction is a matter arising in the relations between states *inter se* or between states and other actors on the 'international plane', it is not clear that it is the fact of presence or occurrence within a territory that provides the underlying basis for a claim of right to govern on the part of a state. Undoubtedly such a territorial connection does exist in many of the cases where a pattern of governance can be detected in the practice of states. But while territoriality may be the accepted or convenient mode of expression of the interest of the state in enforcing its law in the case in question, it is not determinative of the question. A state may rely on the concept of territoriality at times to express its claim to jurisdiction over an offence, or to resist that of another state, but it will not automatically claim jurisdiction over an activity or transaction whenever it takes place within its territory.[9] In addition, it will often claim jurisdiction over events which have occurred in the territory of another state, on grounds other than territorial jurisdiction. Moreover, two or more states may claim 'territorial' jurisdiction over the same event or transaction because all or part of the

[8] Distinguishing it from other international actors.

[9] It was noted in the *Lotus Case* that '[t]he territoriality of criminal law . . . is not an absolute principle of international law and by no means coincides with territorial sovereignty' (1927) *PCIJ*, Ser. A. no. 10 at p. 20.

conduct in question occurred, or is deemed to have occurred, within the territory of the state. While some devices exist to assist in the prioritisation of such claims – the distinction between prescriptive and enforcement jurisdiction serves such a purpose – territorial claims are not definitively exclusive.

An example can be seen in the scenario where a suspected terrorist sought for conspiracy in State A and for the commission of the offence in State B, has taken refuge in State C and A or B requests his extradition. A, B and C all have territorial claims arising out of their own particular legal interests. In the cases of A and B, their respective legal interests arise from the recognised legal right of a state to frame and enforce its criminal law and hence to exercise jurisdiction in respect of criminal actions carried out wholly or partly in its territory. C's interest consists of the more limited right of a state to regulate the admission and expulsion of foreign nationals and the movement of its own citizens and the associated power to deport or extradite the alleged offender.[10] In each case, there are recognised limits to the way in which, or the circumstances in which, such rights can be exercised.[11]

Another example can be seen where different methods are used by different states to calculate the tax due on business operations, as in the long-running dispute between Barclays Bank and the State of California,[12] which culminated in a Supreme Court action in 1994. Here Barclays complained that the use by California of a worldwide reporting system, whereby Barclays' tax base for Californian taxation was calculated according to a formula involving the proportion of the Barclays Group total level of sales, employment and capital investment which occurred in California, was liable *inter alia* to result in excessive double taxation. Their complaint was essentially that this basis of calculating tax was incompatible with the basis used by other taxing jurisdictions, namely the arm's length or separate accounting principle. Each method, though, is merely one way to express the operation of the territorial principle of jurisdiction in relation to the complex set of factual circumstances presented by a large multinational concern such as Barclays. Each method, if applied correctly and consistently to all of the operations of a transnational group, such as Barclays, would amount to no

[10] But note that C's jurisdiction does not arise purely because the offender is present in the territory, but because he is a foreign national, whom C has a right to exclude (deport or extradite) or a national whom C has a right to extradite in certain circumstances.

[11] International law prescribes certain minimum standards for the treatment of foreign nationals by the authorities of another state and outlaws certain practices such as torture in relation to all groups. The authority of a state to use its police authority to enforce its law is generally confined to within its territorial borders. The rights of states in relation to admission and expulsion are also thought to be subject to certain limitations.

[12] *Barclays Bank plc* v. *Franchise Tax Board, an Agency of the State of California* 129 L. Ed. 2d 244 (hereinafter the *Barclays Case*). See further Section 3.2.1, below.

more than all of the Group's income being liable to tax once. By one view, California was simply recognising the reality that in relation to some businesses, their involvement in the jurisdiction cannot adequately be measured by treating each part of the enterprise as a separate independent entity.[13]

Where a claim to jurisdiction on a basis other than territoriality is asserted, there is undeniably recognition of the primacy of the territorial link in enforcement matters; however, the primacy of territory as a basis of prescriptive jurisdiction is simultaneously denied or challenged. This can be seen in the scenario where several states seek to exercise jurisdiction over a terrorist suspect and request the suspect's extradition from a state holding him/her. The making of the request implies recognition of the primary right of the holding state in enforcement jurisdiction and this finds reflection in the international law rule whereby unauthorised action by the representatives of one state within the territory of another will amount to a breach of the principle of non-intervention.[14] Beyond this, however, claims might be made on various grounds, territory, nationality, etc., and there is no rule according priority to territory. Each separate claim reflects a perception of concern on the part of the claimant state in exercising jurisdiction, that is a perception of public interest in the matter.

A further point to be noted is that the form in which the public interest of a state in exercising jurisdiction over a particular event or person is expressed may be no more than a matter of habit or convenience. The use of the concept of territoriality is little more than a convenient label and does little to convey what the perceived interest of the claimant state in pursuing the matter amounts to.

This is particularly so where one or more states base their claim on grounds of territory. In laws affecting transboundary commercial operations, it has increasingly become necessary for states to develop complex criteria and formula to determine precisely when an operation is deemed to fall within the 'territorial' jurisdiction of the state. The central point for the purposes of this argument is that 'territory' is not self-defining. In relation to jurisdictional claims, it is deployed to describe a set of relationships which are deemed to be intimitely connected to the state in a variety of ways. While a physical presence within a given physical space may be a frequent basis for applying the description, this in itself is not always enough and in some cases is not necessary.

Even where there is only one such claim the point holds true. A claim based on nationality, for instance, is normally made only where there is no

[13] For a full discussion of this case see Section 3.2.1, below.

[14] See for instance, the *Lawler Incident, 1 McNair* 78; also the incident concerning Sidney Jaffe, removed from Canada to Florida by 'bounty hunters' in clear breach of international law: Statement by US Secretary of State Schultz to Florida Probation and Parole Commission *78 AJIL* (1984) 207. See generally *Oppenheim* 385–90.

territorial intimacy between the claimant state and the individual in question, or where a contrary territorial connection exists (as where the national is present in the territory of another state). Yet far from being merely an alternative or secondary basis for jurisdiction, as it is often portrayed, the idea of jurisdiction based on nationality serves to undermine the concept of jurisdiction based on territoriality by denying the centrality of the link between state and territory and the same can be said of other bases of jurisdiction. A possible exception is where claims relate to areas not in any case subject to territorial sovereignty, such as the high seas or *terra nullius*, where assertions of jurisdiction will tend neither to reinforce nor deny territoriality as a basis of jurisdiction (or sometimes to reinforce and sometimes to deny it).[15]

Claims to jurisdiction based on grounds other than territoriality may be said to have increased in recent times, reflecting the increasing degree of 'territorial non-coincidence' between economic activity and the nation state.[16]

In addition, claims to 'territorial' jurisdiction do not preclude claims based on other grounds, such as nationality or protection, over the same subject matter. For instance, where jurisdiction over a company based in the territory of and registered with the authorities of a state is involved, no single basis for the jurisdiction claim will necessarily be evident. In fact, when the underlying reasons for attributing a particular relationship or activity to one category rather than another are examined, it can be seen that the deployment of these categories does not depend so much on any essential distinction between them as on custom and practice in the conceptualisation and description of those relationships. While the traditional categories of jurisdictional claim are more than mere labels – they also denote identifiable and established concepts – the task of relating those concepts to facts leaves a great deal of room for argument and dispute.

Thus 'territoriality' as a basis of jurisdiction fails to prescribe, either inclusively or exclusively, the set of relationships which it is commonly used to describe and does not serve to delimit these relationships from others which might commonly be described as subject to jurisdiction on some other basis.

The vertical aspect

This problem can also be examined by looking at the relationships or transactions which form the basis of claims to jurisdiction. Where jurisdiction is asserted over an individual on territorial grounds, a physical link between

[15] The claim to universal jurisdiction against *hostis humanis generis* (denying any supremacy of territoriality) might be contrasted to a claim to jurisdiction based on hot pursuit from territorial waters (affirming).

[16] See further R. Murray 'The Internationalization of Capital and the Nation-State' *67 New Left Review* (1971) 84; S. Picciotto 'Jurisdictional Conflicts, International Law and the International State System' *11 International Journal of the Sociology of Law* (1983) 11.

the individual and the state is normally at the root of the assertion, such as where an activity has taken place (either wholly or partly) within the territory of the state. Where this connection is absent or is less direct, some other ground such as nationality, protection of the state or the 'effects' of the activity on matters deemed to be of concern to the good order of the state may be invoked; otherwise, the matter may be deemed not to fall within the jurisdiction of the state.

However, while it is our habit to conceptualise 'territorial' jurisdiction as being premised on the physical intimacy between the individual and the state, it is questionable whether this conceptualisation will withstand further scrutiny. Typically, it is not the mere presence of the individual within the state, but the occurrence within the state of some activity which arouses the concern of the state. For instance, a state will not normally take jurisdiction over offences which took place outside its own territory merely on the basis of the presence of the offender in the territory. A common exception is where the state asserts the right to deport or extradite an alleged offender to be tried for offences which took place elsewhere or where, rarely, the state claims the right of universal or quasi-universal jurisdiction to try the alleged offender itself. These exceptions are reserved for very serious offences which are regarded as having a highly detrimental effect on the interests of the state, whether domestically of internationally, and it is arguably these potential effects which form the basis of the right to exercise jurisdiction. In such cases the presence of the offender, far from being the key to jurisdiction, is little more than a practicality *sine qua non*.

Nor is it every activity of the individual over which the state claims jurisdiction, in the sense of a right to enforce its law. States subject to governance only a portion of the human activity which occurs within the boundaries of the state. This may be simply due to a sense of propriety, it may be conceptualised in a distinction between public and private spheres, or it may be detailed more precisely in the pertinent constitutional documents and understandings which operate in a particular state. Nevertheless, it is universal. What then determines whether or not activity is of any interest to the state? Clearly, it is not the mere fact of occurrence within the territory of the state, but some perception that the activity is one which ought to be regulated to enhance the good order, however defined, of the state. Moreover, while states have traditionally been recognised as having a great deal of discretion in this area, the regulation of their jurisdiction by the growing body of human rights norms and customary international law rules on the treatment of foreign nationals, together with the expansive collection of voluntary undertakings of states in relation to a wide range of matters, establishes that in principle the jurisdiction of the state in relation to activities within its territory is regulated by international law.

A similar conclusion can be drawn from the practice of states relating to the assertion of jurisdiction over companies. Something more is generally required before jurisdiction will be asserted than the mere physical presence of operations of the company or the carrying out of transactions in the territory of a state. Many states rely on tests involving the place of incorporation or the seat of management to locate the activities of the company within the state's jurisdiction. Indeed, the practice of according recognition to the corporate personality may lead to the opposite result. The conclusion of transactions by a foreign company, or the presence of one of its agents or branches, is often ignored for many purposes. Thus, in many domestic legal systems the recognition of the personality of the foreign company is selective. A company may be recognised where it is deemed important to impose laws designed for the protection of the environment, the consumer or the marketplace, while the profits arising from those transactions are ignored for tax purposes. Again, it is not the physical link between the company and the state which is of importance, but the impact of the activities of the company on the good order of the state which lies at the heart of the jurisdiction claim.

In conclusion, an examination of the transactions and relationships underlying claims to jurisdiction fails to reveal any real reliance by states on territoriality as a basis for jurisdictional claims. While claims may be conceived of as arising out of a general territorial authority, they are in reality reflections of specific recognised legal interests. The concept of territoriality as a ground of jurisdiction, though undoubtedly useful as a descriptive concept, has little use in reality as a prescriptive tool: 'even if states exercise only their own exclusive territorial competence, this could produce overlapping and conflicting effects, due to the multiple geographic contacts of individuals and of interrelated economic activities'.[17]

3.1.2 *Nationality*

A second element of statehood, the requirement of population, is reflected in the nationality principle of jurisdiction, by which a state will claim the right to subject to its jurisdiction individuals and corporate entities on whom it has conferred its jurisdiction. The justification underlying such claims focuses, therefore, on the relationship between the sovereign in its internal capacity as ruler of the state, and the subjects or citizens of the state. As with territory, this justification reflects underlying concepts of the nature of the state. Nationality can be seen to originate in the idea of a personal allegiance between sovereign and subject, which represents the internal dimension of territory. It can probably be said that changing conceptions of the relationship between the sovereign and its subjects have been reflected in state practice in this area. It has, for example, become clear that nationality should reflect the reality of a 'social bond' between the state and the

[17] S. Picciotto *International Business Taxation* (1992) at p. 307.

subject,[18] and the previously wide discretion of states to confer and withhold nationality gradually eroded. Moreover, the shift in emphasis from ties of nationality to human rights issues, which in many respects overlooks or ignores such ties, may have had some influence on the factors to be taken into account in determining nationality. Finally, the growing importance of transnational transactions in goods and services, and the 'internationalisation' of economic actors have also brought into play a range of public policy concerns different to those stemming from an allegiance-centred concept of nationality.

However, determining the precise detail of the 'genuine link' requirement is far from easy, and states continue to use a wide range of tests or concepts to determine whether this exists in different types of cases. The *Nottebohm Case* involved the nationality of an individual in circumstances where the result of the apparent grant of nationality had been to deprive the individual concerned of his original German nationality.[19] In that context, the Court, having examined evidence of the existence of customary law restrictions on such grants, stated the following:

> According to the practice of States, to arbitral and judicial decisions and to the opinion of writers, nationality is a legal bond having as its basis a social fact of attachment, a genuine connection of existence, interests and sentiments, together with the existence of reciprocal rights and duties. It may be said to constitute the juridical expression of the fact that the individual upon whom it is conferred, either directly by the law or as the result of an act of the authorities, is in fact more closely connected with the population of the State conferring nationality than with that of any other State.

While these guidelines may assist in like cases they are unlikely to be of much help where the nationality of a company,[20] or of the child of a refugee or asylum seeker[21] is the issue, or possibly even where the result would be dual nationality.

[18] See the *Nottebohm Case* (1955) *ICJ Rep.* 4 at 23.

[19] Brownlie *Principles, supra* note 3 at p. 401.

[20] Company laws of states utilise a wide range of conditions to be satisfied before incorporation, for instance, can be completed. In addition, there may be some circumstances where states will look behind incorporation when applying particular rules.

[21] Brownlie identifies a wide range of factors relied on in the internal legislation of states as connecting factors, including residence, domicile, immigration *animo manendi* (with an intent to remain permanently), and membership of ethnic groups associated with the state territory: Brownlie *Principles*, p. 385 *et infra.* The vulnerability of the individual may be another relevant factor; see, e.g. the *United Nations Convention on the Rights of the Child*, Article 7(1): 'The child shall be registered immediately after birth and shall have the right from birth to a name, the right to acquire a nationality, and, as far as possible, the right to know and be cared for by his or her parents'. See also Arts 7(2), 8(1) and 8(2).

Even where nationality is recognised (and in reality it is not often at issue in jurisdictional conflicts), the jurisdictional rights which flow from nationality remain to be determined. Since nationals abroad are within the sovereign territory of another state, jurisdictional claims based on nationality must be tempered to accommodate the competing territorial jurisdiction claims of the host state. Oppenheim states:

> A particular problem arises where under the laws of a state its nationals abroad are required to perform (or refrain from performing) acts abroad which, according to the laws of the state where those nationals are, it would be an offence for them to perform there (or refrain from performing) . . . [T]he state of nationality must not require compliance with its laws at the expense of its duty to respect the territorial sovereignty of the state of residence.[22]

Thus, the question would seem to be one of respect for the territorial sovereignty of another state.[23]

The problem would then be not establishing the bond of nationality, but in ascertaining whether the facts are such as to make the claim to jurisdiction 'just and reasonable'.[24] Such a determination would involve an assessment of the interest of the state of nationality, and the interests of any other states in the issue at hand. This would surely involve an enquiry into more than the mere fact of nationality. The relationship between the wider political, economic and commercial interests of the state of nationality as well as the full range of interests of competing states would have to be examined.

However, the question arises whether law, rather than comity, imposes any limits on the use of the nationality principle. The UK government has stated 'The nationality principle justifies proceedings against nationals of the State claiming jurisdiction in respect of their activities abroad only provided that this does not involve interference with the legitimate affairs of other States or cause such nationals to act in a manner which is contrary to the laws of the State in which the activities in question are conducted'.[25]

In some cases the justification for the assertion of jurisdiction lies in the effects within a state's territory of acts performed outside that territory – the 'effects' doctrine. In other cases the justification lies in the implementation of a state's foreign policy or some other such political aim.[26] In the following

[22] *Oppenheim* 464. One example of such a request cited is the application of US regulations made in the aftermath of the hostages crisis which purported to apply the freeze of Iranian deposits in US banks to all their branches and subsidiaries, including subsidiaries abroad. *Ibid.* at note 11.

[23] Bowett 'Jurisdiction', *supra* note 1 at p. 8.

[24] Mann 'Jurisdiction', *supra* note 1 at p. 44.

[25] 1967 *BPIL* 58 at 60.

[26] See for instance the Siberian pipeline case, discussed by A.V. Lowe 'Public International Law and the Conflict of Laws: The European Response to the United States Export Administration Regulations' *33 ICLQ* (1984) 515. See also the Helms–Burton dispute, discussed below at Section 5.3.1.

examination of selected 'long-arm' jurisdiction cases, these justifications will be described in detail and examined.

3.1.3 *Other bases of jurisdiction*

The 'effects' doctrine

The 'effects' doctrine has been relied on particularly by the US courts in anti-trust cases and was first raised in the *Alcoa Case*[27] in 1945. This case concerned an agreement made by aluminium production companies based outside the US to restrict the production of aluminium, an action regarded under US anti-trust principles as a means of providing artificial price support.[28] The Court found that action taken outside the territory of a state, which was intended to produce effects within its territory, had the effect of shifting the burden of proof to the defendants to show that those effects had not in fact resulted.[29] In later cases, a doctrine of judicial restraint has been developed, applying a 'balancing test' to determine whether the US courts should assume jurisdiction. In the *Timberlane Case*,[30] a number of factors to be considered by US courts were identified and these were further refined in the *Mannington Mills Case*.[31] The factors to be considered included:

- the degree of conflict with foreign law or policy;
- the nationality or allegiance of the parties and the location of the corporations;
- the extent to which enforcement by either state can be expected to achieve compliance;
- the relative significance of effects on the US as compared with those elsewhere;
- the extent to which there is an explicit purpose to harm or affect US trade or commerce;
- the foreseeability of such effects;
- the relative importance to the violations charged of conduct within the US as compared with conduct abroad;
- whether litigation is pending abroad;
- effects on foreign relations if the court exercises its jurisdiction;

[27] *US* v. *Aluminum Company of America and Others* 44 F. Supp. 97; 148 F. 2d 416.

[28] The mechanism employed was an agreement to pay royalties to the other companies if production exceeded a certain level. This undoubtedly discouraged production over the agreed quotas.

[29] See also *US* v. *Watchmakers of Switzerland Information Center Inc.*, 133 F. Suppl. 40 (1955); 134 F. Supp. 710 (1955).

[30] *Timberlane Lumber Company* v. *Bank of America* 549 F. 2d 597 (1976).

[31] *Mannington Mills Inc.* v. *Congoleum Corporation* 595 F. 2d 1287 (1979).

- whether, if relief is granted, the party will be placed in the position of being forced to perform an act illegal in another country or be under conflicting requirements;
- whether an order for such relief would be acceptable in the US if reciprocated; and
- whether a Treaty with the affected nation has addressed the matter.

A number of commentators expressed doubts about this judicial exercise, questioning both the justiciability[32] and the comity[33] of the solution offered. The notion that the courts of one country should sit in judgement on the international legal interests of another would seem to offend against the principle of sovereign equality of states, well established in domestic jurisdictions in the form of 'act of state' doctrines and doctrines of state immunity.

The approach of the Supreme Court in *Timberlane* was reflected in the Restatement (Third) of Foreign Relations Law, s. 403(2) and the US Supreme Court returned to the issue again in the case of *Hartford Fire Insurance Co.* v. *California.*[34] In this case, the majority in the Supreme Court was satisfied that the activities complained of had produced 'direct, substantial and forseeable effects in the United States' as required by the Sherman Act.[35] In addition, adopting a very narrow view of the meaning of 'conflict', the majority in the Supreme Court took the view that a conflict would only exist with the laws of another state, where the laws of one required a party to perform some action which the other prohibited. In *Hartford* this was not the case; the regulatory regime in the UK essentially permitted the conduct which was the subject of the case, while the relevant US law prohibited it. Thus, the majority concluded without much discussion that in the present case comity did not require abstention from the exercise of jurisdiction.[36] However, the Supreme Court also cast doubt on whether, where the requirements of the relevent US legislation had been met (that is, where the required effects were shown), jurisdiction should ever be declined on the grounds of comity.[37] The majority thus appeared to cast doubt on the previous case-law of the Supreme Court and the Third Restatement.[38] The minority, by contrast, applying the balancing of interests test as laid down in *Timberlane*

[32] Bowett 'Jurisdiction', *supra* note 1 at p. 22.

[33] A. V. Lowe 'Blocking Extraterritorial Jurisdiction: The British Protection of Trading Interests Act, 1980' *75 AJIL* (1981) 257 at pp. 268–9.

[34] 113 S. Ct. 2891 (1993) (also known as the *Insurance Antitrust Case*).

[35] Sherman Act, 1890; see also Foreign Trade Antitrust Improvements Act 1982.

[36] Justice Souter, 113 S. Ct. 2891 at 2910.

[37] *Ibid.*

[38] See for example A. F. Lowenfeld 'Jurisdiction Issues Before National Courts: The *Insurance Antitrust* Case' in K. M. Meessen (ed.) *Extraterritorial Jurisdiction in Theory and Practice* 1996 at p. 1; A. Robertson and M. Demetriou '"But that was another country . . .": The Extraterritorial Application of US Antitrust Laws in the US Supreme Court' *43 ICLQ* (1994) 417.

and *Mannington Mills*, found that this was a clear case where jurisdiction should be declined. On the majority's narrow construction of 'conflict' with a foreign law, Justice Scalia wrote 'That breathtakingly broad proposition, which contradicts the many cases discussed earlier, will bring the Sherman Act and other laws into sharp and unnecessary conflict with the legitimate interests of other countries – particularly our closest trading partners'.[39]

From the point of view of traders potentially affected by these exercises of jurisdiction, one of the most disturbing parts of the test is that the 'weighing' of interests takes place at the time that the action comes before any court, which may be long after the events which form the basis of the action have occurred. So quite apart from the iniquitous spectacle of the courts of one country determining the balance of interests of that country against those of another, the procedure does not meet the requirement of legal certainty. This uncertainty could itself be damaging to the trading interests of other nations.[40]

As far as jurisdictional principles are concerned, it is interesting to note that the list of factors to be considered include several which focus on the 'connection' between the actors or transactions in question and the (two) states concerned. This would seem to emphasise the origins of the 'effects' doctrine as a policy response to the failure of the traditional jurisdictional principles to address squarely the relationships between the actors or transactions and the state in question, and thus the inadequacy of these principles to protect the interests of the state in seeking to regulate these actors or transactions.

These assertions of jurisdiction have remained controversial. The UK government, for instance, has consistently opposed extra-territorial jurisdiction claims, passing legislation to block actions associated with such claims[41] and has protested regularly about such assertions. At the heart of complaints about 'long-arm' jurisdiction has been that these assertions of jurisdiction infringe British sovereignty. The Shipping Contracts and Commercial Documents Act 1964[42] was concerned to block acts which 'constitute an infringement of the jurisdiction which, under international law, belongs to the United Kingdom'.[43] As Lowe notes,[44] the later Protection of Trading Interests Act 1980[45] focused on acts which 'are damaging or threaten to damage the trading interests of the United Kingdom'.[46]

Thus, whereas the US asserted the right to exercise jurisdiction to defend its 'state interests' even over non-nationals and even over acts which occurred

[39] 112 S. Ct. 2169 at 2922.

[40] Lowe 'Blocking Extraterritorial Jurisdiction', *supra* note 33 at p. 269.

[41] See, e.g. the Shipping Contracts and Commercial Documents Act 1964, C. 87 of 1964; Protection of Trading Interests Act 1980, C. 11 of 1980.

[42] *Ibid.*

[43] See ss. 1(1)(b) and 2(1).

[44] Lowe 'Blocking Extraterritorial Jurisdiction', *supra* note 33 at p. 274.

[45] *Supra* note 41.

[46] *Ibid.*, ss. 1(1)(b) and 1(3).

outside its territory (but which had effects in the US), the UK claimed the right to defend its 'state interests' only in relation to persons 'carrying on business in the United Kingdom' or of UK nationality. Each party's claims are now based on the same grounds – state interests – though the claims in substance are far from reconcilable, as the dispute testifies.

The EC's position in relation to extra-territorial jurisdictional claims remains unclear. While the UK government has remained consistently opposed to such claims, the position of some other Member States[47] and the position of the Commission in relation to anti-trust matters is somewhat different. In the *Dyestuffs Case*,[48] the Commission seemed to base its extension of EC competition (anti-trust) laws to a company based outside the EC on the 'effects' doctrine; the European Court of Justice (ECJ), however, was more cautious. Rejecting the argument of the British government that the separate legal personalities of a parent and a subsidiary company should be respected, the Court treated the two companies as a single economic entity. This enabled the Court, in the circumstances of the case, to attribute the extra-territorial actions of the parent to the subsidiary and hence deem them to have taken place within the EC. The *Woodpulp Cases*,[49] however, presented a problem not so easily resolved. In this case, the activities in question had been carried out, it seemed, entirely by parties based outside the EC and could not be attributed to agents or subsidiaries within the EC. The European Commission argued that the application of competition law rules was justified, first, because the effect of the price collusion at issue was substantial and was intended; indeed it was the primary and direct result of the contested agreements; and, second, because, although the agreements had been entered into outside the EC, they had been implemented inside the EC by parties either trading directly into the EC or through trade involving agents or sales offices within the EC. The ECJ looked to this notion of implementation as the basis for finding jurisdiction, but found it immaterial whether or not agents, sales offices or subsidiaries had been involved. In concluding that the agreements had been implemented within the EC, the ECJ found that the case was covered by the universally recognised territorial principle of international law. However, as numerous commentators have pointed out, this reasoning comes extremely close to the same thing as the 'effects' doctrine; the acts complained of were held to fall within the jurisdiction of the Court and the Commission precisely because of their effects within the EC.[50]

[47] Noteably Germany and Greece cf. Lowe 'The European Response', *supra* note 26 note 36 at p. 529.

[48] *ICI* v. *Commission* [1972] ECR 619. See also the Opinion of the Advocate-General in the *Woodpulp Cases*: Case 89/85 [1988] ECR 5193.

[49] See for instance Case 89/85 [1988] ECR 5193.

[50] See F. A. Mann 'The Public International Law of Restrictive Practices in the European Court of Justice' *38 ICLQ* (1989) 375.

3.1.4 *The inadequacy of the traditional jurisdictional principles*

These disputes exemplify both why the traditional jurisdictional principles have such appeal to the lawyer, and why they are unsatisfactory. The traditional principles appeal because of the illusion of order they create. The set of principles, taken together and coupled with the distinction between jurisaction and jurisfaction, appear to order claims, to avoid conflict and to create some element of certainty. Defined by reference to objectively verifiable criteria – territorial presence or nationality – they appear to stand apart from naked assertions of state power – to provide a legal solution free from political interference. Their apparently disjunctive and reciprocal nature has appeal within a particular state sovereignty paradigm – the 'chunk' schools of sovereignty[51] – which see sovereignty as constituting absolute control within a portion of territory to the exclusion of all others. However, this apparent appeal is also the weakness of the jurisdictional principles. The principles do not accurately represent the concerns of states in relation to persons, property and transactions, and do not in reality provide a sustainable basis for the ordering and prioritisation of claims and therefore fail to meet the needs of the modern international community. An examination of the way these principles are adopted and adapted in practice, and of the disputes between states which persist especially in commercial spheres, illustrates the need for fresh paradigms and new legal concepts which better reflect contemporary values.

3.2 **Limitations on jurisdictions in the field of taxation**

The traditional principles of jurisdiction outlined above have been relied on by states in shaping the external limits within which they exercise the 'right to tax'. The rules derived from these principles are to be found in the domestic and international laws and codes governing taxation. Primarily the pattern has been one of states acting unilaterally to draw limits to their own jurisdictional claims, but this activity has been complemented by the conclusion of a multitude of bilateral arrangements by which states formalise the demarcation of their rights so as to avoid elements of 'double taxation' which would be deterimental to wider trade and investment concerns. Multilateral action at the *legal* level is strikingly absent in the taxation field, though, as shall be seen, model codes have exerted a great deal of influence on the shape and content of bilateral agreements. The OECD is undoubtedly

[51] The description is attributed to Inis Claude. See M. R. Fowler and J. M. Bunck 'The Chunk and Basket Theories of Sovereignty' in W. W. Thompson (ed.) *Community, Diversity, and a New World Order: Essays in Honor of Inis L. Claude, Jr* 1994 at pp. 137–44.

the most influential of the international organisations active in this area, playing an important role in analysing problems with existing practices and in bringing forward proposals for reform which, when adopted, play an important role in co-ordinating the development of new practices among its Members. Picciotto[52] points also to the important influence exerted by a 'community' of international tax specialists, government officials, academic experts and business representatives: 'It was they who devised the model conventions . . . They also negotiated the actual bilateral treaties based on the models . . . Finally, the allocation to national tax jurisdictions of income derived from international bargaining processes (is) also carried out by such specialists'.[53]

An initial analysis might then begin with the observation that the principle of sovereign equality is much in evidence in this area, where states generally regard themselves as having a wide discretion to set and apply their own tax rules. While it is generally assumed that states cannot impose their tax laws on persons or property only transiently within the state, states can extend their tax regimes to nationals, even if resident abroad, and their foreign assets and earnings. Moreover, territorial jurisdiction allows states to tax earnings or assets within their territory owned by foreign nationals or non-residents.[54] As noted above, there are recognised limits on jurisdictional claims in customary international law, though the precise content of these limits is a matter of dispute in some areas. The Barclays dispute, discussed further below, is a clear example of such a dispute in the taxation field. Substantive limits on the state's power to tax derive from two main sources: rules of custom and the multilateral WTO regime. The latter is dealt with separately in Section 4.2.

Customary international law restrictions on tax jurisdiction can be examined under three headings. First, there may be restrictions arising from particular substantive rules of the system, such as the principle of non-intervention, or the rules on the treatment of foreign nationals. Second, there may be restrictions arising from the general principles of jurisdiction outlined above. And, finally, there may be specific restrictions on jurisdiction in the taxation sphere, evidenced by state practice and *opinio juris*.

3.2.1 *Substantive customary law restrictions on tax jurisdiction*

Three candidates fall for consideration under this heading: the principle of non-intervention in internal affairs, the rules on the treatment of foreign nationals and the principle of non-discrimination.

[52] Picciotto *International Business Taxation*, *supra* note 17 at p. xiii.
[53] *Ibid.*
[54] *Oppenheim* 137–9.

Non-intervention in internal affairs

The principle of non-intervention, which can be found in Article 2(7) of the UN Charter and is an important concomitant of state sovereignty, can be regarded as a fundamental principle of international law, and clearly has application in the sphere of economic relations between states. The measure of illegitimate intervention is state sovereignty. In the *Nicaragua Case*,[55] the ICJ stated that this principle 'involves the right of every sovereign State to conduct its affairs without outside interference'.[56] States must be able to 'decide freely', the Court argued, on the choice of a political, economic, social and cultural system; '[i]ntervention is wrongful when it uses methods of coercion in regard to such choices, which must remain free ones'.[57] However, only some of the most serious forms of conduct will constitute unlawful intervention. In dealing with the facts of the *Nicaragua Case*, the Court found itself unable to regard the US economic acts complained of, namely the cessation of economic aid, the reduction of the Nicaraguan sugar quota and eventually a trade embargo, as sufficient to amount to a breach.[58] It would seem highly unlikely, by analogy, that hostile taxation policies could ever amount to an unlawful intervention.

Treatment of foreign nationals

It was seen in Chapter 1 that the customary international law rules relating to the treatment of the property of foreign nationals are rather unsettled. However, there appears to be a requirement that any 'taking' of foreign property does not discriminate on grounds of race[59] and a requirement that 'takings' be compensated. Taxation may be found to amount to a *de facto* taking where it effectively eclipses rights of ownership[60] and in such circumstances would be legal only if it satisfied the requirements outlined above.

[55] *Case Concerning Military and Paramilitary Activities In and Against Nicaragua* (*Nicaragua* v. *United States*), *Merits*, Judgment, *ICJ Reports* (1986), p. 14.

[56] *Ibid.*, para. 202. The General Assembly *Declaration on Principles of International Law Concerning Friendly Relations and Co-operation Among States in Accordance with the Charter of the United Nations of 1970* states: 'No State may use or encourage the use of economic, political or any other type of measures to coerce another State in order to obtain from it the subordination of the exercise of its sovereign rights and to secure from it advantages of any kind.' UNGA Res. 2625 (XXV) of 24 October 1970. The formulation is identical in the earlier *Declaration on the Inadmissibility of Intervention in the Domestic Affairs of States and the Protection of Their Independence and Sovereignty of 1965*, UNGA Res. 2123(XX) of 21 December 1965 and both were relied on as evidence of custom by the ICJ in the *Nicaragua Case*.

[57] *Ibid.*, para. 204.

[58] *Ibid.*, paras 244–5.

[59] See Section 1.1.2 above and references cited therein.

[60] See further *Starrett Housing Corporation* v. *Islamic Republic of Iran*, Award No. ITL 32-24-1 of 19 December 1983, *4 Iran–US CTR* 122. In this case the Iran–US Claims Tribunal stated in relation to management rights: 'measures taken by

Doubts about the cohesiveness of the oft-cited 'public purpose' requirement were discussed fully in Chapter 1;[61] however, it can be noted here that genuine measures of taxation are very likely to satisfy any such requirement, where, for instance, this has been established in a treaty. Taxation is directed to a very wide range of means and normally the discretion of the taxing state would not be questioned. However, it is possible that measures enacted in the form of taxation but motivated by entirely different concerns (extraneous to the regulation of the taxing state) might fall foul of such a requirement.

The individual and international law

In relation to taxation, the traditional perspective of international law holds true that the individual is the object rather than the subject of international law. Individuals on the whole have no role to play in determining whether they become liable to taxation under the rules of a particular state; indeed they have little control over their very visibility in those laws. Casual travellers to states other than their home state often find themselves paying sales taxes, service taxes, etc., occasioned by the conclusion of economic transactions within the territory of the host state. Frontier workers, who live in one state and work in another, will often find themselves liable for income tax on their earnings in the state of employment. Residence within a state may give rise to taxation of various sorts: income taxation on unearned income, local government taxes and 'charges' for specific services. Property ownership or distributions from insurance or pension funds might also produce a liability to taxation either in the state of source or in the host state of the recipient.

To a very large extent these matters are regarded as falling within the domestic jurisdiction of states and are of no concern under international law. This is so even where individuals are liable to taxation in a state other than their own.[62] In practice many states will operate self-restraint, or will enter into a bilateral treaty to reduce or avoid the possibility of 'double taxation'. In some cases, though it would appear to be the exception rather than the rule, individuals might gain a right to challenge incidences of 'double taxation' through domestic tribunals or transnational arbitration procedures. However, these elements of 'protection' of the individual from excessive taxation are within the discretion of the state; customary international law, it would seem, places very little in the way of constraint on the state.

---

a state can interfere with property rights to such an extent that these rights are rendered so useless that they must be deemed to have been expropriated'. *Ibid.*, p. 154. In 1964 the UK government protested to Burma that its 99 per cent taxation of the profits of certain UK companies amounted to expropriation, *BPIL* (1964) 202.

[61] See Section 1.1.4 above and references cited therein.

[62] Subject to customary international law rules regarding the treatment of foreign nationals, see above.

Companies under international law

Many of the thornier problems of international taxation involve the treatment of companies and groups of companies. While corporate entities do not have international legal personality (i.e. they are not bound directly by rules of international law), their corporate identity or status is recognised in a variety of contexts. First, it is recognised that states may confer on companies their nationality, bringing them within the protection of the state under rules of state responsibility and thus giving the state the right to demand from other states a certain level of protection for the company and its assets. Though it is not explicitly stated, it seems likely, as in other areas of international law, that grants of nationality will only be recognised if they are reflective of a 'genuine connection' between the company and the state which claims the company as a national. However, as Brownlie points out, there is no single recognised way to determine the nationality of a company for the purposes of international law. Moreover, states commonly do not themselves explicitly grant nationality, choosing instead to determine on a rule-by-rule basis whether they are bound by relevant aspects of domestic law: '[T]he nationality must be derived either from the fact of incorporation . . . or from various links including the centre of administration and the national basis of ownership and control . . . (and) the content of nationality tends to depend on the context of the particular rule of law involved'.[63] Subject to the possibility of a genuine link requirement, it is therefore accepted that states do have a right to subject companies to their laws, including their tax laws. This right is recognised regardless of the nationality or status of the shareholders in any company; thus, it could be said that international law is cognizant of the fact of recognition of corporate personality in domestic law. In some instances, there will also be a duty on states to regulate the conduct of corporate entities over whom they have recognised control, for instance in order to enforce UN sanctions, or to apply terrorist jurisdiction conventions or environmental protection conventions, and this would appear to go beyond mere cognizance into the realms of prescription.[64] The fact of corporate personality under domestic law has also been recognised in the rules concerning injuries to foreign nationals where in the *Barcelona Traction Case*[65] the ICJ recognised as a general principle of international law the rules common in domestic legal systems that courts will not look behind the corporate veil in ordinary circumstances.[66]

[63] Brownlie *Principles*, *supra* note 3 at p. 422.

[64] Query whether international law rules would demand that a state take jurisdiction over a corporate entity where that entity was not recognised under domestic law rules.

[65] *I.C.J. Rep.* (1970) p. 3.

[66] *Ibid.*

It is, however, one thing to note that states normally recognise the separate corporate personality of a subsidiary company – and treat it as acting at arm's length from its parent – and another to assert that this is required by international law. On the contrary, it can be argued that this practice, though almost universal, may be adopted merely for convenience and devoid of any legal effect. A case which throws this issue under the spotlight is the *Barclays Case*.[67]

The Barclays dispute concerned the taxation method applied by the Californian State government to tax the income of Barclays Bank operations falling within the Californian jurisdiction. Two Barclays concerns operated in California: Barclays Bank of California (Barcal), a Californian banking corporation, and Barclays Bank International (BBI), a UK corporation of which Barcal was a wholly owned subsidiary. Both corporations were in turn part of the Barclays Group of companies, a banking multinational based in the UK and carrying on business worldwide.[68]

During the years in issue, California applied the 'worldwide reporting method' to calculate the tax due to the state from the Californian operations of the companies. Under this method companies are required to pay tax according to a formulary apportionment of the income of the whole group of companies of which they form part. The formula applied by California was an average of the proportions of worldwide (or group) payroll, property and sales located or occurring in California.

This method, by which no attempt is made to measure the actual extent of a company's involvement in a particular jurisdiction on a case-by-case basis, contrasts with the more traditional actual or individual accounting basis under which the tax authorities purport to tax the profits actually arising out of operations conducted in the jurisdiction by the enterprise in question over a particular time period. In the case of related companies, such as within a corporate group, this can of course involve the substitution of actual figures with 'arm's-length' transaction costs, to curb tax avoidance through transfer pricing. This particular aspect ceases to be a problem when the worldwide reporting mechanism is used because under the formula employed, the actual profitability of the various parts of a group is not at issue. The worldwide reporting mechanism in favoured by some states because it appears to them to result in a more equitable division of the tax base (the profits on which liability to taxation is calculated); that is, it appears to produce a level of revenue which reflects more accurately the actual level of business conducted within that state. It is favoured in particular because it catches in the revenue net companies with a high commercial profile, for

[67] *Supra* note 12.

[68] The Barclays Group comprised 220 corporations, conducting more than 98 per cent of their business outside the US. Barcal and BBI, and their successor in action, Barclays Bank plc, are all referred to hereinafter as Barclays.

instance, in sales of goods or financial services, but without any locally incorporated subsidiary. Hence, it is favoured by states such as California where rents are high and which are accordingly vulnerable to a significant disequilibrium in trade; many companies offering goods and services within California would choose to locate their operations elsewhere, so as to avoid these high local rents.

Barclays sought to challenge the application by California of the worldwide reporting method on the grounds that this action was in breach of both the due process and commerce clauses of the US Constitution, in that it imposed an unduly onerous and discriminatory tax compliance burden on the company and that it prevented the Federal government from speaking with one voice on commercial relations involving foreign relations, also in breach of the commerce clause.

The dispute centred on the franchise tax payable by Barcal for its revenue year 1977. In submitting its own assessment, Barcal relied solely on the income from its own operations. The Californian tax authorities, however, determined that Barcal was part of a worldwide unitary business, the Barclays Group. They applied the statutory formula then utilised in California to assess Barcal liable to pay tax on a percentage (0.0003232 per cent) of the total income of the Barclays Group for the year in question. A similar exercise was carried out to assess the tax liability of the parent company, BBI, whose liability was calculated to be based on 0.0139032 per cent of the Group's income. The tax liability so calculated exceeded the figure submitted by the respective companies in each case. The companies sued for refunds and succeeded in the lower courts in California, but not when the matter reached the Californian Supreme Court.

Meanwhile, the case had also been raised in the international arena. California's worldwide reporting tax formula had met with a degree of opposition from a large number of foreign state governments. Many, including the UK government, had made diplomatic protests to the US Federal government over the action of California. The UK government had also enacted retaliatory legislation under which dividends due to US corporations from their UK subsidiaries would be liable to corporation tax.[69] The matter had been addressed at Congressional Committee hearings[70] and representations

[69] Finance Act 1985, s. 54 and Schedule 15, para. 5, now Income and Corporation Taxes Act 1988, s. 812 and schedule 30, paras 20–1 (not in force). This legislation, though never enacted, has been used to put pressure on the US government to persuade California to modify its legislation.

[70] Judgment, *supra* note 12, at note 23, and citations therein. As early as 1965, the Special Subcommittee on Interstate Commerce of the House Committee on the Judiciary recommended that States should use formula apportionment as between themselves, but that they should refrain from taxing any income exempt from federal taxation. Though Congress has returned to the matter often, no legislative action has been taken.

had been made by the Federal government to the Californian State government on the subject, expressing concern at the potential impact of the State's action on foreign relations.[71] When the case finally came before the US Supreme Court, *amicus curiae* briefs in favour of the petitioners (Barclays) were submitted by the UK and by a group of twenty OECD states comprising the Member States of the EC along with Australia, Austria, Canada, Finland, Japan, Norway, Sweden and Switzerland.[72]

California had also in the meantime made concessions to foreign corporations in its franchise tax law, partly at least in response to pressure from the Federal government. A 1986 amendment introduced the option of a 'water's edge' election, whereby foreign corporations could elect to exclude from their combined report companies in the group whose presence in the US fell below a stated threshold level. This election involved the payment of a substantial fee and could be disregarded by the California Franchise Tax Board in certain circumstances. These new provisions, however, were felt by foreign governments, including the UK, not to have gone far enough and the conditions attached to the water's edge election were felt to be unacceptable. In 1993, with the UK having set a deadline for implementation of its retaliatory measures and accordingly under increased pressure from the Federal government, California further modified its tax law to allow the water's edge assessment as of right and without payment of the fee. While this was enough to prevent the implementation of retaliatory legislation in the UK, that government and the group of twenty OECD states collectively persisted in their opposition to the use by California of the worldwide reporting mechanism.

In 1994, the *Barclays Case* reached the Supreme Court where it was joined with the case of *Colgate-Palmolive Co.*, a Delaware corporation doing business throughout the US and the rest of the world. The Court was thus in a position to adjudicate on the legitimacy of the Californian measures complained of in respect of both domestic and foreign multinational corporations.

The legal argument

The Californian State measures in question in Barclays had been the subject of litigation in an earlier Supreme Court case, *Container Corp. of America* v. *Franchise Tax Board.*[73] This case involved a US-based corporation with

[71] See for instance the letter from Secretary of State Schulz to Governor of California of 1986, quoted in the *Amicus Curiae* Brief of the UK: 'In an environment in which separate accounting is the federal policy and the generally accepted international rule, state taxation on a worldwide unitary basis creates a clear risk of double taxation . . . this risk of double taxation may distort investment decisions, thereby reducing the overall flow of investment into the United States'.

[72] The US Federal government, which had sided with Barclays at earlier stages in the litigation, submitted a brief in support of the respondents (California), but were equivocal in their support for the use of the worldwide reporting mechanism in the circumstances.

[73] 463 US 159, 77 L. Ed. 2d 545, 103 S. Ct. 2933, hereinafter *Container Corp.*

a number of foreign subsidiaries, and the Supreme Court found that the tax was not unconstitutional in these circumstances. Specifically, the Court in *Container Corp.* rejected the argument that the foreign subsidiaries in the US-based group were exposed as a result of California's action to a risk of multiple international taxation. While accepting in that case that some double taxation may have occurred, the Supreme Court found that this was not an inevitable result of the Californian use of the worldwide reporting mechanism and that the use of an arm's-length standard would not eliminate the risk of such double taxation.[74]

In *Container Corp.*, the Supreme Court reserved judgment as to whether the same view would be taken of a foreign-based group. Thus, the task faced by Barclays in presenting their case before the Supreme Court was to show that the argument relied on in *Container Corp.* was displaced by the varying or additional considerations arising in the case of a foreign-based group. For this reason their attention focused on the foreign policy dimension (the one-voice argument), the *aggravated* risk of double taxation over and above that faced by a US-based corporation, and the discriminatory compliance burden faced by a foreign-based corporation for which worldwide-combined reporting was not the norm.

As indicated above, Barclays argued that the Californian State action was unlawful because it prevented the Federal government from speaking with one voice, in breach of the commerce clause.[75] Under this clause, state action specifically sanctioned by Congress could not be impugned; however, the commerce clause has been interpreted as also having a dormant aspect, so that state action might be deemed unlawful even in areas where Congress had not acted. In the earlier case of *Complete Auto Transit, Inc.* v. *Brady*,[76] the Supreme Court had ruled that a state tax on inter-state commerce would breach the dormant commerce clause if it either:

- applied to an activity lacking a substantial nexus with the taxing state;
- was not fairly apportioned;
- discriminated against inter-state commerce; or
- was not fairly related to the services provided by the state.

Although in this respect the case dealt with inter-state commerce in the US domestic context, there are clear parallels with issues which would arise in the international context (and which in fact underpinned the objections of other states).

[74] *Container Corp.* 188 *et infra.*

[75] The commerce clause (Art. 1, s. 8, clause 3, US Constitution) gives power to Congress to regulate commerce with foreign nations and has been relied on in the Supreme Court to claim protection from state action inimicable to national commercial interests, even in situations where Congress has not acted.

[76] 430 US 274, 51 L. Ed. 2d 326, 97 S. Ct. 1076 (1977).

The Supreme Court in *Barclays* also referred to the 'special need for Federal uniformity'[77] in matters of foreign commerce, another issue with a parallel in international tax practice, and cited two additional concerns to be addressed in cases where the tax affected foreign commerce: first, the enhanced risk of multiple taxation argued to be present for foreign companies (this was relied on by the petitioners to distinguish the case from *Container Corp.* and to import a foreign policy dimension); and, second, the importance of ensuring that state action did not impair the ability of the US government to speak with one voice.[78]

The Court proceeded on the basis that this was an area in which the dormant commerce clause applied and hence proceeded to see whether the test laid down in the *Complete Auto Case* and the additional requirements indicated above were satisfied. As might have been expected following the earlier judgment in *Container Corp.*, the Supreme Court had little difficulty in holding that Barclays had failed to demonstrate that any of the four conditions in *Complete Auto* were satisfied.

On the nexus argument, the UK government had argued in its *amicus curiae* brief that there was no meaningful contact between the activities of Barclays members operating entirely outside the US (whose income would form part of the tax base under the full-blown worldwide reporting mechanism used prior to 1986, though not after that if a water's edge basis was used). The Court described the principle of treating affiliated business enterprises as a single unitary business as 'settled jurisprudence' and endorsed the theory underlying unitary taxation that within a group of companies 'certain intangible "flows of value" . . . link the various members together as if they were essentially a single entity'.[79] Thus, the nexus requirement was found to be satisfied by the business that each of the taxpayer companies had carried out in California, and the state was justified in treating the whole group as a single unitary business.

On the question of apportionment, the Court had already concluded in *Container Corp.* that the worldwide reporting method, if applied on an appropriate basis, constituted a reasonable way to determine the portion of the income of a business which had arisen within the jurisdiction. They maintained this view, noting that 'if applied by every jurisdiction, "California's method" would result in no more than all of the unitary business' income being taxed'.[80] Their attention therefore focused on the claim by

[77] Judgment, *supra* note 12 at p. 258, quoting *Wardair Canada Inc.* v. *Florida Dept. of Revenue*, 477 US 1; 91 L. Ed. 2d 1 at p. 8.

[78] *Ibid.*

[79] *Ibid.*, p. 258, note 10. Neither Barclays nor Colgate had disputed that they were a unitary business.

[80] *Ibid.*, p. 259, quoting from judgment in *Container Corp.*, *supra* note 73 at p. 169.

Barclays that the tax was discriminatory, in that it imposed an unduly onerous compliance burden by forcing a foreign-based group to convert its financial records into the unitary form required by California, where this was not the accounting method normally used by foreign-based groups. The Court recognised that compliance burdens could, in some instances, fall foul of the commerce clause, but found that Barclays had failed to establish that the Californian rules resulted in systematic overtaxing of the business. Further, on Barclays' claim that the imprecision of the rules in certain areas breached the due process clause, the Court found that this was an inevitability in areas of law dealing with such complex subject matters (and noted that the 'approximations' complained of were a common feature in separate accounting systems to determine 'arm's-length' prices): 'We refused in *Container Corp.*, "to require California to give up one allocation method that sometimes results in double taxation in favour of another allocation method that also sometimes results in double taxation".'[81] Thus, the US Supreme Court took the view that the wealth of international practice establishing the arm's-length accounting method as the standard accounting method for taxation purposes held no normative value; that it was a matter merely of convenience rather than one of obligation.

The instability threatened to international tax practice resulting from this ruling cannot be understated. The use of a worldwide reporting mechanism would only be no more likely to lead to double taxation if it were uniformly adopted by all states, employing the same formula. And, while one particular formula may seem to produce a better result for one state, it is unlikely that consensus would emerge quickly between a group of states, each competing for their share of revenue. Above all, the case emphasises that the underlying question of what links a company to a state, such as to justify making it liable to pay taxation, is a philosophical question with significant economic and political ramifications, not susceptible to being resolved by unilateral determination. The arm's-length method, and the underlying concept of separate corporate personality may be failing states in the global marketplace, where a company can employ a host of modern technological and commercial devices to market and sell their products without establishing a subsidiary or branch. But the task of renewing and replacing these traditional legal concepts is a formidable one.

Controlled foreign corporations and anti-avoidance measures

States have moved beyond the general position outlined above at times in order to effect workable anti-avoidance provisions. One such example concerns arrangements involving the use of Controlled Foreign Corporations

[81] *Ibid.*, p. 263. The Court then turned to the question of whether California's taxing method breached the commerce clause by preventing the nation from speaking with one voice in matters of commerce.

(CFCs). The CFC problem can be summarised by postulating the case of a company A, resident in X, which holds a controlling interest in a foreign subsidiary, C, resident in Z. Under the residence principle, A will be liable in X to taxation on dividends and other income received from C.[82] In order to defer this liability, A transfers its holding in C to B, a wholly owned subsidiary resident in Y, a low-tax jurisdiction.

To counter this sort of tax avoidance, many developed countries have adopted rules under which the payment of dividends to B is treated as a payment to A, making A once again liable to tax on this income in X. Though the corporate personality of B is still formally recognised, the provisions effectively lift the corporate veil from B to expose the tax avoidance. This is, however, the exception to the rule, and will be done generally only in carefully and tightly prescribed circumstances. Such provisions are increasingly common among developed states and the OECD has encouraged their use.

3.2.2 *Restrictions arising from the general principles of jurisdiction*

The first major restriction on the exercise of jurisdiction flows from the distinction between prescriptive and enforcement jurisdiction or *jurisaction* and *jurisfaction*. Prescriptive jurisdiction (*jurisaction*) is the power to make rules or decisions, whereas enforcement jurisdiction (*jurisfaction*) refers to the power to enforce those rules or decisions. States generally cannot take action on the territory of another state to enforce their rules or decisions, except where the consent of the other state has been obtained. It therefore follows that states cannot compel the payment of taxes or disclosure of relevant information by individuals or institutions located in the territory of another state. In exercise of their prescriptive jurisdiction, however, they may frame their laws so as to make such persons liable to taxation or disclosure obligations. This can be done provided that there is an adequate basis for jurisdiction under one of the principles outlined above. So economic activities occurring within the territory of the state, persons resident in the state and nationals (individuals or companies) of the state are regularly subjected to its fiscal jurisdiction, for instance under sales tax, income or corporation tax and taxation of foreign earnings rules. There may be further discretion in relation to acts which impact in some way on the state, either under a legal fiction, such as the *subjective* or *objective* territorial principles, or possibly under an *effects* doctrine. These are less common, sometimes controversial and not frequently encountered in the taxation sphere. However, 'long-arm' jurisdiction has been utilised in the framing of

[82] C may of course already have paid tax on its profits to the host state, Z, and in such a case A must look to bilateral provisions or unilateral rules in X for relief from double taxation: see further Section 4.1.2 below.

anti-avoidance measures, though as Picciotto notes, with some regard to jurisdictional issues.[83] Generally speaking, the discretion of states is wide in relation to taxation and there is no obligation to practise forbearance, for instance to avoid double taxation or to grant 'tax sparing' relief, though many states do so unilaterally or by agreement. Thus, there is no obligation to recognise the primacy of territorial jurisdiction (indeed the *residence*, as opposed to the *source* principle does exactly the opposite), or to avoid undermining the economic policies of other states. Nor is there any closed set of categories of 'taxation' which will be recognised as legitimate: new environmental, local, windfall or other taxes are a constant feature of modern regulatory systems. Academic views are divided on the question as to whether the international rules on state jurisdiction require in principle that there must be some recognised underlying basis for the exercise of fiscal jurisdiction, and no purpose would be served by rehearsing those arguments again here.[84] The tax jurisdiction of states is certainly wide. It is possible to state in principle that if there was no substantial and *bona fide* connection between the taxing state and the persons, transactions or assets to be taxed, then any enforcement action which could be said to amount to a 'taking' of property would amount to an expropriation, rather than a legitimate exercise of taxation powers. However, this arises not from any inherent limitation on jurisdiction to tax, but from the existence of the separate body of rules on the treatment of foreign nationals, discussed at Section 2.2.1.

It is not possible to argue that specific rules relating to fiscal jurisdiction have emerged which have acquired the status of customary international law. States will not normally enforce other states tax demands, but may do, for instance under a co-operation agreement. Many arrangements exist for

[83] Picciotto, *International Business Taxation*, *supra* note 17 at pp. 145–6. Picciotto notes that, in framing rules to deal with CFCs, states have generally accorded with three broad principles for anti-avoidance rules established by the OECD Fiscal Committee: states should seek only 'to maintain equity and neutrality of national tax laws in an international environment' and should therefore (1) target only income that is genuinely passive; (2) target base companies in low-tax jurisdictions only, not companies in countries with comparable taxation; and (3) not treat the base company as non-existent where it has been established in accordance with the laws of another state. *Ibid.*, p. 154. See further OECD Committee on Fiscal Affairs *International Tax Avoidance and Evasion. Four Related Studies* 1987.

[84] Compare Knechtle: 'to the present there has been no internationally recognised principle in public international law which limits the sovereignty of States in fiscal matters' to Martha or Albrecht: A. Knechtle *Basic Problems in International Fiscal Law* 1979 at p. 37; A. R. Albrecht 'The Taxation of Aliens Under International Law' *29 BYIL* (1952) 145 at p. 152 *et infra*. For a discussion see R. S. J. Martha *The Jurisdiction to Tax in International Law: Theory and Practice of Legislative Fiscal Jurisdiction* 1989, Chapters 1 and 2; A. H. Qureshi 'The Freedom of a State to Legislate in Fiscal Matters Under General International Law' *Bulletin for International Fiscal Documentation* (1987) 14; Picciotto, *International Business Taxation, supra* note 17 at pp. 307–8.

the exchange of information, but there are no customary international legal obligations to co-operate in such matters. And though many double taxation treaties have been concluded along the lines of the OECD Model or the UN Model, thus producing patterns of similar provisions, there is no *obligation* to recognise the underlying principles and there are many variations within this body of practice as well as many cases where such treaties have not been concluded. They do not therefore add up to a body of customary international law.[85] The absence of generally accepted obligations in the fiscal sphere underlies the *Barclays Case* discussed above, and is also at the root of the the problems presented by tax havens.[86]

[85] Qureshi, *ibid.*, at p. 19. In any case, the interpretation of such patterns of state behaviour, and the value of such as evidence of 'state practice' within the meaning of Article 38, Statute, ICJ, is problematic. Lillich was fiercely critical of the ICJ's view of the value of lump-sum settlements of international compensation claims in the *Barcelona Traction Case*, R. Lillich 'The Rigidity of Barcelona' Editorial Comment *65 AJIL* (1971) 522. More directly analagous is the question of whether Bilateral Investment Treaties (BITs) have given rise to firm principles of customary international law. This was discussed in Chapter 2, at Section 2.1. See further references cited therein.

[86] Tax havens are beyond the scope of this study. See, however, the discussion on harmful tax competition and the absence of effective co-ordination in Section 5.2.1 below.

4

Taxation of transnational business

4.1 General principles

On the whole, states have preferred to enact limits to their fiscal sovereignty by the conclusion of bilateral treaties, where elements of reciprocity can perhaps be taken into account. Attempts to enact multilateral treaty regimes have been resisted, particularly by the developed states. As noted above, it is not possible to identify any consensus on the extent to which the principles adopted by states in their bilateral voluntary arrangements have become accepted as more generally binding rules of customary international law.[1] Indeed, against the background of such an extensive network of bilateral treaties it could be argued that the question is largely of academic interest only.[2] However, the rules adopted by states in their voluntary undertakings reveal a great deal about the concept of the state and the perceptions of the 'state interest' which underlie their claims of 'right to tax' and their jurisdictional claims. These attitudes and perceptions of the states themselves form an important part of the environment against which current rules and proposed changes should be assessed.

An examination of the rules used by states in the tax sphere can thus be informative not only as a description of current practice, but also to gain insight into the legal and non-legal constraints within which the current regime operates. Certain of these constraints may have to be removed to effect change.

Although domestic law rules for the taxation of transnational business are typified by their detailed complexity, they are underpinned for the most

[1] Section 3.2.2, *supra*.

[2] Note though that the question of the extent to which repetitive practice had led to the formation of a rule of customary international law was at the heart of the dispute between the UK and the US over the unitary tax system employed by California. See further the *Barclays* dispute at Section 3.2.1, *supra*.

part by a small group of relatively simple concepts. These concepts are employed singly or in combination, and adapted to meet the needs of a vast range of practical and legal circumstances. The two primary tasks for taxation regimes are the definition or description of the tax base and the allocation of taxable income or wealth between tax authorities, and it is with these tasks that the basic concepts described here are concerned.

Similarly, rules relating to the taxation of international business have accepted the concept of separate corporate personality.[3] Domestic law provisions concerning the ambit of the state's tax provisions have approached the issue as a jurisdictional one, focusing on the question of whether a particular corporate entity satisfies the criteria which will attract liability to taxation. Commonly states levy taxes on companies which are 'resident', or have their 'seat of management' within the jurisdiction, which are 'established' in the jurisdiction, or which are 'citizens', by virtue of incorporation.[4] These criteria may vary from one form of taxation to another within the same state, with income tax, for instance, typically being applied on a different basis from sales taxes or taxes on employment. Typically, the question of profits distributed to shareholders is dealt with as a separate jurisdictional question, with the effect that the personality of the company and that of the shareholders are recognised as distinct.

Once the threshold criteria are deemed to be satisfied so that the entity is subject to the state's tax provisions, the task begins of determining what income exactly is attributable to that corporate enterprise. This is immensely difficult to determine in some cases where the company is part of a group of companies, not all of which are situated within the jurisdiction. Complex and detailed provisions are commonly employed to determine the question, and to combat avoidance action on the part of the corporate group. Some of these issues are discussed further below.

4.1.1 *Basic tax principles*[5]

The first of these is the concept of *residence*, employed by all jurisdictions to some extent in relation to at least some types of income. Taxation by residence involves taxing income regardless of where it arose at the point of residence of the person, actual or legal, to whom that income accrues. In the UK, for example, income and corporation taxes are levied on the basis of

[3] See further *Barcelona Traction, Light and Power Co. Case (Second Phase), ICJ Reports* (1970) 3.

[4] These concepts do not enjoy uniform interpretations.

[5] See generally A. R. Albrecht 'The Taxation of Aliens in International Law' *29 BYIL* (1952) 145; A. A. Knechtle *Basic Problems in International Fiscal Law* English edn, 1979; S. Picciotto *International Business Taxation* 1992; R. S. J. Martha *The Jurisdiction to Tax in International Law: Theory and Practice of Legislative Fiscal Jurisdiction* 1989.

residence of individuals and of corporations, and residence is defined for this purpose in the tax statutes, case law and decisions of the tax authorities. Companies are regarded as resident if their central management and control are in the UK or if they are incorporated in the UK.[6]

The residence principle stands in opposition to the *source* principle, by which tax is levied on income in the jurisdiction in which the income-producing activity or transaction takes place. It is also commonly used in relation to income tax, recognising the interest that a state has in business transactions taking place within its territory; the UK, for instance, taxes the income of non-residents earned in the UK. Clearly, when these two principles – residence and source – are combined, there is immediate potential for double taxation. Hence, double taxation treaties normally contain a provision whereby one state will recognise up to a certain level the tax liability imposed by the other. The source principle underpins the imposition of sales taxes, levied either at the point of production or at the point of retail sale; in either case, the state is claiming a right to tax the economic activity taking place within its jurisdiction.

Though both the residence and source principles express in a general way the perceived interest of the state in taxing the income or activities in question, neither is self-defining. The residence principle invokes in some way a connection between the individual taxpayer and the state of residence, though this could be justified by reference to some concept either of allegiance or of benefit. Whichever of these notions provides the underlying justification, detailed provisions need to be employed to determine exactly how residence is to be established and how the income accruing to a resident is to be assessed.

Similarly, the source principle depends in its application on a complex array of criteria to determine when income can be said to have arisen in the territory of a particular state. The question is very difficult where the actors have only a transitory presence or no presence at all within the territory of a state. Under traditional 'arm's-length' accounting procedures, heavy reliance is placed on the existence of a permanent establishment within the territory of a state, and an attempt then made to disentangle the transactions of connected businesses to determine which are properly attributable to the activities of that permanent establishment. By contrast, under unitary accounting methods, where formulae incorporating factors such as percentage sales, capital investment and payroll[7] are used to determine the level of economic involvement of a company in a particular jurisdiction, the reliance on the existence of permanent establishment to identify the actor as a taxpayer loses much of its obvious utility. Though modern technology has perhaps undermined the utility of the concept of permanent establishment,

[6] Income and Corporation Taxes Act 1988, ss. 334–6.

[7] See further Section 3.2.1, *supra.*

by vastly extending the possibilities of carrying out business within a jurisdiction while remaining physically outside it, the arm's-length accounting method is still by far the most prevalent.[8]

4.1.2 *Principles employed in the avoidance of double taxation*

In the allocation of taxes between jurisdictions, the most commonly used concepts are those of *tax exemption, tax credit* and *tax sparing*. These concepts are employed both in unilateral measures and in bilateral double taxation treaties and implicitly give priority to the claim of one state to tax the income in question over that of the other. Where this is done on a reciprocal basis, it could be argued that the use of these concepts is influenced only by considerations of convenience, though this argument appears weak in the face of the vast body of practice giving rise to set patterns of deployment of these methods. Where priority is accorded by one state to another unilaterally, clear indications are given as to the perceived 'interest' of the state in taxing the income or transactions in question.

Tax exemption involves one state exempting from its tax regime all or part of the income of a taxpayer, leaving the other to tax the income in question. Frequently, this means in relation to income tax that the state of residence of the taxpayer will forgo taxation of foreign income in favour of the source state, thus ensuring that the resident does not suffer double taxation. The exemption system 'provides an economic incentive for residents to invest in low-tax countries and not to invest in those with high tax rates'.[9] To prevent the taxpayer from utilising such provisions to avoid incurring taxation of part of his/her income at higher marginal rates of taxation, the whole of the taxpayer's income may be used to calculate the extent of the exemption due (exemption with progression).

The *tax credit* method involves the second (residence) state giving the taxpayer credit against his/her tax bill for taxes already paid in source states. Such credit may be partial or full, or may mean only that the second state will calculate tax due on an amount *net* of taxes due or paid in the first state.

[8] See further W. Hellerstein 'Are Days of World-Wide Unitary Taxation by States Limited?' *72 Journal of Taxation* (1990) 172; R. M. Hammer 'Will the Arm's Length Standard Stand the Test of Time? The Specter of Apportionment' in H. H. Alpert and K. van Raad (eds) *Essays on International Taxation* 1993 at p. 201; Picciotto *International Business Taxation, supra* note 5, Chapter Nine; K. Vogel 'World-wide v's Source Taxation of Income – A Review and Reevaluation of Arguments' in C. E. McLure, H. Sinn, P. B. Musgrave *et al. Influence of Tax Differentials on International Competitiveness* 1990, at p. 115.

[9] J. A. Roin 'The Grand Illusion: A Neutral Tax System for the Taxation of International Transactions' *75 Virginia Law Review* (1989) 919 at p. 925 (footnotes omitted). See also UNCTC *International Income Taxation and Developing Countries* (1988), UN Doc. ST/CTC/56 (1988), p. 18.

Depending on the precise system in operation, the tax credit system removes or reduces any incentive for the investor to seek out low-tax jurisdictions for investment.[10] Hence the tax credit method may produce greater neutrality in investment decisions. Arguably, while tax exemption explicitly accords to the first state a 'right' to tax (in the moral or legitimacy sense), tax credit merely recognises the reality that the first state has already exercised its *de jure* power to tax.

Tax sparing, like tax exemption, gives explicit recognition to the legitimacy of the tax policies of the first (source) state, in this case by recognising that that state might wish to offer tax concessions or tax breaks to an enterprise. Under tax sparing provisions the second state, the state of residence, treats the enterprise as if it had already suffered tax at the normal rate in the source country, giving (for example) tax credit on the tax notionally forgone as well as on that levied, since otherwise the policy underlying the offer of a tax break would be undermined by the second state, in whose benefit it would ultimately operate. Recently the practice of tax sparing has come under scrutiny by the OECD and has been questioned on efficiency grounds.[11]

A similar motivation underlies the concept of *withholding* taxes, used in relation to payments of dividends by companies. Typically, company profits are subjected to tax as they arise. However, considerations of equity between taxpayers have led many states to impose further tax if and when profits are distributed to shareholders in the form of a dividend and this is seen by many as establishing a disincentive to companies to distribute profits. Thus dividends, or the company profits from which they derive, may be exempted in part or in whole from tax to prevent the double taxation which would otherwise result and hence to encourage the distribution of profits and potential reinvestment in the market.[12] However, this goal will clearly not be met if dividends are removed from the jurisdiction and as in the case of tax sparing provisions, the state of residence of the taxpayer would receive the benefit of the exemption in such cases. Accordingly, many countries impose withholding taxes which are taxes charged on dividends paid to non-residents.[13]

[10] Roin, *ibid.*, p. 927; UNCTC, *ibid.*, pp. 20–1.

[11] OECD *Tax Sparing: A Reconsideration* 1998. See further Section 5.2.1 below.

[12] In the UK this is done by crediting shareholders with a proportion of the Advance Corporation Tax already paid by the company, which taxholders can then set against their tax bill. This system allows for the maintenance of marginal tax rates vis-à-vis shareholders.

[13] Within the EU, for instance, Directive 435 (1990) provides that witholding taxes shall not be applied to payments of dividends from a company resident in one Member State to a parent company resident elsewhere in the EU, provided that the parent owns at least 25 per cent of the capital of the subsidiary. In addition, the Directive requires that Member States give exemption from tax or full tax credit to all distributions of profits.

4.1.3 *Double taxation treaties*

The existing network of double taxation treaties is extensive – over 1500 such treaties exist worldwide – and the provisions of these agreements can vary considerably. However, most follow the general approach adopted in the OECD Model Double Taxation Agreement.[14]

Chapter One of the Model lays down the scope of the Treaty, both personal and material. The Treaty covers all 'persons' (individuals, companies or other bodies) resident in one or other state, or both; it relates to income taxes, including corporation taxes, and capital taxes such as capital gains taxes, as well as taxes on wages or salaries paid by enterprises. The relevant taxes of each state are generally listed and the list updated annually.

The definitions section in Chapter Two establishes the principal concepts employed in double taxation agreements. The most important of these are 'fiscal domicile' (Article 4) and 'permanent establishment' (Article 5). The 'fiscal domicile' of an individual or company is the state where it is liable to taxation by virtue of 'domicile, residence, place of management or . . . similar' (Article 4(1)) and the Article lays down rules to determine which of the two state parties' claims will be given precedence. Thus, it gives recognition to the state where the person has a permanent home, or failing that the state with which his or her personal and economic relations are closest, or failing that the state where he or she has a habitual abode, or failing that, the state of which he or she is a national (Article 4(2)). Companies 'resident' in both states are deemed to be resident at the place where 'effective management' is situated.

'Permanent establishment' means 'a fixed place of business in which the business of the enterprise is wholly or partly carried on' and includes a place of management, a branch, office, factory, workshop, mine, quarry or building site or similar which exists for more than twelve months. Using these core concepts, the Model adopts the *residence* basis for taxation as its principal tool, then provides for a range of exceptions in relation to different situations and different types of income.

Chapter Three of the Model gives recognition to some common situations where taxation will not be confined to the state of residence: immoveable property may be taxed in the state in which it is situated, business profits attributable to a permanent establishment may be taxed in the state in which the permanent establishment is situated, and dividends and interest payments paid by a resident of one state to a resident of another may be taxed in that other state. Further provisions cover royalties, capital gains,

[14] The first OECD Model Agreement was adopted in 1963. The most recent version is available at the OECD web pages: http://www.oecd.org. A Commentary is also attached. Only the major provisions of the Model Agreement are summarised here. The Model provisions may be amended substantially in negotiations between particular pairs of states.

payment for personal services, directors' fees, the earnings of artists and athletes, pensions and payments to students. Chapter Four (Article 22) gives recognition to the situations where capital will be taxed otherwise than in the state of residence of its owner; capital which is immoveable, or is part of the property of a permanent establishment may be taxed in the state where the property or the permanent establishment respectively is situated.

The operative provisions of the Treaty follow. Chapter Five (Article 23A and B) provides for the use of either the tax exemption or the tax credit method to avoid double taxation. Chapter Six provides for application of the non-discrimination principle to prohibit nationality-based discrimination, to the limited extent that the nationals of one Contracting Party may not be subjected by the other Contracting Party to taxation or tax-connected burdens more onerous than those to which nationals of that state are or may be subjected 'in the same circumstances' (Article 24). Thus, while *direct* discrimination is prohibited, the double taxation agreements do nothing to tackle *indirect* discrimination in the many cases where there are relevant differences in circumstances.[15] This, as will be seen, is one of the areas where the ECJ has been able to progress further in certain respects than individual states in eliminating discrimination and hence levelling the playing field for transnational taxpayers.[16] Discrimination between nationals of different foreign states is often outlawed by the inclusion of an MFN clause in a Protocol.

On the administrative front, the Model makes provision for a Mutual Agreement procedure (Article 25) where, in the event of double taxation, the taxing authorities of the two states can try to reach a satisfactory accommodation, and provision for the exchange of information between the taxing authorities of the two states for the purposes of the Convention (Article 26).

In respect of business taxation, the OECD Model thus affirmed the principle of taxation by *residence*, but the impact of this was significantly abated by the recognition of the *permanent establishment* as a taxable person in its own right. Arm's-length accounting between headquarters and permanent establishment was thus required, and a division of expenses incurred centrally on behalf of or for the purposes of the permanent establishment. The treatment of dividends was an important item which had divided developed

[15] Some of these are specifically recognised in the Model Convention. In relation to the non-discriminatory taxation of permanent establishment, for instance, the Model provides 'This provision shall not be construed as obliging a Contracting State to grant to residents of the other Contracting State any personal allowances, reliefs and reductions for taxation purposes on account of civil status or family responsibilities which it grants to its own residents'.

[16] See further Section 6.2.1 below. For a discussion of the strains imposed on the arm's-length accounting method by the creation of free trade areas, see P. R. McDaniel 'NAFTA and Formulary Apportionment: An Exploration of the Issues' in H. H. Alpert and K. van Raad (eds) *Essays on International Taxation* 1993 at p. 293.

and developing states; companies commonly received a credit or refund of taxation paid on profits which was then distributed and taxed again in the hands of shareholders. However, there was understandable reluctance on the part of capital-importing states to allow this where the dividends were to be paid to foreign shareholders. It now became common to apply a witholding tax, applied when dividends, interest, fees and royalties were remitted out of the jurisdiction. However, the Model Agreement encouraged limits to be placed on this, allowing the state of residence to have a further bite at the cherry after remittance.[17] In respect of dividends, the suggested limit was 15 per cent, but in practice rates vary.

The arm's-length or separate taxation approach of the OECD Model has been heavily criticised in some quarters. Vann argues that it is non-neutral in its impact on taxpayers' behaviour and that subjecting different types of income to different taxation regimes 'encourages taxpayers to recharacterise income to obtain the best tax result'.[18] In particular, the Model is inadequate to deal with the group structure of corporate groups. Separate treatment of related companies causes the problem of treaty shopping and is inadequate as a basis from which to attack the practice of transfer pricing.[19]

A further criticism made by Vann relates to the 'reciprocity' approach advocated by the OECD Model, by which identical tax rates are agreed by both parties, regardless of their internal tax rates or the structure of the trade and commerce between them. This formal reciprocity is obviously far removed from substantive reciprocity in many situations and probably also leads to inequitable differences between the treatment of different taxpayers.

Vann also argues that the Model Tax Treaty and the network of bilateral treaties which it spawns create an illusion that some element of equality and restraint has been introduced into inter-state relations, which he says is not reflected in practice:

> Nations are encouraged to think that the Model will produce formal equality and will restrain more powerful countries in pursuing their self-interests. In fact international tax policy is no different from international policy generally. In the creation of the Model in the first place the policies of the more powerful countries are likely to be dominant, which is certainly the case with the OECD Model. While some restraining influence is no doubt exercised by treaties concluded pursuant to the Model, more powerful countries can still thumb their noses at treaty obligations where political imperatives so dictate. Small countries in particular need to consider whether there are any significant benefits in bilateral tax treaties that cannot be obtained in other ways.[20]

[17] Model Agreement, Commentary.

[18] R. J. Vann 'A Model Tax Treaty for the Asian-Pacific Region?' *Bulletin for International Fiscal Documentation* (1991) 99–111; 151–63.

[19] See further Sections 4.1.4 and 5.2.1 below.

[20] Vann 'A Model Tax Treaty', *supra* note 18 at p. 111.

Dissatisfaction with the emphasis on residence-based taxation of foreign investment in the OECD Model was voiced by developing countries and increasingly within developed states. As noted in Chapter 1, foreign investment was regarded under the classical view as a growth engine for less developed economies, which had the capacity both to stimulate the local economy and to bring increased revenue to the state. However, '[t]o the extent the burden of relieving double taxation fell on the source countries, the developing countries, it translated into a direct loss of revenues and foreign exchange for them'.[21] There was therefore a root contradiction between the policy of encouraging the promotion and protection of foreign investment, and the continued preference for taxation by residence, since the tax receipts gained from foreign investor profits were one of the supposed incentives for the adoption of an open-door policy towards investors. Thus, as Picciotto describes, there was inherent tension over the source/residence question between, on the one hand, the foreign affairs interests of capital-exporting states, the capital-importing states and business interests, and on the other hand, the revenue authorities of capital-exporting states.[22] And despite the fact that Double Taxation Treaties concluded along the lines of the OECD Model had become commonplace between developed states by the late 1960s, developing states remained on the whole rather reluctant participants. In 1967, the UN established a Group of Experts to consider the special problems relating to tax treaties between developed and developing states. After more than a decade of deliberation, the work of this Group culminated in the publication of a UN Model Treaty.

The UN Model Treaty follows very closely the OECD Model, both in form and substance, though with some significant modifications; it retains the central principle of taxation by residence, but broadens many of the definitions used so as to extend the tax base of the source country. For instance, the taxation of a permanent establishment is not confined only to that establishment's activities, but is extended by a 'force of attraction' concept to include other sales by the parent company in the host state of 'goods or merchandise of the same or similar kind as those sold through the permanent establishment'. Similarly, the activities of independent agents, even legally independent foreign subsidiaries engaged in export activities, can at times be treated as activities of the permanent establishment.[23] However,

[21] UNCTC *International Income Taxation and Developing Countries*, *supra* note 9 p. 16. See also C. Irish 'International Double Taxation Agreements and Income Taxation at Source' *23 ICLQ* (1974) 292.

[22] Picciotto *International Business Taxation, supra* note 5, Chapter Two.

[23] For a full discussion of the differences between the OECD and UN Models, see S. S. Surrey 'The UN Group of Experts and the Guidelines for Tax Treaties Between Developed and Developing Countries' *19 Harvard ILJ* (1978) 1. For a discussion of problems reconciling the 'force of attraction' principles with GATT obligations, see J. Fischer-Zernin 'GATT versus Tax Treaties? The Basic Conflicts

these modifications do not constitute any radical departure from the OECD Model. Moreover, the outcome reinforces, rather than addresses, the bilateral treaty approach.

4.1.4 *Transfer pricing and other abuses – combatting avoidance and evasion*

For states' tax laws to be effectively implemented, the general principles outlined above have to be tempered to address the beheviour of tax-payers, who will resort to avoidance and/or evasion strategies to minimise their tax liabilities.

Corporate groups have long presented a major challenge to the established system of treating each incorporated entity separately, and taxing them as they would be taxed if operating at arm's length. The separate taxation of permanent establishment raises similar problems. The first issue which arises is the attribution to the separate entities within a corporate group of both income and expenses incurred by one 'member' on behalf of the group as a whole or other members. This might include expenditure on group headquarters and headquarter functions, or on research, development or marketing which benefits other members of the group, or income such as royalties on assets vested in the parent company but effectively arising from the activities of a subsidiary. The second issue concerns the transparency of intra-group transactions, and this raises the issue of transfer pricing. Transfer pricing occurs when assets, goods or services are passed from one group member to another at a price which varies from that which would have been set had the two entities been dealing at arm's length, with the objective of shifting losses and profits between jurisdictions to obtain tax advantages. Though provisions exist to combat transfer pricing by imposing arm's-length bargaining prices for tax calculation purposes,[24] there are real difficulties for countries in obtaining full information about the operations of groups and in assessing the validity of the prices indicated in company accounts. In some cases, this occurs because of a lack of information or because the taxing state is unable to devote sufficient resources to the problem. In other cases there may be, due to nature of the trade or the MNE in question, no free market in the sorts of goods or services provided by one part of the organisation to another. Additionally, where transfer pricing is tackled, there may not be agreed accounting principles which can be used to the satisfaction of all parties.

Thus the solution embodied in the OECD Model whereby states make unilateral adjustments to the tax liabilities of companies is far from ideal,

---

between International Taxation Methods and the Rules and Concepts of GATT' *21(3) JWTL* (1987) 39 at pp. 56–8.

[24] See, e.g. Article 9, OECD Model.

even if it is accompanied by a provision allowing the company to seek a parallel adjustment in the accounts presented to other interested states.

A number of measures of varying force have been adopted within the OECD to improve upon this situation. First, it should be noted that the OECD Guidelines for Multinational Enterprises[25] provided that enterprises should 'refrain from making use of the particular facilities available to them, such as transfer pricing which does not conform to an arm's length standard, for modifying in ways contrary to national laws the tax base on which members of the group are assessed'. These Guidelines have no binding force and there are no measures for monitoring or otherwise assessing the compliance of enterprises with these standards. In 1995, the OECD approved a set of Transfer Pricing Guidelines for Multinational Enterprises and Tax Administrations,[26] which seek to guide both MNEs and the tax authorities of different states towards consistency in the handling of a range of transfer pricing issues. In addition, the guidelines provide for a monitoring process whereby the OECD Committee on Fiscal Affairs will examine the laws and practices of OECD Member States for consistency with the guidelines, and will identify both good practice and problems to be tackled in the future. Again these are non-binding, though this does not of course necessarily mean that they are ineffective in securing change.

4.2 **Taxation under the World Trade Organisation**

Taxation is implicated as a potential trade barrier under several different WTO obligations. As the WTO now has 135 Members and 36 observers, the obligations arising from WTO obligations are an important source of limitations on tax jurisdiction, regardless of whether WTO rules reflect in any respects customary international law limitations on tax jurisdiction.

4.2.1 *The General Agreement on Tariffs and Trade*

The General Agreement on Tariffs and Trade 1994, concerning trade in goods, requires respect for the 'national treatment' (Article III) and the 'most favoured nation' (Article I) principles in trade between states. Thus, aside from the tariffs agreed in the appropriate schedules to GATT (Article II and Annexes), importing states must refrain from using taxation in ways which breach these obligations directly or indirectly. Exceptions may be

[25] OECD *Declaration and Decisions on International Investment and Multinational Enterprises* 1992. For a discussion see Section 2.2.2, *supra*.

[26] These have since been extended to cover more types of transactions and updated by two annexes (on Monitoring Procedures and of Examples) and a revised Glossary. These developments are discussed further at Section 5.2.1 below.

permitted where these fall within the scope of one of the exceptions to GATT rules contained in Article XX.

While Article I principally concerns customs duties, it extends to 'charges of any kind imposed on or in connection with importation or exportation or the international transfer of payments for imports or exports'. Any tax which flows from importation or exportation will be caught by this provision; in other words, it will be regarded as a disguised customs duty or related 'charge'.[27] The MFN principle requires equality in treatment between imports from different WTO Members, though in certain circumstances more favourable treatment may be extended to less developed states.

Article III:1 deals with internal taxes, charges, laws, regulations and requirements affecting the sale, transport, distribution and use of products and quantitative restrictions concerning the composition of products and provides that such measures must not be protectionist of domestic products or production. Article III:2 provides (first sentence) that imported products will not be subject to any internal taxation or other internal charges in excess of those imposed on like domestic products and (second sentence), that internal taxes and charges will not in any other way afford protection to domestic products. This would be the case where, for instance, an imported product was subject to taxation where a directly competing or substitutable domestic product was not.[28] Article III:4 requires that imported products are treated no less favourably than like domestic products in matters relating to sale, transport, distribution or use.

Thus, whereas customs duties are unlawful only where they exceed tariff bindings in relation to bound products, or where they breach the MFN principle, taxes are unlawful if they discriminate in favour of like domestic production.[29] Generally, the purpose of such taxes is irrelevant, a point affirmed by the Panel Report on *United States – Taxes on Petroleum and Certain Imported Substances* (the Superfund dispute).[30] This prevents the use of the taxation system for a variety of public purposes if the result is discrimination between imported and domestically produced goods. However, GATT Panels have established that in determining whether 'like products' are involved, the limited anti-protectionist objectives of the Article should be borne in mind:

> the purpose of Article III is thus not to prevent contracting parties from using their fiscal and regulatory powers for purposes other than to afford protection to domestic production. Specifically, the purpose of Article III is not to prevent

[27] Panel Report on *United States Customs User Fee*, adopted 2 February 1988, *BISD Supp. 35* 245.

[28] Interpretative Note Ad Article III.

[29] Panel Report on *EEC – Regulation on Imports of Parts and Components*, adopted 16 May 1990, *BISD Supp. 37* 132 at 191–2.

[30] Adopted 17 June 1987, *BISD Supp. 34* 136.

contracting parties from differentiating between different product categories for policy purposes unrelated to the protection of domestic production.[31]

As the US Superfund dispute served to demonstrate, the imposition of a 'green' surcharge on imports to compensate for lower environmental protection standards in other countries would not fall foul of Article III, provided the tax did not exceed the tax which domestically produced products would have borne.[32]

The prohibition on discriminatory taxation in Article III:2 (first sentence) has been found to be absolute and not dependent on proof of trade distortion or nullification or impairment of benefits accruing under other Articles. The provision thus protects 'competitive expectations', that is the relationship between like products in the market, rather than trade volumes or other 'national' concerns. This can be compared with the prohibition on other measures falling under Articles III:1 or III:2 (second sentence), which are prohibited only if protectionist; in relation to such a complaint, the protectionist effect of the measure between imports, actual or potential, and domestic 'like products' would need to be explored.[33] An example can be found in the Panel Report on *Japan – Customs Duties, Taxes and Labelling Practices on Imported Wines and Alcoholic Beverages*.[34] The Japanese system of levying duty on alcoholic beverages according to their 'raw material' content led to differential tax rates on like products, which would be permitted provided the result was not discriminatory. However, since the result was that imported goods were subject to higher rates than domestically produced rates, the system fell foul of Article III:2 (first sentence).[35]

The GATT, and particularly its MFN provision (Article I), applies principally to the treatment of goods rather than traders and hence tends to implicate indirect taxes rather than direct taxes. However, the treatment of manufacturers and traders can have an indirect effect on trade in goods and this is recognised in Article III. However, it is nowhere made clear whether

[31] Panel Report on *United States – Measures Affecting Alchoholic and Malt Beverages*, adopted 19 June 1992, *BISD Supp. 39* 206 at 276. The Panel later notes that the purpose of Article III 'is not to harmonize the internal taxes and regulations of contracting parties'. *Ibid.*, at 293–4.

[32] The Panel noted that the tax on affected imported substances equalled in principle the amount of tax which would have been imposed on the chemicals used in their manufacture if those chemicals had been sold for such a purpose in the US. *Supra* note 30, para. 5.2.9. The national treatment requirement was therefore satisfied. However, a provision for a higher penalty rate of taxation calculated by reference not to the price of the chemicals used in production, but on the value of the imported substances did not satisfy the requirement. *Ibid.*

[33] GATT *Analytical Index: Guide to GATT Law and Practice* 6th edn, 1994 (hereinafter *Analytical Index*) pp. 130–2.

[34] Adopted 10 November 1987, *BISD Supp. 34* 83.

[35] *Ibid.*, at 120–1.

differences in treatment stemming from the existence, or absence, of bilateral arrangements for the avoidance of double taxation fall foul of GATT provisions. This exemplifies the inherent clash between the non-discrimination basis of WTO MFN and national treatment provisions and the more limited reciprocity approach which underlies many international obligations, 'Bilateral treaties, to the extent that they affect international trade, tend to run counter to the GATT most-favoured-nation (mfn) principle, which requires the handling of trade distortions on a multilateral, non-discriminatory level, and stipulates an automatic and unconditional application of trade preferences granted by a GATT state to any other GATT member'.[36]

In some cases, lower rates of taxation or exemptions from taxation, though discriminatory, may be justifiable as permissible subsidies under Article XVI. The Agreement on Subsidies and Countervailing Measures[37] provides that a subsidy exists *inter alia* if 'government revenue that is otherwise due is foregone or not collected (e.g. fiscal incentives such as tax credits)' and a benefit is thereby conferred (Article 1). Article 3 prohibits subsidies contingent in law or in fact upon export performance or on the use of domestic over-imported goods. Other subsidies are actionable if they produce adverse effects; that is, if they cause injury to the domestic industry of another WTO Member, cause nullification or impairment of any benefits accruing to another WTO Member or cause serious prejudice, actual or threatened, to another WTO Member (Articles 5 and 6). Non-specific subsidies, and subsidies for research activities, regional regeneration and environmental improvements are non-actionable, provided certain requirements are met (Article 8).

The Illustrative List of Export Subsidies annexed to this Agreement includes a number of taxation measures. The Agreement provides for a system of notification and regulates the use of countervailing measures by other WTO Members to eliminate the adverse effects of subsidies.

The recent Foreign Sales Corporation (FSC) dispute between the EU and the US involves an alleged export subsidy. The alleged subsidy is paid to FSCs, normally subsidiaries of US corporations based in tax havens such as the Virgin Islands, Barbados or Guam. US firms exporting through such subsidiaries qualify for income relief, provided that a large part of the product is manufactured in the US. Payments by the FSC to its US parent are not subject to US tax, nor are distributions from the FSC to the parent

[36] J. Fischer-Zernin 'GATT versus Tax Treaties? The Basic Conflicts Between International Taxation Methods and the Rules and Concepts of GATT' *21(3) JWTL* (1987) 39 at p. 58.

[37] GATT *The Results of the Uruguay Round of Multilateral Trade Negotiations: The Legal Texts* 1994 at p. 264. For an account see T. Collins-Williams and G. Salembier 'International Disciplines on Subsidies. The Gatt, the WTO and the Future Agenda' *30(3) JWT* (1996) 5.

company, causing the EC Commission to complain that up to 64 per cent of the parent firm's foreign trade income was exempt from tax. The EU lodged a complaint under the WTO Understanding on Dispute Settlement (DSU) regarding this tax exemption, which it argued constituted an export subsidy of $2 billion per year to US firms. Following the failure of consultations, the dispute was referred to a panel in July 1998. In August 1999, it was reported that the Panel's interim report found mainly in favour of the EU and that the US would be given until 1 October 2000 to adapt its laws.[38] The US appealed against the findings of the Panel and the Appellate Body's report was circulated in February 2000. The Appellate Body stressed that it was not ruling that a WTO Member must choose one kind of tax system over another. However, it upheld some of the Panel's findings, including the principal finding that the FSC measure was in breach of Article 3.1(a) of the Agreement on Subsidies and Countervailing Measures and certain provisions of the Agriculture Agreement.

Thus, taxation measures, though discriminatory, may be justified as 'non-actionable subsidies' or maintained as 'actionable subsidies' against which suitable measures may be taken by other WTO Members. Only those most clearly export oriented are prohibited.[39] This helps to clarify the range of possibilities for using the taxation system to pursue public policy goals, most clearly by providing examples in the range of 'non-actionable subsidies' contained in Article 8.

More generally contracting parties may, ultimately, be authorised to suspend GATT concessions or obligations vis-à-vis another party if they consider that any benefit accruing under GATT is being nullified or impaired (Article XXIII). The nullification or impairment is actionable, whether it stems from breach of a GATT obligation, the *application of any measure* or *any other situation*. The *measure* or *situation* may be a fiscal rule[40] or procedure, so that as well as avoiding breaches of specific GATT obligations through fiscal rules, WTO Members need to consider the impact of their fiscal rules and policies vis-à-vis concessions granted within the WTO system.

4.2.2 *Exceptions, variability and historic preferences*

Historically GATT included a range of provisions allowing contracting parties to depart from GATT's basic obligations in a range of situations where genuine national policy concerns, permanent or temporary, arose and these

[38] CCH *Trade Regulation Newsletter*, Issue 6, 1999.

[39] The tax treatment of export earnings was the subject of GATT Panel investigations in four related cases in the 1970s: cf. Panel Reports on *United States Tax Legislation (DISC) BISD Supp. 23* 82, on *Income Tax Practices Maintained by France, ibid.*, 114, *by Belgium, ibid.*, 117 and *by the Netherlands, ibid.*, 137.

[40] A. H. Qureshi 'Trade-Related Aspects of International Taxation. A New WTO Code of Conduct?' *30(2) JWT* (1996) 161 at pp. 161–2.

have been maintained in GATT 1994. Article XX provides a range of general exceptions allowing contracting parties to adopt measures relating to public needs, such as the need to protect public morals, or to protect human, animal or plant life, provided that arbitrary or unjustifiable discrimination does not result,[41] while Article XXI provides an exception in relation to national security. Article XII provides for temporary use of quantitative restrictions on imports to redress balance of payments difficulties[42] and Article XIX allows contracting parties to take temporary and proportionate 'safeguarding' measures against sudden surges of imports which threaten domestic producers.[43] A second feature of GATT is its preservation in certain provisions of historic protections, preferences and/or existing benefits accorded on the basis of reciprocity. This approach is reflected in the concept of 'grandfather rights', in Article I.2, III.6 and elsewhere. Though subject to 'standstill' – leading to the description of GATT as a one-way street in which parties can only move closer to compliance – this results in further fragmentation of GATT obligations. Another feature of GATT historically was the menu approach taken to supplementary understandings and provisions, whereby contracting parties could choose whether or not to accept additions to the original GATT provisions on a case-by-case basis.[44] The Uruguay Round departed from this by obliging all WTO Members to accept all parts of the package, which are presented as annexes to the WTO Agreement. This important development does much to unify the GATT regime, as indeed does the establishment of the WTO itself[45] and the development of a single dispute resolution process.[46]

[41] GATT Article XX. See GATT *Analytical Index* p. 517 and references therein; also the Agreement on the Application of Sanitary and Phytosanitary Measures, GATT *The Results of the Uruguay Round of Multilateral Trade Negotiations: The Legal Texts* 1994, p. 69 *et infra*.

[42] GATT *Analytical Index* p. 327 and references therein. See the Understanding on Balance-of-Payments Provisions of the General Agreement on Tariffs and Trade, GATT *The Results of the Uruguay Round of Multilateral Trade Negotiations: The Legal Texts* 1994, p. 27 *et infra*.

[43] GATT *Analytical Index* 477 and references therein. See the Agreement of Safeguards, GATT *The Results of the Uruguay Round of Multilateral Trade Negotiations: The Legal Texts* 1994, p. 315 *et infra*.

[44] For example the Antidumping Code of 1967 *BISD Supp. 15* 24.

[45] Marrakesh Agreement Establishing the World Trade Organisation, GATT *The Results of the Uruguay Round of Multilateral Trade Negotiations: The Legal Texts* 1994, p. 6 *et infra*.

[46] Understanding on Rules and Procedures Governing the Settlement of Disputes, GATT *The Results of the Uruguay Round of Multilateral Trade Negotiations: The Legal Texts* 1994, p. 404 *et infra*. Reservations may still be used in some circumstances, and many provisions retain an element of flexibility. For a general discussion see, e.g. J. Whalley 'Developing Countries and System Strengthening in the Uruguay Round' in W. Martin and L. A. Winters (eds) *The Uruguay Round and the Developing Economies*, World Bank Discussion Papers 307, 1995, at p. 305.

4.2.3 *The General Agreement on Trade in Services*

The General Agreement on Trade in Services (GATS) concluded during the Uruguay Round establishes a framework for the progressive liberalisation of trade in services. It seeks to ensure respect for the MFN principle, i.e. that there is no discrimination between service suppliers from different third countries (Article II). It also seeks to tackle protectionist national regulations on the supply of services by requiring these to be 'based on objective and transparent criteria, such as competence and the ability to supply the service' (Article VI 4(a)) and 'not more burdensome than necessary to ensure the quality of the service' (Article VI 4(b)). The agreement also promotes the adoption of multilaterally agreed criteria for recognition of service providers and the adoption of common international standards for service provision. In addition to these general provisions, each WTO Member is committed to according 'national treatment', that is treatment no less favourable, to services and service suppliers in the areas listed in its Schedule.[47]

The regime thus created is less well developed than that pertaining to goods, for instance in relation to subsidies which are to be revisited (Article XV). In addition, Article II 2 provides for the maintenance of exemptions from the MFN principle, and a number of service sectors were wholly excluded from the ambit of the agreement.

Subject to these limitations, taxation measures are subject to restrictions under GATS where they discriminate in breach of the MFN principle, where there is a scheduled 'binding' to accord national treatment or where restrictions on the recognition of service providers or on the terms of provision of services do not satisfy the 'objective justification' criteria established in Article IV.[48] Because the commitments extend to both the provision of services and the treatment of 'service suppliers', direct as well as indirect taxes are implicated. However, as opposed to the silence on this matter in GATT, GATS specifically provides that inconsistency with Article II (MFN principle) will not constitute a breach if it stems from the application of an agreement on the avoidance of double taxation (Article XIV (e)). Otherwise, GATS provides a range of exceptions similar to those operable in the GATT framework.

4.2.4 *The Agreement on Trade-Related Investment Measures*

Policies designed to promote inflows of foreign investment into a state, or to promote or protect existing investments, are capable of having distortive

[47] See further Section 7.4 below.

[48] See further Qureshi 'Trade-Related Aspects', *supra* note 40; P. Sauve 'A First Look at Investment in the Final Act of the Uruguay Round' *28(5) JWT* (1984) 5.

effects on trade, and in 1982 a complaint launched by the US against Canada in respect of certain provisions of its Foreign Investment Review Act of 1973 highlighted the relationship between such policies and GATT provisions.[49] This was followed by the inclusion of trade-related investment measures (TRIMs) as a negotiating item in the Uruguay Round[50] and the conclusion of a separate Agreement on Trade-Related Investment Measures[51] at the outcome of that Round.

The TRIMs Agreement commits parties not to utilise TRIMs which are in breach of GATT Articles III (national treatment) or XI (quantitative restrictions). It covers matters such as local content requirements and trade-balancing requirements, ties between import volumes and foreign exchange inflows and export restrictions.[52] Any attempt to use the tax system to confer benefits along such lines would fall foul of these provisions and the basic GATT Articles to which they relate. It is probably safe to conclude that the Agreement on TRIMs adds little to the restrictions on fiscal sovereignty already imposed by GATT itself. Some clarification is introduced by the Agreement on TRIMs and, perhaps, some markers for the future. Article 9 establishes a commitment to return to this area within five years and to consider, as part of a review, whether this Agreement should be complemented with provisions on investment policy and competition policy.

4.2.5 *The Agreement on Trade-Related Aspects of Intellectual Property Rights*

Under GATT Article XX(d) measures may be taken to secure compliance with national laws relating *inter alia* to 'the protection of patents, trade marks and copyrights', subject to the requirement that 'such measures are not applied in a manner which would constitute a means of arbitrary or unjustifiable discrimination . . . or a disguised restriction on international

[49] Panel Report on Canada – Administration of the Foreign Investment Review Act, adopted on 7 February 1984, *BISD Supp. 30* 140; see further Section 7.1 below.

[50] F. Beveridge 'Privatisation and Deregulation – Changing Agendas in the International Law of Private Investment' in J. McEldowney (ed.) *National and International Perspectives on Law and Privatisation* 1999, at p. 168; E. M. A. Knaw '"Trade Related Investment Measures" in the Uruguay Round: Towards a GATT for Investment?' *16 NCJ Int'l L. and Com. Reg.* (1990) 309; T. S. Shenkin '"Trade-Related Investment Measures" in Bilateral Investment Treaties and the GATT – Moving Toward a Multilateral Investment Treaty' *55 U. Pitt. L. Rev.* (1994) 541.

[51] GATT *The Results of the Uruguay Round of Multilateral Trade Negotiations: The Legal Texts* 1994, p. 163, hereinafter the TRIMs Agreement. See further Section 7.3 below and references cited therein. Also P. Low and A. Subramanian 'TRIMs in the Uruguay Round: An Unfinished Business?' in W. Martin and L. A. Winters (eds) *The Uruguay Round and the Developing Economies*, World Bank Discussion Papers 307, 1995, at p. 413.

[52] See the Illustrative List annexed to the TRIMs Agreement.

trade'. However, in the decade preceding the commencement of the Uruguay Round it became clear that while the use of intellectual property laws as disguised protectionism was a potential problem, the absence of any adequate protection for intellectual property was a far greater concern, at least to the US.[53] Hence, Trade-Related Aspects of Intellectual Property Rights (TRIPs) became a negotiation topic in the Uruguay Round[54] and an Agreement on Trade-Related Aspects of Intellectual Property Rights[55] was concluded.

The TRIPs Agreement provides for the application of both the MFN (Article 4) and the national treatment (Article 3) principles in respect of intellectual property protection. The TRIPs Agreement builds on existing Intellectual Property Conventions[56] and to avoid conflict between the approach adopted in these conventions allows departure from the national treatment principle where that was already permitted under these pre-existing agreements. The MFN principle does not feature in these earlier intellectual property agreements and an extensive network of existing agreements provides for a higher standard of protection to be accorded between the Contracting Parties.[57] The TRIPs Agreement provides for these exceptions to be recognised where they derive from pre-existing treaty commitments or as a function of the treatment accorded in another country.[58]

[53] M. C. E. J. Bronkers 'The Impact of TRIPs: Intellectual Property Protection in Developing Countries' *31 CMLR* (1994) 1245; G. E. Evans 'Intellectual Property as a Trade Issue. The Making of the Agreement on Trade-Related Aspects of Intellectual Property Rights' *18 World Competition* (1984) 137.

[54] Ministerial Declaration on the Uruguay Round, GATT Doc. MIN.DEC (20 September 1986, reproduced in *25 ILM* (1986) 1624; T. Stewart (ed.) *The GATT Uruguay Round: A Negotiating History (1986–1992) Vol. II: Commentary* (1993) at p. 2245.

[55] GATT *The Results of the Uruguay Round of Multilateral Trade Negotiations: The Legal Texts* (1994) 336, hereinafter the TRIPs Agreement.

[56] The *Paris Convention for the Protection of Industrial Property*, as revised 14 July 1967, *828 UNTS 305*; the *Berne Convention for the Protection of Literary and Artistic Works*, as revised 24 July 1971, *828 UNTS 221; International Convention for the Protection of Performers, Producers of Phonograms and Broadcasting Organisations*, adopted at Rome on 26 October 1961, *496 UNTS 43*; and the *Treaty on Intellectual Property in Respect of Integrated Circuits*, adopted at Washington on 26 May 1989.

[57] R. Dhanjee and R. L. Boisson De Chazournes 'Trade-Related Aspects of Intellectual Property Rights (TRIPs): Objectives, Approaches and Basic Principles of the GATT and of Intellectual Property Conventions' *24(5) JWT* (1990) 5 at p. 12.

[58] See further J. Reinbothe and A. Howard 'The State of Play in the Negotiations on TRIPs (GATT/Uruguay Round)' *5 EIPR* [1991] 157; Dhanjee and Boisson De Chazournes 'TRIPs' *ibid.*; D. L. Booton 'The Introduction of an Agreement on Trade-Related Intellectual Property Rights into the GATT Framework: International Protection of Patents and the Implications for Developing Countries' (unpublished LL.M. thesis, University of Liverpool, 1994).

Taxation is not explicitly mentioned in this agreement. Article 3 refers to 'treatment . . . with regard to the protection of intellectual property', while Article 4 refers to any 'advantage, privilege or immunity granted' with regard to the protection of intellectual property. It would seem safe to assume that tax treatment of intellectual property matters, such as taxation of royalties, stamp duties on licences, etc., would be included within the purview of these provisions, and that where, for instance, such matters are dealt with in bilateral double taxation treaties or trade treaties between Members departures from the MFN and national treatment principles will be tolerated to the extent detailed in the TRIPs Agreement.

It can therefore be concluded that there are a number of areas where the WTO Agreements restrict the fiscal sovereignty of WTO Members. The main focus of these restrictions is protectionism and this finds expression in the MFN and national treatment principles in each of the areas addressed by the main WTO Agreements. In relation to domestic fiscal policy, the major restraints arise from the obligation to avoid unjustifiable protection of domestic economic activity vis-à-vis foreign competitors, and in particular the restrictions on subsidies. To date, however, only the most clearly trade-distorting practices have been addressed through the WTO Agreements and many national policy concerns are recognised through the range of exceptions, preservation of historic preferences and provisions for departure from WTO obligations in defined circumstances.

5

Challenges to the international legal order

Introduction

The current provisions for the protection and regulation of foreign investment and for the taxation of transnational business, outlined in the previous chapters, are riddled with flaws, whether viewed from an economic, political or legal perspective. In this chapter, a number of the most important criticisms of these provisions will be examined in greater depth, first in relation to foreign investment, then in relation to taxation. In the final section of the chapter, some of the problems common to those provisions will be addressed.

5.1 International law and foreign investment: a critique

5.1.1 *The distinction between direct and indirect investments*

In Chapter 1, it was seen that international law has hitherto only addressed problems faced by *direct* foreign investment, leaving aside the issue of protection of *indirect* investments. Practicality rather than logic dictates that this should be so. There is no reason in principle why claims arising from an injury to a company should not vest in and be handled by the several or many states of whom the shareholders are nationals. Large-scale expropriations involving many investors often will affect nationals of several different states in similar ways, and incidents such as riot or terrorist attack where actionable may also share this feature. Thus it is plausible that separate claims could be pursued by the shareholders' states of nationality. Though this would overlook the 'corporate personality' of the company, it would ensure that all investors were similarly treated in relation to protection and claims, regardless of the particular form of the investment. Arguably it would give due recognition to modern investment forms where the 'indirect' or portfolio investor and the institutional shareholder play a major part in the capitalisation of companies. In addition, it is arguable that a move from recognition of corporate personality to recognition of shareholder interests would reflect a shift in the concerns of states from protection of their own (national) economic interests towards ensuring the free movement of capital more generally. In other words, it would reflect both the trend towards globalisation of capital investments and a growing concern on the part of states that capital movements be unrestricted.[1]

This trend towards establishing a right of free movement for capital is discussed further in Chapters 6 and 7.

5.1.2 *The system of diplomatic protection*

The system of diplomatic protection, stemming from an outmoded notion of allegiance to the sovereign and an associated notion that nationals fall under the protection or 'peace' of the sovereign, seems ill-suited to the reality of modern commerce. The first complaint is that the direct involvement of the home state of the investor serves in most cases merely to politicise the dispute unnecessarily. Indeed many of the initiatives examined in Chapter 1[2] to improve dispute settlement processes follow a strategy of minimising the involvement of the home state by creating instead a right of action, usually under arbitration, for the disgruntled investor. The direct involvement of the home state can be viewed as undesirable from three standpoints.

From the standpoint of the host state, the claim of the home state appears as an attempt to intervene in the state's internal economic policy and hence as an unwanted intrusion on its sovereignty. Moreover, in the negotiation and settlement of a claim between two sovereign states, many factors may come into play, widening the dispute beyond its substance: the claims settlement process is inevitably power rather than rule oriented. A further effect of dealing directly with a foreign government may be to weaken or embarrass the host government at home, since opponents are bound to exploit the issue to claim that the government is weak.

From the standpoint of the home state, the need to place weight on the complaints of an investor who has suffered injury abroad may not be high on the list of priorities of the government; thus the pursuit of claims, though regarded as important from a deterrent perspective, also acts as a disruption to 'normal' diplomatic relations and may not be welcomed. The home state will inevitably have many 'live' issues in its dealings with another government and may be unwilling to risk jeopardising negotiations on some of these by pressing too hard for the settlement of claims. Depending on the nature of the dispute, the home government may not think highly of a particular

[1] See further M. Sornarajah *The International Law on Foreign Investment* 1994 at p. 6 *et infra.*

[2] See further Section 1.3, *supra.*

claim and this may also affect the attitude adopted. The government of the home state may also stand to lose domestically where the investor's expectations are unmet, as opponents attempt to make political capital out of the government's position. While the position of the investor vis-à-vis the home state may vary from state to state, it is clear under the classical international law rules that the international claim is that of the state itself, and the investor itself has no say in the pursuit or settlement of the claim.[3]

From the investor's point of view, the involvement of the home state appears as something of a mixed blessing. In a situation where there seems to be no way that the investor can resolve the matter of the dispute amicably, the home state may be able to bring some weight to bear. There is, however, a risk, that their involvement will serve to escalate the dispute, and render settlement less likely, or bring adverse publicity to the investor who may be intent on protecting its interests in other neighbouring or allied states. The involvement of the home state may also reduce the settlement options available to the investor. In some cases at least, investors might prefer to negotiate directly a new arrangement with the host state, whereby the nature of their holding, or their long-term relationship with the enterprise, can be altered to retain a long-term involvement with the host state, but at the same time satisfying the host government that its concerns have been met: '[u]nless the expropriation is considered part of a generalised attack on foreign capital, most investors would prefer quiet business negotiations, sometimes accompanied by low-key commercial diplomacy . . . as multinational firms take a more self-reliant approach to political risk, they rarely try to raise investment disputes to the intergovernmental level'.[4]

There are many examples where this has been achieved in the past, not least in the oil industry in the Middle East during the 1970s, when the policy of concluding participation agreements in favour of state oil companies was pursued successfully by several OPEC members.[5] In general, the involvement of the home state may make such an outcome less likely. Thus it might be argued that the system of diplomatic protection is too clumsy to serve adequately the needs of the parties in foreign investment disputes.

A more fundamental criticism of the system of diplomatic protection flows from its reliance on the concept of nationality to provide the link between the investor and the home state. Besides the fact that there is no

[3] This is mirrored in UK law, where the Courts have made clear that the matter falls within the Crown Prerogative and cannot be challenged: *Anisminic* v. *Foreign Compensation Commission* [1969] 2 AC 147; *R* v. *Secretary of State for Foreign and Commonwealth Affairs, ex parte Pirbhai* 129 SJ 756, transcript on Lexis.

[4] C. Lipson *Standing Guard. Protecting Foreign Capital In The Nineteenth and Twentieth Centuries* 1985 at p. 123.

[5] Boyd 'Expropriation', *supra* Chapter 1, note 2, Chapter 3 and references cited therein; L. Allen *OPEC Oil* 1979.

uniformity of practice on incorporation, the very notion of the nationality of a company sits uneasily with the move towards the realisation of global capital markets. The latter carries with it the implication that MNEs will form and reform themselves regularly, purely for economic gain, with the place of incorporation, siting of headquarters or place of exercise of central management functions being chosen merely for efficiency and expediency. The practice of companies of operating through locally incorporated subsidiaries and of buying and selling these companies in open financial markets adds to this perception of the nature of the contemporary investment scene.[6] Against this scenario, the link of nationality would appear to carry little meaning, such that continued reliance on this as the basis of diplomatic protection can hardly be justified. The effective and genuine link postulated as the basis of nationality in international law[7] is merely a fiction in relation to the multinational of this scenario, and it should be asked whose interests it serves. Of course this scenario does not correspond entirely to reality; indeed, some would argue that the notion of 'globalisation' in fact provides a smoke screen. Susan Strange points out that labels such as 'multinational' may be misleading, serving to give a company the appearance of operating globally and hence of not being exclusively attached to one particular state, when in fact there is a large coincidence of interests between the home state and the company.[8] Under this scenario, the company, though organised in a group structure with many foreign subsidiaries, continues to advance the interests of the state by coincidentally promoting other national companies (e.g. by using their products or services), by serving the interests of their consumers (by sourcing materials or manufacturing goods cheaply abroad) and of course by paying taxes on their global profits at least in part to the home state. Yet even under this scenario, there would seem little reason to acknowledge a claim for the home state where a foreign subsidiary suffers at the hands of a host state. By comparison with the individual traveller or migrant, the 'multinational' company is very well equipped to anticipate, analyse and protect itself against the political risks encountered in the pursuit of commercial interests.

[6] For a discussion of MNE organisational issues see P. T. Muchlinski *Multinational Enterprises and the Law* 1995, Chapter 3 'Business and Legal Forms of Multinational Enterprise: Towards a Theory of Control' (pp. 57–89). Muchlinski observes that legal forms may not coincide with business organisation within a firm: 'This may lead to a mismatch between the firm's control structures and the legal structures through which the firm is sought to be regulated, to the detriment of effective regulation'. *Ibid.*, p. 57. See also T. L. Brewer and S. Young *The Multilateral Investment System and Multinational Enterprises* 1998 at pp. 11–13.

[7] For a discussion see Section 3.1.2, *supra*.

[8] S. Strange '*Cave! Hic Dragones*: A Critique of Regime Analysis' in P. F. Diehl (ed.) *The Politics of Global Governance: International Organisations in an Interdependent World* 1997, p. 41 at p. 46.

In addition there is an unpalatable asymmetry between continued recognition of the right of diplomatic protection over companies operating abroad, and the adamant rejection by the OECD of any duty to impose binding obligations on those same companies in respect of their foreign operations.[9]

5.1.3 *International protection discourages localisation*

A third argument against the current system for the protection of foreign investments is that it discourages localisation of firms and hence weakens the ability of the host state to ensure that the benefits flowing from the foreign investment are maximised. This argument is based on the assumption that the priorities of the local subsidiary or branch of a multinational are determined by or in the interests of the firm, and that this is so even where greater opportunities exist within the host economy from which the subsidiary or branch operating alone could benefit. An example is where the group structure determines that the local subsidiary should specialise in a small number of products, possibly though not necessarily for export, whereas the local economy offers great diversification opportunities which do not accord with the group corporate priorities and which are hence ignored. Though in a perfect market situation another investor would step in to take those opportunities, this is not a reality, especially in many less developed countries where investment capital is in short supply. The argument extends to political as well as commercial gains. Where a locally incorporated firm is in fact responsive to a command centre or network outside the jurisdiction, rather than (or in addition to) the local rulers, it may be harder to persuade the firm to respond to political pressure, whether from within or outside the government. Thus campaigners on social, environmental and consumer issues, as well as governments, may regard the delocalised nature of foreign investment as a barrier to effective governance of the local subsidiary or branch.[10] Of course, the constantly updated international perspective of the firm, together with the advantages in marketing, access to technology and fluid financial arrangements, contributes to the frustration of local preferences by making exit from the host state an ever-present threat. The economic reality is that the priorities of the firm are determined elsewhere already.

Against this background, it should be asked whether it is inevitable that systems for the protection of foreign investment should recognise and possibly reinforce this aspect of reality, or whether they should attempt to mitigate it. Legal recognition of the interests of the home state in such circumstances originated in the ages of discovery, conquest and colonisation; a re-examination of its role in the contemporary world is called for.

[9] See Section 2.2.2, *supra*.

[10] M. H. Shuman 'GATTzilla v. Communities' *27 Cornell ILJ* (1994) 527.

One response would be that without the element of delocalisation or 'internationalisation' which systems for the protection of foreign investment bring, investors would be wary of committing their capital in other jurisdictions, to the detriment of those states and also of their home states. Yet it is not clear that investors are affected at all by the existence of systems for their protection in ways to which the market could not respond, for instance through insurance. After all, the existence of international legal guarantees about standards of treatment do not guarantee anything, not even compensation, in the event of a breach.

5.1.4 *The focus on property aspects of the investment relationship*

Until very recently, international law has been concerned almost exclusively with the question of expropriation, as noted in Chapter 1, and has ignored wider questions about the regulation or treatment of foreign investment. Where wider issues have been addressed, in the OECD and in UNCTAD, it has not been possible to agree on binding legal obligations; rather non-binding Codes of Conduct have been adopted. There has therefore been a strong focus on property aspects of the foreign investment relationship, at the expense of other aspects of both MNE behaviour and the treatment of foreign investment by governments. This has had consequences for the way in which debates over the treatment and regulation of foreign investment have been conducted. The focus on property aspects of the relationship has placed in the centre of the global stage a particularly Western legal concept of property and this has highlighted tensions between legal cultures, rather than goals they may share. In addition, the concept of the sanctity of property, harnessed together with the classical view of foreign investment as a 'good' thing, have served to discourage disaggregation of the 'good' and the 'bad' in foreign investment relationships. There has been a tendency to view these relationships as 'property' relationships, rather than as economic or social relationships. Thus wider issues of social and environmental protection and of consumer protection have not been accommodated readily in legal discourse regarding the protection and regulation of foreign investment, and more generally the debate about foreign investment has not assimilated current notions of 'good governance' either in relation to companies or governments.

5.2 International law and taxation: a critique

The international patterns of taxation of transnational enterprises are characterised by loose co-ordination, rather than any strategic co-operation or harmonisation. Moreover, it is hard to detect any coherent policy objectives of states in the international arena, besides the rather vague aspirations to protect their own tax base, while avoiding undue distortions in capital movements through double taxation. A major problem facing the international community, and one which makes very difficult the task of setting policy objectives, is the 'free rider' problem, epitomised by the tax haven, but in reality endemic in a system where competition between states to attract investment and to secure their own individual tax bases is largely unfettered. In addition, the current 'system', the product of unilateral and bilateral action, steered in some areas by loose co-ordination, has developed with scant attention to issues of equity between states, and this is of particular concern to developing states as they seek to develop coherent fiscal discipline.

5.2.1 *The absence of effective co-ordination*

Taxation policy is subject to a degree of co-ordination at the international level, most noticeably evidenced by the vast network of double taxation treaties which the OECD and UN Model Double Taxation Treaties have spawned. Though not uniform, these treaties produce a plethora of bilateral arrangements similar in form and in the underlying principles deployed. Tax rates applying to various types of activity are subject to negotiation under the Models, but the guidance exerted by the Models, combined with competitive forces, has produced cluster patterns of similar rates at or above the 'norms' established in the Models.

However, there remain many differences, both major and minor, between the tax laws of different states affecting foreign investment and this raises a number of distinct questions.

First there is an obvious point that investors operating in several different states will face an array of different provisions, so that compliance is expensive. While many investors will seek to maximise their profits by utilising the differences between states' laws to their advantage, there is clearly also a loss of efficiency stemming from these differences, which erodes profits and hence taxes.[11] Little, if anything, has been done which directly aims at reducing this 'double burden' element in the current regime; indeed any suggestion that this should be done would seem superfluous at present, given the wide disparities between national regimes.

A second consequence of the lack of effective co-ordination is that the 'solution' hitherto adopted by many states attempting to give coherence to their treatment of foreign investment is a defensive or sub-optimum strategy in which each state tries to protect its own tax base in the face of intense competition from other states keen to attract foreign investment, increasing globalisation of capital and capital movements and the increasing sophistication of foreign investors themselves. Yet the demand to improve the efficiency of the international tax system to maximise the benefits flowing from the foreign investment may conflict with the desire of states to retain sovereign

[11] Thus investors, host state and home state all stand to lose.

power. Moreover, the equation is not the same for all states – improved co-operation could not necessarily be achieved without greater equity, which would produce winners and losers.

The body able to exert the greatest influence on taxation policy has proved to be the OECD.[12] The OECD is composed of the richest states in the world and currently has a membership of twenty-nine. Members have to demonstrate their commitment to the principles of the market economy, pluralist democracy and respect for human rights. Under Article 2 of the OECD Convention, Members undertake to ensure economic growth and external and internal stability, to reduce obstacles to trade in goods and services, to liberalise movements of capital and to contribute to the economic development of all the world's countries.[13] The OECD's Committee on Fiscal Affairs has played a very significant role in the co-ordination of state action in relation to Double Taxation Agreements and has conducted many studies into the implications and effects of the current arrangements for taxation of transnational business. The greatest contribution of the OECD has undoubtedly been the establishment and periodic amendment of the OECD Model Double Taxation Convention. More recently, the OECD has extended its interest into a wider range of tax matters, attempting to take a lead in addressing these issues at a global level (despite its limited membership).

In 1995, the OECD produced substantially revised *Transfer Pricing Guidelines*.[14] The *Transfer Pricing Guidelines*, first published in 1979, aim to assist both companies and tax administrators to develop a uniform and consistent approach to the problem of transfer pricing. Based on the arm's-length principle, the Guidelines seek to ensure that competition principles are respected by substituting 'market' prices for those agreed between associated enterprises. In 1998, the original Guidelines were supplemented by an annex on monitoring procedures[15] and an annex containing examples to illustrate the operation of the Transfer Pricing Guidelines.[16]

[12] Between 1920 and the Second World War, significant work was done by the Financial Committee of the League of Nations and their Committee of Technical Experts and, from 1928, by the League's Fiscal Committee: S. Picciotto *International Business Taxation* 1992, Chapter One.

[13] Convention on the Organisation for Economic Co-operation and Development (OECD), Paris 1960 and Associated Protocols, *888 UNTS* 179, as amended. Members also undertake to supply each other and the Organisation with information necessary to the Organisation's work, to enable consultations, studies and projects and to co-operate closely including, where appropriate, in co-ordinated action: *ibid.*, Article 3.

[14] Transfer Pricing Guidelines for Multinational Enterprises and Tax Administrations (OECD, 1995).

[15] Transfer Pricing Guidelines for Multinational Enterprises and Tax Administrations, Annex: Guidelines for Monitoring Procedures on the OECD Transfer Pricing Guidelines and the Involvement of the Business Community (OECD, 1998).

[16] Transfer Pricing Guidelines for Multinational Enterprises and Tax Administrations, Annex: Examples to Illustrate the Transfer Pricing Guidelines (OECD, 1998).

Two more recent themes to be addressed by the OECD are tax sparing and tax competition. In relation to tax sparing, an OECD study published in 1998 concluded that the practice of a number of countries of including tax sparing clauses in Double Taxation Agreements was increasingly problematic. Besides their acknowledged distortive effects, tax sparing clauses were *inter alia* vulnerable to taxpayer abuse, they might in some circumstances undermine the goal of attracting foreign investment (and reinvestment of profits) by encouraging repatriation of profits and they are a rather blunt and inefficient method of granting foreign aid.[17] The study included a number of best practice guidelines to be observed in the negotiation of tax sparing clauses and led to the adoption by the OECD of a Council Recommendation endorsing the findings of the report.[18] This recommends to OECD Members *inter alia* that they restrict the use of tax sparing clauses to the poorest states, possibly with a 'sunset clause' built in; in addition, it is suggested that investors should only be able to benefit for a fixed number of years. Perhaps most important of all, a number of recommendations are made which are directed at combating abuse by investors and host states alike. In addition, the Recommendation instructs the Committee on Fiscal Affairs to continue its work in this area and to develop a dialogue with non-Member states 'with the aim of developing a more coherent position on the granting and design of tax sparing'.[19]

The approach of the OECD to this issue is therefore non-binding. This is in keeping with the general approach of the OECD, which generally can only take binding Decisions by 'general consensus' and which often prefers the non-binding Recommendation.[20] This consensus-based approach has only rarely been departed from[21] by the OECD and may be viewed as particularly appropriate in an area where full compliance can only be achieved through the renegotiation of a plethora of Double Taxation Agreements.[22]

[17] OECD *Tax Sparing: A Reconsideration* (OECD, 1998); also OECD 'Is there a need to re-evaluate Tax Sparing' http://www.oecd.org/daf/fa/MATERIAL/c_sparg.HTM.

[18] Recommendation of the Council on the Granting and Design of Tax Sparing in Tax Conventions (OECD, 1998).

[19] *Ibid.*, III.

[20] OECD Convention, *supra* note 13, Articles 5 and 6. Provision is made for the abstention of a Member from a vote on a Decision or Recommendation: in such a case the Decision or Recommendation is valid but is not applicable to the abstaining Member (Article 6).

[21] The alternative course of action open to the Organisation is to negotiate the text of a multilateral treaty to which its members can then accede, such as was proposed in the unsuccessful Multilateral Agreement on Investment (MAI) negotiations; see further Section 7.4 below. This approach has not been used in relation to fiscal matters except in the Council of Europe/OECD Convention on Mutual Administrative Assistance in Tax Matters 1988, *ETS No. 99*.

[22] Some states will be in a position to effect compliance, in part at least, through unilateral action; i.e. by amending their tax laws and/or practices. However a

Moreover, the OECD seeks to extend its influence beyond its membership, exercising a global co-ordinating function, so that the issue of whether the Guidelines are binding vis-à-vis its Members is not crucial to the attainment of the OECD's objectives. However, while perhaps indicating the appropriateness of the OECD's approach to the policy environment in which they operate (albeit by choice), these factors underline both the absence of any strong central force for change and the clumsiness of the resultant arrangements when a collective will for change is demonstrated. There is nothing even approaching a legislative technique, still less a legislature, in the field of international law and taxation. Nor is there any formal arbitration or adjudicative mechanism to fall back on if Members subsequently dispute the meaning of any Decision or Recommendation. Any such matters would have to be referred back to the full OECD membership for resolution under the 'general consensus' approach, unless resolved by informal or *ad hoc* mechanisms.

A further area to come under scrutiny in the OECD recently is 'harmful' tax competition; that is, the operation of tax havens and preferential tax regimes in ways which are 'harmful'. An important study *Harmful Tax Competition: An Emerging Global Issue* was published by the OECD in 1998 and was accompanied by the adoption of Guidelines in this area.[23] The notion of 'harm' is central to the OECD's work on tax competition, and, arguable, to the OECD's work on taxation and investment more generally, so this report is of wider interest than to its immediate audience of tax administrators. Harm is placed in the context of increasing globalisation and liberalisation (particularly of capital movements), which are cornerstones of the OECD's work and which are recognised as providing increased opportunities for tax evasion and avoidance, leading in turn to increased resort to tax havens and sharper competition between governments to attract economic activity. The report argues that this requires a response from states '[i]f nothing is done, governments may increasingly be forced to engage in competitive tax bidding to attract or retain mobile activities. That "race to the bottom", where the location and financing decisions become primarily tax driven, will mean that capital and financial flows will be distorted and it will become more difficult to achieve fair competition for real economic activities'.[24] The consequences of this are then related to the economy of individual states:

---

significant proportion of the issues are covered by Double Taxation Agreements or by the co-operation agreements and co-operative practices which facilitate their implementation.

[23] Council Recommendations and Guidelines for Dealing with Harmful Tax Practices *OECD C(98)17* (OECD, 1998).

[24] *Harmful Tax Competition: An Emerging Global Issue, Synthesis and Summary of Recommendations*, http://www.oecd.org/daf/fa/tax_comp/taxcomp.htm.

> it will become more difficult to collect taxes on income from mobile activities. If spending is not reduced to make up for this revenue loss there is a real risk that taxes on labour, consumption and non-mobile activities will need to be increased. This shift will make tax systems less equitable and, by narrowing the tax base, will introduce further distortions. By increasing non-wage labour costs, it may also have a negative impact on employment.[25]

The report differentiates between three situations where there are differences in tax burdens on geographically mobile activities:

1 where the first country is a tax haven, i.e. imposes no or only nominal tax on income;
2 where the first country collects significant revenues from individual or corporate income, but has in its tax system preferential features which allow particular income to be subject to low or no taxation;
3 where the first country collects significant revenues from individual or corporate income, but the effective tax rate is lower than that applicable in another country.

The report adopts the view that the first two situations are harmful, whereas the latter is not, presumably falling within the scope of 'acceptable' competitiveness.[26]

The report further identified four 'key factors' which would assist in identifying harmful preferential tax regimes:

1 the regime imposes a low or zero effective tax rate on the relevant income;
2 the regime is 'ring-fenced';
3 the operation of the regime is non-transparent; and
4 the jurisdiction operating the regime does not effectively exchange information with other countries.

Regimes would be evaluated as harmful which had the low or zero tax rates referred to in (1), combined with one or more other factors. It is noticeable that only (1) relates to the substance of harmful tax competition; the remaining three factors relate more to the 'trappings' of tax havens than to any notion of unfair competition *per se.* As will be seen, the validity of these criteria was challenged by two OECD Members, Luxembourg and Switzerland, both highly concerned about the implications for bank secrecy.[27]

[25] *Ibid.*

[26] This view was not shared by Switzerland, which thought the second situation also should be viewed as beneficial competition.

[27] Recommendation 7 requires countries to review their laws, regulations and practices relating to bank secrecy 'with a view to removing impediments to the access to such information by tax authorities'. Recommendation 8 addresses the issue of information exchange between tax authorities.

The OECD's response, a set of non-binding guidelines, builds to a large extent on existing national and bilateral measures (the network of Double Taxation Conventions). As was noted in relation to transfer pricing, this approach highlights the clumsy nature of the current arrangements, since both national and bilateral arrangements may be slow and difficult to reform. However, a new body, the OECD Forum on Harmful Tax Practices, is established to oversee the required reforms and the implementation of any future recommendations in this area. The Forum will also engage in a dialogue with non-Member states, where appropriate using the fora offered by other tax organisations, with the aim of promoting the Recommendations to those non-Member states.

There is nothing surprising in the way in which the notion of harm is discussed in *Harmful Tax Competition* – as noted, it falls squarely within the dominant economic ideology favoured by the OECD. Moreover, by focusing on the potential economic detriment to states, whether OECD Members or not, the report provides the rationale for compliance with the guidelines. However, this report and the Recommendations and Guidelines for dealing with Harmful Tax Practices contain a clearly censorious message, which is new. The OECD's activities have normally rested on mutual self-interest. The conclusion of Double Taxation Agreements, for instance, was promoted as a means to encourage foreign investment, thereby boosting levels of economic activity. In any case, the same result could be achieved by states acting unilaterally, and this was regarded as an acceptable alternative strategy. Moreover, failure to tackle actual or potential double taxation by one means or another, while it might hurt some foreign investors, would ultimately hurt the host and home states involved more. Thus, where there was reciprocity in investment flows, the losses involved in agreeing to abate taxing powers would partly be addressed by reciprocal application of the agreed principles, and even in the absence of reciprocity of investment flows the losses would in theory be cancelled out by the indirect benefit of increased flows of foreign investment stemming from the increase in investor confidence and security. In summary, Double Taxation Agreements were good for foreign investment and foreign investment was good for states.

The report on *Harmful Tax Competition* and the Recommendations and Guidelines for dealing with Harmful Tax Practices move away from this mutual self-interest approach. These measures carry the suggestion that failure to implement the Guidelines will in itself be construed as anti-social behaviour, thus introducing a new, more directive tone to OECD policy. Interestingly this new tone is also applied to the 1995 Guidelines on Transfer Pricing[28] through Recommendation 6,[29] which states that countries should 'follow the

[28] *Supra* note 23.

[29] That is, the Recommendations and Guidelines for dealing with Harmful Tax Practices, *supra* note 23.

principles set out in the (Transfer Pricing Guidelines) and thereby refrain from *applying or not applying* their transfer pricing rules in a way that would constitute harmful tax competition'.[30] This more directive tone is evident also in the establishment of the OECD Forum on Harmful Tax Practices, which will play an active role in promoting the OECD's policies in this area and in the setting within the Guidelines[31] of deadlines for the removal by Members of harmful features of their own tax regimes.[32]

Thus it seems that the OECD is beginning to give more shape to community concerns over the fiscal policies of some states, whether Members or non-Members, and to initiate action to address these concerns. At present the OECD favours 'soft' instruments such as resolutions and guidelines which are of limited legal effect, depending for their effectiveness more on consensus. However, the restricted membership of the OECD and the current popularity of the liberalisation agenda have enabled the OECD to reach agreement across a range of specific areas, including those referred to above.

Note, though, that two Member states, Luxembourg and Switzerland, were not parties to the consensus on the issue of harmful tax competition. Both objected to the focus of the Committee on Fiscal Affairs on geographically mobile activities such as financial and other service activities, arguing that a more comprehensive approach was required, both *in abstracto* and according to the Committee's mandate. Luxembourg in particular seemed to regard the Recommendations as an attack on bank secrecy, a view shared by Switzerland. Switzerland also objected to the criterion adopted in the report for the identification of harmful preferential tax regimes, arguing that not enough recognition was given to the positive effects of tax competition:

> The Report recognises that each State has sovereignty over its tax system and that levels of taxation can differ from one State to another. However, that same Report presents the fact that tax rates are lower in one country than in another as a criterion to identifying harmful preferential tax regimes. This results in unacceptable protection of countries with high levels of taxation, which is, moreover, contrary to the economic philosophy of the OECD.[33]

[30] *Ibid.*, Recommendation 6, emphasis added.

[31] Guidelines for Dealing With Harmful Preferential Tax Regimes in Member Countries. These guidelines are an integral part of the document Recommendations and Guidelines for Dealing with Harmful Tax Practices, *supra* note 23, and appear in a 'box' between Recommendations 15 and 16.

[32] Guideline 3. Members are also guided to refrain from introducing any new harmful measures (Guideline 1). The OECD Forum on Harmful Tax Practices will maintain a list of such practices (Guideline 2) which 'will be reviewed annually to delete those regimes that no longer constitute harmful preferential tax regimes' (Guideline 3). Thus OECD Members whose own laws and practices do not conform to the Guidelines will be 'named and shamed', a pragmatic stance, perhaps, in light of the intention of the Organisation to seek to export its policies to non-Members.

[33] OECD *Harmful Tax Competition, supra* note 24, Statement by Switzerland. Luxembourg and Switzerland abstained.

The recent OECD initiatives on tax sparing and on harmful tax competition demand normative action on the part of Members and seek also to influence non-Members. It remains to be seen whether the OECD is successful in its goal of providing a strong impetus for greater co-operation. It also remains to be seen how effectively the OECD and its Members are able to export its solutions to non-Members.

5.2.2 *Issues of equity between states*

The issue of equity between states refers to the underlying moral question of which state(s) should receive tax revenue from the various activities of particular economic actors. Characteristics of both the act and of the actor may enter the equation. The issue of equity in taxation is extensively discussed by political theorists; however, the majority of these writings focus on the internal or domestic context, asking questions essentially of equality of treatment of taxpayers similarly situated (horizontal equity) or differently situated (vertical equity). The extension of the scope of domestic tax regimes to cover non-resident earners or the foreign-earned income of residents is normally addressed by extending existing domestic concepts of equity, for instance by pointing to the unequal tax burden between taxpayers if foreign earnings were not taxed. This issue was of particular concern also from an economic perspective; businesses focused on the lack of neutrality and were particularly concerned, for instance in the UK, that foreign firms might gain an unfair advantage.[34] The underlying concept of horizontal equity is also the concept behind the notion of 'double' taxation.[35] However, equity here is defined very narrowly, looking only at the income of the taxpayer and not at its source. The question is often put whether an imaginary taxpayer in Kansas will understand why his neighbour, who receives the same income but from foreign sources, pays less tax. Vogel challenges the narrow focus of this question, arguing that there are relevant differences between the two taxpayers which ought to be taken into account; moreover, he suggests, the neighbour in Kansas would understand these differences if apprised of the facts.[36]

Focus on the issues of *inter-personal* equity – that is, the issues of equity arising between two taxpayers – reduces equity to a very limited formal role, though of course there are important and troubling questions about how equality between taxpayers is to be assessed. Moreover, the question is normally put in the context of a self-contained state. Questions of equality

[34] S. Picciotto *International Business Taxation* 1992, Chapter One.

[35] The notion of 'double taxation' sets up a comparison between the taxpayer who pays 'normal' levels of tax and the taxpayer who pays 'double'. It has therefore taken on a pejorative implication.

[36] K. Vogel 'World-wide v's Source Taxation of Income – A Review and Reevaluation of Arguments' in McLure, Sinn, Musgrave *et al. Influence of Tax Differentials on International Competitiveness* 1990, p. 115 at 156–8.

of treatment between taxpayers in different states are not regarded as apt, because the principle of state sovereignty includes the right of each state to determine its own tax rates and system (and thus, apparently, legitimises differences in treatment between taxpayers in different states). But questions of the treatment of foreign earnings, or the taxation of non-residents, cannot be addressed merely by comparing the income of different taxpayers; consideration must be given to the relationship between the taxpayer and the state, the vertical relationship. Thus 'equity' in these situations can only really be addressed by examining the underlying justifications for taxation, since it is only by assessing the moral basis of the state's assertion of a right to tax that equality of treatment can be assessed. Equity in this wider sense might encompass notions of substantive, as opposed to merely formal, equality.[37] In situations where more than one state has a legitimate fiscal interest in the activities or income of a particular taxpayer, the extent of their respective interests can only be determined by examining the nature of their relationships to the taxpayer, and by comparing the two relationships. *A priori* if equity can be realised in the vertical relationships between taxpayers and states, inter-personal equity will have been achieved.

Inter-nation equity, however, has a further dimension. Superficially, it might appear that if states have taxed individuals only to the extent justified by the nature of their relationship with the taxpayer, then the resulting distribution of revenue between states will be equitable. However, equity in the broader sense outlined above might necessitate some redistributive function; preferential treatment for developing countries in the use of tax sparing clauses is one example of this in practice.

It is, however, an exception, rather than the rule, that such considerations of equity are explicitly addressed in current international tax practice. The absence of effective co-ordination or of coherent policy goals means that there is no general capacity in the international tax system for any redistributive function to be addressed. While double taxation treaties, by allocating tax competences between states, play a significant role in determining how revenues fall to be divided, it should be remembered that they are only a part of the picture, governing only a fraction of transnational fiscal relationships. It is through the principles of jurisdiction discussed in Chapter 3, as applied through established taxation practices and methods, that the issue of equity is currently mediated.

Yet it was seen in Chapter 3 that existing principles of jurisdiction fail to prescribe either inclusively or exclusively those relationships which they seek to govern, either in a horizontal or a vertical dimension. Similarly, Vogel reminds us that the concepts of 'source' and 'residence' used to determine

[37] It is anyhow arguable that vertical equity, as traditionally posed, necessitates considerations of substantive equality; the different levels of tax burden to be imposed on taxpayers differently situated cannot be set without reference to some broader distribution policy.

the right of states to tax particular persons or activities are not self-defining; thus a discussion of inter-nation equity needs to supply its own definitions.

5.3 **Structural limitations of the international legal system**

The development of an effective regime in relation to either the regulation or taxation of foreign investment depends on both the emergence of a consensus over the rules to be followed and on the effective implementation of those rules. Yet in recent years there has been abundant evidence that states still seek to defend their own narrowly conceived state interests over wider community interests. Two specific problems are pertinant in this context. The first is the problem of one state seeking to impose its political viewpoint on other states in a way that contravenes established international law rules. Epitomised by the Helms–Burton dispute between the US and many of its major trading partners, the problem is particularly acute when the state in question is a powerful one and is one which is prepared to adopt measures having extra-territorial effect. An account is given below of the Helms–Burton dispute and of the legacy it leaves in relation to the negotiation of future disciplines on the regulation and taxation of foreign investment.

A second and more general problem relates to the position of the 'free-rider', the state which seeks to remains free from the obligations entailed by participation in a legal regime or network of obligations, but which nevertheless benefits from such participation by other states. The concept of sovereign equality and the doctrine of sovereign equality of states means that this is an intractable problem in international economic relations. But there are growing indications that states which perceive their interests to be damaged by such states are increasingly prepared to adopt courses of action which make the free rider's position at least uncomfortable if not untenable.

5.3.1 *Unilateralism – the Helms–Burton dispute*[38]

The US Helms–Burton Act[39] was introduced in July 1996. The Act provided for a broad package of measures to be taken against Cuba to encourage

[38] B. M. Clagett 'Title III of the Helms–Burton Act is Consistent With International Law' *90 AJIL* (1996) 434; K. J. Kuilwijk 'Castro's Cuba and the US Helms–Burton Act' *31(3) JWT* (1997) 49; A. V. Lowe 'US Extraterritorial Jurisdiction: The Helms–Burton and D'Amato Acts' *46 ICLQ* (1997) 378; S. Smis and K. van der Borght 'The EU–US Compromise on the Helms–Burton and D'Amato Acts' *93 AJIL* (1999) 227; J. L. Snyder and S. Agostini 'New US Legislation to Deter Investment in Cuba. A First Glance' *30(3) JWT* (1996) 37; B. Stern 'Can the US Set Rules for the World?' *31(4) JWT* (1997) 5; O. Q. Swaak-Goldman 'Who Defines Members' Security Interests in the WTO?' *9 Leiden JIL* (1996) 361.

[39] US Cuban Liberty and Democratic Solidarity (Libertad) Act of 1996, Public Law 104–114-Mar. 12, 1996, reproduced at *35 ILM 357* (1996) (hereinafter Helms–Burton Act).

democratisation, economic reform, respect for human rights and free movement of persons. Through this Act the US applied pressure not only to Cuba, but to third states whose more active support was sought for US Cuban policy.

Title I of the Helms–Burton Act provides for the strengthening of international sanctions against Cuba over a wide field. The acts of the Castro government 'including its massive, systematic, and extraordinary violations of human rights' are determined to present a threat to international peace and the President is instructed to seek the imposition of UN sanctions in the form of an embargo.[40] The Cuban government is also warned that the completion of a nuclear power facility in Cuba or the provocation to flee of any further 'wave' of refugees to the US will be regarded as an act of aggression. In addition, the President is urged *inter alia* to encourage other countries to restrict trade and credit relations with Cuba, and to use sanctions to this end,[41] to tighten the scope and enforcement of the existing US embargo on trade with Cuba,[42] to oppose Cuban membership of international financial institutions until change is instituted in Cuba,[43] to continue to oppose Cuban participation in the Organisation of American States,[44] and to suspend aid to any of the independent states of the former Soviet Union determined to be engaged in inappropriate trade or financial dealings with Cuba.[45]

Title II authorises various types of assistance to Cuba, particularly support to groups working for democratic change.

Title III relates to property once owned by US nationals in Cuba, but claimed to have been expropriated without compensation by the Cuban government. Various provisions are made to allow US nationals so affected to bring claims in US courts relating to such properties and to penalise individuals who 'traffic' in such property. In some cases, the penalty for 'trafficking' in such assets can include triple damages.[46] Such actions could be brought against 'any person',[47] the US apparently relying on the 'effects' doctrine to justify the wide scope thus created for its provisions.[48]

[40] Helms–Burton Act, s. 101.

[41] *Ibid.*, s. 102.

[42] *Ibid.*

[43] *Ibid.*, s. 104.

[44] *Ibid.*, s. 105.

[45] *Ibid.*, s. 106.

[46] *Ibid.*, s. 302.

[47] See, e.g. *Ibid.*, s. 302(a)(1).

[48] *Ibid.*, s. 301(9) provides: 'International law recognises that a nation has the ability to provide for rules of law with respect to conduct outside its territory that has or is intended to have substantial effect within its territory'. The 'trafficking' in confiscated property is said to have the effect of undermining the foreign policy of the US towards Cuba and its efforts to protect the claims of US nationals. *Ibid.*, s. 301(6).

The provisions of Title III were particularly controversial. As noted in Chapter 1, expropriation is not *per se* unlawful. Moreover, compensation had already been paid by Cuba in accordance with its Constitution[49] to most states whose nationals had been affected.[50] However, the US argued that this fell short of the standard of 'prompt, adequate and effective' compensation which it insisted was required under international law. The operation of Title III was initially suspended.[51]

Title IV of the Act permits foreign nationals to be barred from the US where they themselves have been involved in a confiscation of US property by Cuba or in its conversion for personal gain, have 'trafficked' in such confiscated property or are a corporate officer, principal or shareholder with a controlling interest in an entity which has done any of these things. The spouses, children and agents of such persons can also be excluded.[52]

The Helms–Burton Act provoked strong reactions from a number of third states, particularly because of the extra-territorial reach of several of its provisions. Protests were made by the European Commission, for instance, even before the legislation was enacted.[53] A number of states and the EU responded with blocking measures to counteract the effects of the Helms–Burton Act.

The response of the EU was twofold. On the one hand, blocking legislation was adopted in the EC to counter certain of the extra-territorial effects of the US measures.[54] Within a couple of weeks of the adoption of this legislation the Council of Ministers, acting under Article J2 of the Treaty on European Union, also adopted a Common Position on Cuba which emphasised the need for improvement in respect of democracy, human rights and living standards in Cuba.[55] The Common Position pledged a more active stance on the part of the EU on this issue.[56]

[49] The relevant Article of the Constitution provided that compensation should be paid in twenty-year fixed-term bonds with an annual interest rate of 4.5 per cent.

[50] Agreements had been reached, apparently, with Canada, France, Italy, Mexico, Spain, Sweden and the UK: *Prada* 1995.

[51] *Ibid.*, s. 306, note also the Statement by the President on Suspending Title III of the Helms–Burton Act, 3 January 1997, in which this suspension was extended by six months *36 ILM* (1997) 216.

[52] *Ibid.*, s. 401.

[53] See the Statement by a Delegation of the European Commission of 5 March 1996, *35 ILM* (1996) 397.

[54] Council Regulation (EC) No. 2271/96, Protecting Against the Effects of the Extra-territorial Application of Legislation Adopted by a Third Country, 1996 *OJ L309 39*, and the accompanying Joint Action adopted pursuant to Articles J.3 and K.3, TEU, under which Member States are to take further measures deemed necessary to protect the interests of natural and legal persons under their jurisdiction.

[55] *Ibid.*, Art. 1.

[56] *Ibid.*, Arts 3 and 4.

Canada also adopted measures to block the Helms–Burton Act,[57] amending its earlier legislative provisions in a number of ways. Mexico followed suit with *Ley Antidoto* or the 'Antidote Act'.[58]

In November 1996, a WTO panel was established at the request of the EU to consider the compatibility of the US Helms–Burton Act with WTO disciplines. Cited in particular were GATT Articles I, III, XI and XIII and GATS Articles II, III, VI, XVI and XVII. The US indicated that it regarded the matter as one of national security, falling presumably under GATT Article XXI (GATS XIV). However, it also indicated that it would not participate in WTO panel proceedings, such were the national sensitivities over this issue. Statements issued by senior US officials suggested the view that matters covered by the 'national security exception' in WTO disciplines could not be considered by a dispute settlement panel; in other words, that there should be auto-interpretation of this clause. Such a view accords neither with accepted international practice on this issue in other fields, nor with the *travaux préparatoires.* A better view is that it is open to a WTO panel to determine whether an 'emergency in international relations' does exist, and if so, whether the measures taken in response can be justified, that is, whether they are proportionate.[59] However, this action was suspended at the behest of the EU in April 1997 while negotiations took place between the two sides. Under a deal struck in May 1998, EU companies were exempted from the possible effects of the measure and hence the action was withdrawn from the WTO, though on the understanding that it would be revived if the agreement was later breached.[60]

The Helms–Burton case serves as an important reminder of the willingness of some states, and particularly the immensely powerful US, to bring a wider political agenda to bear in the foreign investment area. In so doing, they relied in this instance on the 'national security' exception, a constant feature of legal instruments in international economic law. While the legality of their action remains moot, in respect of both WTO rules and customary international law, this is an important reminder of the challenges faced by those who would develop multilateral rules on foreign investment.

[57] Foreign Extraterritorial Measures Act, C F-29, 1996, *36 ILM* (1997) 111. This legislation was adopted on 9 October 1996.

[58] Act to Protect Trade and Investment from Foreign Norms that Contravene International Law of 23 October 1996, *36 ILM* (1997) 133.

[59] Proportionality is a general requirement for resort to reprisal or self-defence under customary international law: *Nicaragua* v. *US* (*Merits*) *ICJ Rep.* (1986) para. 176; 'Advisory Opinion on the Legality of the Threat or Use of Nuclear Weapons' *ICJ Rep*. (1986) para. 41.

[60] See further Smis and van der Borght 'The EU–US Compromise', *supra* note 38. The Helms–Burton Act was at issue again in the MAI negotiations, when the US insisted that a country-specific exception to the general principles of that text be recognised in respect of this legislation: see Section 7.4 below.

6

The challenges of free trade: issues arising from the treatment and taxation of foreign investment in the EU and NAFTA

Introduction

As was seen in the preceding chapters, patterns of state activities in relation to the treatment and taxation of foreign investment have been strongly influenced by the traditional international law concept of sovereignty and the related principles of mutuality and consent. Where efforts have been made to develop or strengthen multilateral regimes, these principles have dominated and remain much in evidence. Above all, it has proven difficult if not impossible to move beyond patterns of behaviour based on competition between states to policies based on a perceived global or community interest. In terms of legal obligations adopted, it can be seen that states have tended to prefer sub-optimal solutions in which state sovereignty is preserved, over the optimal solution which would require the pooling of sovereignty in the hands of a supranational power. Indeed all the standard-setting efforts reviewed in Chapters 1 and 2 can be characterised, in contrast to some other areas of international activity,[1] by the absence of international organisations or by the preferment of a co-ordinating rather than a governing role for such institutions.

Against this background, certain regional free trade areas are worthy of close examination, since it is in the context of free trade areas that the greatest inroads have been made in the economic field in securing both the pursuit of a higher, community interest and, to this end, the subjugation of state interests to the authority of supranational institutions and to the rule of law.

The objective of this chapter is to illustrate some of the challenges which the pursuit of a 'free trade' goal raises for traditional international economic

[1] Trade provides an excellent example in the economic field, the contrast being with the WTO institutions and agreements. In the non-economic field, human rights laws and institutions provide a marked contrast.

law in relation to the treatment and taxation of foreign investment. Two free trade areas in particular are considered, the EU and NAFTA, the two in which the subjugation of state interests to supranational institutions and laws is greatest.

The EU presents both strengths and limitations as a case study of the issues. On the one hand, the extent and depth of co-operation between states, the degree of integration achieved, the extent to which this is underpinned by legal change and the ability of the EU institutions to instigate or implement wholesale legal change are unmatched elsewhere among sovereign states. While 'laboratory conditions' cannot be created in international relations, the economic outlook of the Member States, their level of development and their commitment to the goal of economic integration and hence to the project of the EU are very similar in relative terms. Thus the capacity for change in the regulation and taxation of foreign investment within the EU is great, since many of the factors which on a global level militate against co-operation and co-ordination of efforts are absent or diffuse in the EU.

On the other hand, this group of states is not 'typical' from a global perspective and cannot necessarily therefore serve as a model for wider co-operation. EU Member States are relatively closely aligned in terms of economic ideology and economic development; they necessarily share a peculiarly European conception of co-operation and integration; and their actions in relation to foreign investment are inevitably tempered by other EU objectives, as well as by the individual goals of the Member States.

Most noticeably, perhaps, the efforts of the EC Commission to harmonise direct taxes, which in the past have floundered when faced with resistance from Member States reluctant to concede sovereignty in this sensitive area, have now become intricately linked to Economic and Monetary Union and to the financial disciplines which this entails.[2]

NAFTA is a trilateral free trade agreement between Canada, Mexico and the US. It was closely modelled on the earlier US–Canada Free Trade Agreement of 1988.[3] In relation to investment, the earlier treaty was specifically targeted towards securing liberalisation of the regime for US investors in Canada. NAFTA builds on and develops the established rules to provide general rules for investment for general application between the parties, subject to an extensive array of country-specific exceptions.[4]

As a case study, it too has strengths and limitations. On the one hand, NAFTA is dominated by the US, an immensely powerful and aggressive

[2] See Title VII of the EC Treaty. For an explanation of the legal obligations arising from these provisions, see, e.g. S. Weatherill and P. Beaumont *EC Law* 3rd edn, 1999 pp. 767–83.

[3] *27 ILM* (1988) 281.

[4] For an overview of the investment provisions of the two agreements, see P. T. Muchlinski *Multinational Enterprises and the Law* (1995) at pp. 239–45.

advocate of free trade. Accordingly, NAFTA disciplines are extremely influential as a model for developments on a global scale. Moreover, the relatively small number of participants means that there is in theory at least a relatively high capacity for adaptation and change. In addition, the two smaller participants in NAFTA, Canada and Mexico, present in microcosm some of the same problems encountered on a global scale:

- the disparity in wealth between, for example, the US and Mexico;
- the danger of social and environmental dumping (e.g. in Mexico) if insufficient measures are taken to avoid this;
- fear of economic and cultural domination by a more powerful neighbour (e.g. in Canada) if protectionist measures are wholly dismantled; and
- political differences over issues such as environmental protection.

On the other hand, the domination of the US in NAFTA may mean that solutions are developed there which cannot readily be exported beyond the narrow confines of NAFTA. Moreover, though the wealth gap between the US and Mexico is immense, NAFTA trade rules, like those of the EU, have been developed without thought for the situation of the poorest states.

The discussion is divided into three distinct parts. In the first part of the chapter, issues concerning the treatment of foreign investment, both inward and outward will be explored. In the second part, issues concerning the taxation of foreign investment will be considered. In the final part, a number of issues concerning dispute resolution mechanisms will be addressed.

6.1 The treatment of foreign investment in a free trade area

6.1.1 *The international law context*

Free trade areas such as the EC and NAFTA are founded on a departure from the central non-discrimination and MFN principles of the WTO Agreements as seen, for example, in Article III, GATT 1994.[5] Under Article XXIV of GATT 1994, free trade areas can be established provided that:

1 the duties and other regulations of commerce between its Members are *not on the whole higher or more restrictive* than the corresponding duties and other regulations of commerce existing in the same constituent territories prior to the formation of the free trade area,[6] and

[5] For discussion and commentary, see, e.g. GATT, *Analytical Index* 6th edn, 1994 p. 735 *et infra*; J. H. Jackson, W. J. Davey and A. O. Sykes, Jr *Legal Problems of International Economic Relations: Cases, Materials and Text* 3rd edn, 1995 p. 464 *et infra*.

[6] GATT 1994, Art. XXIV(5)(b).

2 that all duties and other restrictive regulations of commerce are *eliminated on substantially all the trade between the constituent territories.*[7]

The EU has gone substantially beyond the requirements of GATT in respect of internal trade by creating an 'internal market characterised by the abolition, as between Member States, of obstacles to the free movement of goods, persons, services and capital'.[8]

Thus EC law[9] addresses the question of free movement of the factors of production and does not contain any explicit concept of 'investment' or 'investor'. The legal provisions which give effect to this approach recognise as 'fundamental' four specific freedoms: the free movement of goods (Article 28EC), the free movement of workers (Article 39EC), the freedom to establish an economic enterprise (Article 43EC) or provide services within the territory of another Member State (Article 49EC) and the free movement of capital (Article 56EC). All of these provisions, along with rules on competition and on procurement, affect the situation of investors from within and outside the EU. Since the EC Treaty itself casts the four freedoms only as very broad general principles, much of the detail regarding their effect and meaning has been developed through secondary legislation, and by the ECJ through the process of litigation.

NAFTA is a free trade agreement between Canada, Mexico and the US which, together with side agreements on labour and the environment, regulates trade between the three states. NAFTA contains specific provisions on investment and addresses directly some of the barriers and risks which can be encountered by foreign investors in a host state. Thus, as far as investment is concerned, NAFTA follows the general approach of BITs; however, it goes further than the current generation of BITs in its identification of potential problems faced by foreign investment. Litigation has been less

[7] GATT 1994, Art. XXIV(8).

[8] EC Treaty, Art. 3(c).

[9] This refers to the relevant provisions of the EC Treaty and the *acquis communitaire* or body of law developed thereunder (comprising principally regulations, directives and the jurisprudence of the ECJ). The current version of the EC Treaty is that embodied in the Treaty of Amsterdam, which entered into force on 1 May 1999. Though the substance of the relevant free movement principles was largely unchanged, they were all renumbered in the Treaty of Amsterdam. All references to the EC Treaty are to the version as amended by the Treaty of Amsterdam, unless otherwise stated. The terms EC Treaty and EC law refer to the provisions of the 'first pillar' of the EU, a body with wider scope embracing also the second pillar (Common Foreign and Security Policy) and a third pillar (Police and Judicial Cooperation in Criminal Matters). For an explanation of the three pillar structure, see, e.g. D. Curtin 'The Constitutional Structure of the Union: A Europe of Bits and Pieces' *30 CMLR* (1993) p. 17; P. Demaret 'The Treaty Framework' in D. O'Keeffe and P. Twomey (eds) *Legal Issues of the Maastricht Treaty* 1994, p. 3; for an explanation of the changes introduced by the Treaty of Amsterdam, see D. O'Keeffe and P. Twomey (eds) *Legal Issues of the Amsterdam Treaty* 1999.

important as a means of clarifying the scope of the obligations under NAFTA than in the EC to date, but there are some important recent cases which will be examined below.

6.1.2 *Foreign investment in the EC*

Free movement and the non-discrimination principles

As noted above, the rights of free movement of the factors of production (goods, workers, services, capital) throughout the territory of the EU are regarded as of fundamental importance in EC law. However, in reality these issues are governed only in part by EC law, since the Member States also retain power to act in relation to many aspects of free movement. To adopt the formal legal terminology, the EC has exclusive competence in relation to such matters, to the extent that this is expressly or impliedly granted by the Treaty and to the extent that the EC has 'occupied the field', that is, made use of the powers granted to it. Member States have competence to the extent that their historic powers under international law to regulate the treatment and taxation of investment are unaffected by the EC Treaty (i.e. outside its scope) and in fields which though potentially within the scope of EC law have not yet been 'occupied' by the EC.

For instance, in relation to the right of an EC national to establish a company or firm on the territory of another Member State, Article 43EC provides that there is a freedom to do so, subject to 'the conditions laid down for its own nationals by the law of the country where such establishment is effected'. This freedom is directly effective, meaning that it can be relied on and enforced in the national courts of a Member State,[10] and it is regarded as a fundamental freedom, which means in effect that it weighs heavily in any case involving a balancing of interests.[11] In addition, the EC institutions are empowered to introduce legislation with the aim of abolishing, or moving towards the abolition of, barriers to establishment in another Member State (Article 44EC). This has been done, for instance, in relation to banking[12] and insurance,[13] and in relation to the matters covered by the relevant legislation, Member States have no legal competence. Yet in other

[10] Case 26/62 *Van Gend en Loos* v. *Nederlandse Administratie der Belastingen* [1963] ECR 1. For a discussion, see, e.g. J. A. Usher *EC Institutions and Legislation* 1998, Chapter Eight.

[11] See further, e.g. Weatherill and Beaumont *EC Law*, *supra* note 2, especially Chapter Nineteen; P. Craig and G. de Burca *EC Law: Text, Cases and Materials* 2nd edn, 1998, especially Chapter Seventeen. This applies whether EC interests (i.e. of the institutions) or Member State interests are at stake.

[12] A. Arora and X. Favre-Bulle 'The Single European Market and the Banking Sector' in G. G. Howells (ed.) *European Business Law* 1996.

[13] A. McGee (ed.) *The Single Market in Insurance* 1995; R. Merkin and A. Rodger *EC Insurance Law* 1997.

areas Member States retain the competence acknowledged in Article 43EC to lay down conditions governing the operation of businesses and firms, provided that they do not discriminate unlawfully between nationals of other Member States and their own nationals.[14] The main objective of most of the litigation concerning the application of Article 43EC, and hence the subject-matter of most of the ECJ's jurisprudence on this Article, has been clarification of the continuing right of host Member States to lay down such conditions, when the result is direct or indirect discrimination against the nationals of another Member State.

The question of direct discrimination has in practice given rise to little difficulty in relation to foreign investors. Individuals, companies or firms who wish to establish within the territory of another state will generally be permitted to do so,[15] and to enjoy freedom of movement of capital to enable them to do so. If they choose to incorporate there, or to create a partnership or other business organisation under the laws of the host state, they will normally thereby assume a separate legal personality having the status of 'national' and henceforth face no further discriminatory treatment. Even where this is not done, such as where a company establishes a branch rather than a subsidiary, that branch will be entitled to 'national treatment'. That is, it should face burdens and demands in relation to its business operations no less favourable than those imposed by the host state on its own nationals engaged in the same or similar activities.

However, a number of exceptions have been recognised, where the regulatory regime applied by the host state may involve an element of direct discrimination, but such discrimination is recognised to be 'objectively justifiable'.[16] First, it may be acceptable to require 'residence' or incorporation

[14] An exception exists in relation to activities which are connected with the exercise of public authority. In addition, Member States retain a discretion to exclude foreign nationals on grounds of public policy, public security or public health, even where this would interfere with their right of establishment; cf. Council Directive 64/221 and the relevant case-law, discussed by S. Hall 'The ECHR and Public Policy Exceptions to the Free Movement of Workers under the EEC Treaty' *16 EL Rev.* (1991) p. 466; D. O'Keeffe 'Practical Difficulties in the Application of Article 48 of the EEC Treaty' *19 CMLR* (1982) 35.

[15] Case 2/74 *Reyners* v. *Belgium* [1974] ECR 631.

[16] The concept of 'objective justification' is employed in EC law in relation to goods, services, establishment and workers and can be broken down into a number of distinct elements; the objective pursued much be legitimate, the measures must be part of a general policy which is pursued consistently in relation to nationals and non-nationals, the means employed must satisfy the principle of proportionality and must not disrupt the free market more than is necessary. Other less disruptive means should be preferred if available. Though national courts are encouraged to control such measures themselves, the ECJ will adjudicate upon this issue if called upon to do so. The concept of 'objective justification' can be described as a requirement of coherence and rationality in state regulation and is used to considerable effect to tackle disguised protectionism.

within the territory where services are to be provided, even though this increases the burden on enterprises and effectively deprives them of the right contained in Article 49EC (the right to provide services), where there is no less onerous way of meeting the needs of the state.[17] The needs in question are public policy considerations recognised as legitimate and pursued by measures which are 'proportionate'.[18]

Establishment is generally taken to be constituted by a permanent presence within the territory of a Member State. What precisely constituted establishment was the subject of some discussion after the ECJ held in *Commission* v. *Germany* that regulatory authorities were entitled to consider a business to be established, even if their presence 'does not take the form of a branch or agency, but consists merely of an office managed by the undertaking's own staff or by a person who is independent but authorised to act on a permanent basis for the undertaking, as would be the case with an agency'.[19] They also indicated that the establishment provisions of the EC Treaty could be applied to 'a person providing services whose activity is entirely or principally directed towards [the territory of the host state]'.[20] Here the concern was to allow states to prevent abuse of the freedom to provide services (Article 49EC) by someone whose objective was to avoid the rules of professional conduct to which he would be subject if established in the territory.[21]

The ruling demonstrates the difficulty faced in drawing a clear line for the purposes of regulation between the concept of establishment (or foreign direct investment (FDI)) and the trans-boundary provision of services. Edward notes the pressures placed on the Treaty concepts by the growth of modern telecommunications and of business practices which exploit the new technology:

> at the time when the Treaty was drafted, it was easy, conceptually, to distinguish between establishment and services. Except in frontier areas, the slowness of travel and communication made it difficult for a person to carry on activities in more than one state at a time. Even for companies and firms, the setting up of a branch or agency in another country was relatively speaking, a major step to take . . . Today a professional consultant can conduct a multinational practice from his own home and from hotel rooms around the world . . . he may find it convenient, when he has a long job in another country, to take

[17] Case 33/74 *Van Binsbergen* v. *Bestuur van de Bedrijfsvereniging Metaalnijverheid* [1974] ECR 1299; Case 205/84 *Commission* v. *Germany (Re Insurance Services)* [1986] ECR 3755.

[18] The proportionality principle is of immense significance in determining the acceptability of the measures in question. See further *Commission* v. *Germany, ibid.*; Case C-384/93 *Alpine Investments BV* v. *Minister van Financien* [1995] ECR I-1141.

[19] *Commission* v. *Germany, ibid.*, judgment paras 20–1.

[20] *Ibid.*, para. 22.

[21] *Ibid.* See also *Van Binsbergen, supra* note 17.

> a short lease of office space and install a secretary there with a telephone, a word-processor and telecopier. In the case of a small company, the best way of breaking into a new market, *before* deciding whether the market justifies a permanent establishment, may be to open a small office to which enquiries can be directed, or to strike up a relationship with a local intermediary. . . . But physical propinquity or access to the provider of services is becoming increasingly unimportant.[22]

The concepts of establishment and services are rooted in the concept of territorial sovereignty which, as noted in Chapter 5, is increasingly under strain as the basis for economic regulation. Edward reinforces this observation, '[i]n such a world, regulation of professional and corporate activity calls for the development of new concepts and new methods. The idea that there can be effective control by proliferation of national agencies based on a criterion of territorial location flies in the face of the facts'.[23] Edward is however highly critical of the ECJ's permissive stance which would seem to encourage Member States to use extended (and overlapping) concepts of 'establishment' in future, a development which would be hardly conducive to the development of competition and hence of market integration. He suggests instead that the difficulty is one which can only be effectively addressed by the institutions, that is at the supranational level. It is notable, in this context, that the definition of 'services' adopted in GATS is significantly wider than that of EC law and encompasses some forms of foreign investment.[24]

Where a company or firm does decide to establish itself in the 'host' state (i.e. in the state where it wishes to provide its services), it must do so under the relevant laws of the state. Thus it may be required to submit to authorisation or licensing procedures,[25] headquarters requirements,[26] tax laws and all the usual array of legal requirements faced by businesses. Though 'national treatment' is the benchmark, it is recognised that treatment may reflect genuine differences in circumstances[27] so that, for instance, branches of firms based outside the jurisdiction, whose profits are remitted to the company, may be subject to a different tax regime from branches of firms incorporated within the territory, whose profits can be taxed by the host state as part of the company's profits.[28]

[22] D. Edward 'Establishment and Services: An Analysis of the Insurance Cases' *12 ELRev.* (1987) 231 at pp. 252–3.

[23] *Ibid.*

[24] See Chapter 7 below. See also T. L. Brewer and S. Young *The Multilateral Investment System and Multinational Enterprises* 1998, p. 126.

[25] *Van Binsbergen*, *supra* note 17; *Commission* v. *Germany*, *ibid.*

[26] Case 81/87 *R* v. *HM Treasury, ex parte Daily Mail* [1988] ECR 5483.

[27] Case C-107/94 *P. H. Asscher* v. *Staatssecretaris van Financien* [1996] ECR I-3089.

[28] See further Section 6.2.1 below.

Indirect discrimination arises where the national laws, though 'indistinctly applicable' (applying without distinction between nationals and non-nationals) can be seen to give rise to a double or additional burden for non-nationals. An example would be where a company which has already undergone an authorisation procedure in the home state has to undergo such a procedure again in the host state in respect of the operations of a branch situated there. In *Commission* v. *Germany*, the ECJ ruled that the host state could impose such requirements provided they could be 'objectively justified'.[29] Moreover, it is recognised that a Member State is entitled to pursue higher standards than are required by others, so that 'the fact that one Member State imposes less strict rules than another Member State does not mean that the latter's rules are disproportionate and hence incompatible with Community law'.[30] However, the authorisation procedure must take account of the authorisation already obtained and could not be used merely to verify the same facts again.[31]

These cases concern the freedom of establishment and/or the right to provide services, directly relevant to the question of regulation of foreign investment, but the ECJ is also informed by its jurisprudential approach in relation to other areas, notably the area of free movement of goods (Article 28EC, ex 30).

In a series of 'hard cases', the ECJ has been called upon to address the central problem of drawing a line between Member State regulatory measures which can be 'objectively justified' and those which cannot, and hence constitute an unlawful disguised restriction on trade. Examples of such cases include the *Cineteque*,[32] *Danish Bottles*[33] and *Sunday Trading*[34] *Cases*, which, together with *Commission* v. *Germany*, do a great deal to illustrate the nature of the ruling which has to be made and to identify considerations relevant to such a ruling. But they also serve to emphasise that the decision is ultimately a question of fact in each case and one on which opinions will differ according to the view taken of the desirable level of state intervention in the particular market sector in question.

In addition, the *Cassis de Dijon Case* makes clear that the list of 'mandatory requirements' is never closed. Therefore this question too is left open ended and liable to be interpreted differently according to differing

[29] *Supra* note 17, Judgment paras 30–3. Objective justification depends on the existence of 'imperative reasons relating to the public interest which justify restrictions'.

[30] *Alpine Investments, supra* note 18, Judgment para. 51.

[31] *Commission* v. *Germany, supra* note 17, Judgment paras 34–41.

[32] Cases 60, 61/84 *Cinetheque* v. *Federation Nationale de Cinemas Francais* [1985] ECR 2605.

[33] *Case 302/86 Commission* v. *Denmark* [1988] ECR 4607.

[34] Case 145/88 *Torfaen Borough Council* v. *B & Q plc* [1989] ECR 765; Case C-169/91 *Stoke-on Trent and Norwich City Councils* v. *B & Q* [1992] ECR I-6457; Cases C-267 and C-268/91 *Keck and Mithouard* Joined [1993] ECR I-6097.

underlying viewpoints about the respective weights to be attached to the Member State objectives in question and the integrationist objectives of EC law. Nevertheless, the ECJ has firmly fixed these questions within a normative framework and the very nature of the judicial process ensures that Member State regulatory action can be subjected to public scrutiny by a judicial body.

Investors from other Member States may also be subjected to the competition laws and policies of the host state. Under Article 81 EC, for instance, anti-competitive practices such as price fixing and market sharing are prohibited and companies based outside the EU may be required to notify the European Commission of certain types of agreement or supply information requested in the course of an enquiry when they trade within the EU.[35]

Though Member States retain a degree of freedom in relation to the treatment of investors from other Member States, the non-discrimination or national treatment principle is firmly established in EC law and has been used effectively to tackle barriers to establishment. Additionally, in some areas, such as public procurement, the EC has developed policies specifically aimed at liberalising access to the host economy for investors from other Member States.

Finally, it can be noted that in the *Rush Portuguese Case*[36] the ECJ acknowledged that a Member State was entitled to apply its own labour regulations to the staff of an EC company providing temporary services in its territory.[37]

Free movement and investment from third states

Investors from third states cannot automatically rely on the provisions of EC law, since the rights created under the four freedoms are the preserve of EC nationals. Article 48EC confines the application of the free movement provisions of the Treaty to companies or firms 'formed in accordance with the law of a Member State and having their registered office, central administration or principal place of business within the Community'.[38] As Muchlinski notes, this means that potential investors lacking any legally recognised presence in the EU cannot use the provisions of the Treaty to gain access, whether as an investor or as a provider of services.[39] An additional

[35] See, e.g. C. Bellamy and G. Child *Common Market Law of Competition* 4th edn, 1994.

[36] Case C-113/89 *Rush Portuguese* v. *Office National d'Immigration* [1990] ECR-I 1417.

[37] Though it was precluded from requiring that work permits be obtained for non-EU employees of a company established in the EU and providing temporary services in the territory of another State (see below): *Rush Portuguese, ibid.*

[38] Article 48EC provides further: '"Companies or firms" means companies or firms constituted under civil or commercial law, including co-operative societies, and other legal persons governed by public or private law, save for those which are non-profit-making'.

[39] Muchlinski *Multinational Enterprises, supra* note 4, p. 247.

barrier might arise from the fact that a right of access to a Member State to establish a business would not necessarily be accompanied by a *Rush Portuguese*-type right to gain access for key personnel.[40] Immigration from third states remains largely a matter for Member States and policies vary widely, though following the conclusion of the Treaty of Amsterdam the EC has acquired competence to adopt measures concerning both the conditions of entry and residence for third country nationals and the procedures adopted by Member States in these matters,[41] and measures concerning the rights of third country nationals legally resident in one Member State to take up residence in another.[42]

The competence to establish legal conditions for entry into or operation within the EU is split between the Member States and the EC institutions. Member States have by far the greatest role, retaining competence to negotiate and conclude international treaties in relation to investment[43] and to determine unilaterally to which areas of their economy third country investors can gain access and under what conditions. While all the Member States operate, to a greater or lesser degree, an 'open door' policy (in keeping with the OECD Liberalization Codes[44]) the levels of restriction still vary considerably between Member States and from sector to sector. In relation to financial services, for instance, some states have been particularly sensitive about access by investors from outside the EU and this is reflected in the relevant EC legislation;[45] other examples include the UK's sensitivity about issues such as control of the media, while for France the cultural industries remain sensitive.

Member State governments and the European Commission can each act in their respective spheres of competence to regulate competition within the EC and can therefore act to exclude or restrict takeovers or mergers by investors from third states. However, beyond this, the legal role of the EC in relation to inward investment from third states is negligible and stands in marked contrast to the exclusive competence which it possesses in relation to trade in goods from third countries and related matters, such as the imposition of anti-dumping or countervailing duties on such imports. Though explicable in terms of the historic focus of the international community on

[40] Such a right is provided, however, in many Association Agreements: cf. M. Cremona 'Community Relations with the Visegrad Group' *ELRev.* (1993) 345.

[41] Art. 63(3)EC.

[42] Art. 63(4)EC.

[43] See the *WTO Opinion*, Opinion 1/94 [1994] ECR I-5267, in relation to TRIMs.

[44] See Section 2.2, *supra.*

[45] The Second Banking Directive, for instance, provides that an EC Banking licence can be denied to subsidiaries of credit institutions of third states which fail to grant national treatment to EC credit institutions: Directive 89/646/EEC *OJ* [1989] L 386/1 30 December; a similar provision exists in the Investment Services Directive: Council Directive on investment services in the securities field 93/22/EEC *OJ* [1993] L 141/27; Muchlinski *Multinational Enterprises, supra* note 4 at p. 247.

trade in goods, this distinction between trade and investment makes little sense today. Economic actors themselves recognise the link and may, for instance, see direct investment in an EU Member State as a desirable alternative to trade, since it can be used as a means to circumvent both import duties[46] and the rigours of the EC's anti-dumping and subsidies disciplines. Moreover, the close relationship between these areas is increasingly recognised in international institutions.[47]

Investors from third states entering the EC benefit from two distinct sets of rules. First, they can rely on restrictions arising from WTO obligations, or from other international treaties to which the EC or the Member States are party (such as the Energy Charter Treaty[48]). As noted in Chapter 1, there were historically very few restrictions under GATT 1947 on the treatment of foreign investment. GATT essentially addresses trade in goods rather than investment *per se* and focuses on tariffs and non-tariff barriers to trade in goods. However, in the 1980s a groundbreaking action was raised by the US against Canada, protesting at Canada's policy of imposing requirements on foreign investment relating, for instance, to the sourcing of component parts, which, it was argued, indirectly disadvantaged US producers of certain goods.[49] This important case arguably played an important role in establishing that GATT could be used to tackle investment restrictions on investments from other contracting parties. However, the approach used is somewhat tangential as far as protection of foreign investment is concerned and thus restricted in its scope. Nevertheless, the case raised an important new agenda and this was pursued by the US in the Uruguay Round negotiations, resulting in the conclusion of TRIMs.[50] Moreover, GATS also imposes obligations regarding the treatment of foreign investment in relation to the provision of services. These developments are examined in Chapter 7.

The second body of rules from which foreign investors can benefit is the body of EC law itself. Foreign investors stand to benefit greatly by establishing themselves within a Member State through a subsidiary which will then assume an EU nationality and thus acquire the protection of EC law. Companies established within a Member State cannot be discriminated against on the grounds of their foreign parent company. Rather the

[46] The very detailed WTO rules on the origin of goods are designed to prevent abusive use of such a strategy through 'screwdriver' operations.

[47] Two working groups established by the WTO in connection with the TRIMs review (see Chapter 7) have remits which cut across the historic separation of treatment of trade and investment: the group on the relationship between trade and investment and the group on the relationship between competition policy and trade; see T. L. Brewer and S. Young 'Investment Issues at the WTO: The Architecture of Rules and the Settlement of Disputes' *1 JIEL* (1998) 457 at 467.

[48] See further Chapter 7 below.

[49] The *FIRA Case*, discussed below at Section 7.1.

[50] See further Section 7.3 below.

non-discrimination principle entitles them to buy and sell goods throughout the EU, recruit and employ workers from any Member State and in any Member State and to establish subsidiaries, branches or offices or to provide their services on a temporary basis in any Member State, on the same terms as other nationals of that state.[51] Some of the implications of this are demonstrated in the cases outlined above.

6.1.3 *Foreign investment in NAFTA*

Specific provisions on investment are contained in Chapter Eleven of NAFTA and offer protection to investors of the three states and their investments in the territory of the other parties. Article 1102 contains the national treatment principle requiring for investors of another Party and their investments treatment no less favourable than that accorded by a Party to its own investors. This applies to establishment, acquisition, expansion, management, conduct, operation and sale or other disposition.[52] Specifically, states are prohibited from requiring that a minimum of equity be held by their own nationals[53] or requiring the investors of other Parties to divest by reason of their nationality.[54] Nor can it be required that senior management positions be filled by individuals of any particular nationality,[55] though nationality and residence requirements can be imposed on the Board of Directors and its committees 'provided that the requirement does not materially impair the ability of the investor to exercise control over its investment'.[56] Article 1103 provides for MFN treatment, requiring that the investors and investments of another Party be accorded treatment no less favourable than that accorded to investors of another Party or non-Party. Three specific areas of treatment are dealt with more specifically under NAFTA: expropriation, payments and capital transfers and performance requirements.

Expropriation is dealt with in Articles 1105 and 1110. Article 1105 contains general provisions requiring for the investors and investments of another Party treatment in accordance with international law 'including fair and equitable treatment and full protection and security'.[57] Particularly following armed conflict or civil strife, non-discrimination is required in measures relating to losses.[58] Expropriation is prohibited except in accordance with

[51] For an account of the rules, see, for example, S. Weatherill and P. Beaumont *EC Law* 3rd edn, 1999 Chapter Nineteen.
[52] NAFTA Art. 1102(2).
[53] Other than nominal qualifying shares for directors or incorporators of corporations: Art. 1102(4)(a).
[54] Art. 1102(4)(b).
[55] NAFTA Art. 1107(1).
[56] NAFTA Art. 1107(2).
[57] NAFTA Art. 1105(1).
[58] NAFTA Art. 1105(2).

these conditions and where it is for a public purpose, non-discriminatory and compensated.[59] The provisions on compensation basically require that the Hull formula of 'prompt, adequate and effective' compensation is adhered to, but specify the importance of the going concern value in valuation and the requirement of interest.[60] The requirement of effectiveness, that is, that compensation be freely transferable into other currencies, is tied to the general provisions on payments and capital transfers (free movement of capital) in Chapter Eleven. This basically provides that all transfers and international payments relating to an investment of an investor of another Party be freely permitted.[61] The article provides a non-exhaustive list of transactions covered and a list of exceptions: these include measures relating to bankruptcy, insolvency and protection of creditors, securities transactions, criminal law measures and measures concerning the satisfaction of court judgments and matters concerning the reporting of currency movements.[62]

Performance requirements are dealt with in Article 1106. This provision can be regarded from a global perspective as an important step in giving legal shape to the US policy of attacking the use of performance requirements where these impacted on foreign investment and trade, the policy which inspired the *FIRA Case* (above) and was later to be taken up in the Uruguay Round of Multilateral Trade Negotiations. Indeed, the provisions of NAFTA go further towards dismantling performance requirements than it proved possible to go in the WTO Agreements.

Article 1106 prohibits the imposition of requirements, or the enforcement of commitments or undertakings, whereby an investor undertakes:

> (a) [to] export a given level or percentage of goods or services;
> (b) [to] achieve a given level or percentage of domestic content;
> (c) [to] purchase, use or accord a preference to goods produced or services provided in its territory, or to purchase goods or services from persons in its territory;
> (d) to relate in any way the volume or value of imports to the volume or value of exports or to the amount of foreign exchange inflows associated with such investments;
> (e) to restrict sales of goods or services in its territory that such investment produces or provides by relating such sales in any way to the volume or value of its exports or foreign exchange earnings;
> (f) to transfer technology, a production process or other proprietary knowledge to a person in its territory, except when the requirement is imposed or the commitment or undertaking is enforced by a court, administrative

[59] NAFTA Art. 1110(1).
[60] NAFTA Arts 1110 (2)–(6).
[61] NAFTA Art. 1109.
[62] NAFTA Art. 1109(4)(a)–(e).

tribunal or competition authority to remedy an alleged violation of competition laws; or

(g) to act as the exclusive supplier of the goods it produces or services it provides to a specific region or world market.[63]

The Parties are also prohibited from making the availability of any advantage conditional on such trade-distortive requirements.[64]

Importantly, investors of Parties and of non-Parties are covered by these provisions. This is because the object of the exercise is to remove trade distortions which might adversely affect the investors of the Parties, whether or not they are directly subject to such requirements, not merely to guarantee a certain minimum standard of treatment for investors of the Parties.

The apparently broad application of these provisions is in practice heavily restricted by the use of reservations and exceptions, provided for in Article 1108. This Article operates in two ways. First, it establishes broad general exceptions which in practice are significant in reducing the scope of the rest of the Chapter Eleven of NAFTA: public procurement and subsidies, for instance, are exempt from the national treatment and MFN requirements, while certain types of performance requirements can be used in relation to export promotion schemes and foreign aid programmes, in public procurement and in relation to preferential tariff rates and quotas. Second, Article 1108 provides for reservations by individual states, to the extent laid out in their national schedules of commitments. Article 1108(1) provides that states need not apply the national treatment or MFN principles, nor the disciplines on performance requirements and nationality requirements for senior managers, where these are already subject to restrictions,[65] or can be 'grandfathered' under existing restrictions,[66] and are listed in a party's schedules of commitments.[67]

It can therefore be seen that NAFTA, like EC law, introduces far-reaching changes in the rules governing the treatment of foreign investment from within another Contracting State. Three areas in particular are of significance. First, NAFTA introduces between the State Parties the principle of 'national treatment' in respect of the treatment of foreign investment. This standard, previously pursued in some US BITs,[68] is amplified in a number of further provisions,[69] providing for market access and outlawing between the parties the use of strategies such as compulsory joint ventures

[63] NAFTA Art. 1106(1).

[64] NAFTA Art. 1106(3).

[65] NAFTA Art. 1108(1)(a).

[66] NAFTA Art. 1108(1)(b) and (c). 'Grandfather' rights allow existing restrictions to be renewed or amended, provided that they do not become more restrictive.

[67] NAFTA Art. 1108(1)(a)(i). Restrictions maintained by local governments need not be so listed, however: NAFTA Art. 1108(3).

[68] See further Section 2.1, *supra*.

[69] See text at notes 50–3, *supra*.

or indigenisation, regarded under customary international law as legitimate tools of sovereign states.[70] Second, as noted above, NAFTA establishes a set of specific prohibitions in relation to performance requirements. This approach of specifically enumerating prohibited practices stands in marked contrast to the rights-based approach which is the cornerstone of EC law, where by and large it has been left to the ECJ to determine whether similar sorts of practices infringe the trade rights of EC nationals.[71] The enumerative approach of NAFTA was subsequently followed in TRIMs, discussed in Chapter 7.[72] Third, NAFTA sets these rules within a framework under which, in reality, the commitments of an individual state are determined by its reservations and by the pattern of exclusions and exceptions. In reality, the regime for foreign investment established under NAFTA is a GATT-like one-way street in which states must not increase restrictions in the areas identified in the provisions, but where they have established a framework for negotiation over liberalisation, under which states will be under pressure to make concessions on a reciprocal basis. As will be seen in Chapter 7, in this respect NAFTA effectively established a model for the liberalisation of investment regimes.[73]

NAFTA also established specific procedures for the settlement of disputes between investors and host states – these are examined below.[74] In the present context, however, it can be noted that since those dispute settlement procedures are presented as arbitral in nature and have certain features characteristic of arbitration, including confidentiality in respect of negotiations and/or awards, the dispute settlement process does not serve any role in the development of authoritative interpretation and/or progressive development of the provisions of NAFTA.[75]

6.2 The taxation of foreign investment in a free trade area

6.2.1 *Taxation of foreign investment in the EU*

Taxation arises as an issue in EU law because the differences and interplay between the tax regimes of different Member States has the potential to distort the market and in the process to discriminate between economic

[70] See further Section 1.1, *supra*.

[71] See further Section 6.1.1, *supra*.

[72] See further Section 7.3 below.

[73] In particular GATS and the Draft MAI: on GATS see Section 7.4 below and on the Draft MAI, see Sections 7.5–7.9 below.

[74] See Section 6.3 below.

[75] Though it may of course introduce an element of self-censorship on the part of government parties and has been criticised in this respect: see further Section 6.3 below.

actors in ways which are deemed unacceptable. At the macroeconomic level, the tax practices of Member States can threaten the integration goals of the EU, while at the microeconomic and legal level they can threaten the free movement rights contained in the EC Treaty by discriminating between economic actors. However, while the EC value-added tax (VAT) system is well established and goes a long way towards the elimination of trade distortions caused by indirect taxation, the progress of the EU towards the harmonisation of direct taxes has been much slower. Notable in the field of taxation is the absence of provisions for the harmonisation of direct taxation.[76] The issue of double taxation has generally been addressed by requiring Member States to resolve disputes with taxpayers through co-operation.[77] To this end, taxpayers can refer to arbitration disputes which result where one state has made an adjustment to declared profits or losses to tackle alleged 'transfer pricing', but no corresponding adjustment has been made by the other (host or home) state concerned.[78]

Efforts to tackle trade-distorting differences between national fiscal regimes have led to some legislation. In 1990, directives were enacted to harmonise the treatment of cross-border dividends between parent and subsidiary companies[79] and to deal with cross-border mergers and divisions.[80] However, substantial difficulties have been encountered whenever the Commission has turned its attention to harmonisation of the tax base or of tax rates and there has been little progress on these issues.[81]

It has therefore been left to the ECJ to decide according to the accidents of litigation how the principles of EC law, of which the fundamental freedoms

[76] See generally P. Farmer and R. Lyal *EC Tax Law* 1994; B. J. M. Terra. and P. J. Wattel *European Tax Law* 1993; F. Vanistandael 'The Limits to the New Community Tax Order' *CMLR* (1994) 293; D. W. Williams *EC Tax Law* 1998.

[77] In 1977, a directive was passed to enhance the basis for mutual co-operation: Council Directive of 19 December 1977 concerning mutual assistance by the competent authorities of the Member States in the field of direct and indirect taxation, Directive 77/799/EEC, *OJ* 1977 L 336/15, as amended.

[78] Convention 90/463/EEC on the elimination of double taxation in connection with the adjustment of profits of associated enterprises, *OJ* 1990 L 225/10. See further Farmer and Lyal *EC Tax Law*, *supra* note 76 at pp. 300–8; Williams *EC Tax Law, supra* note 76 at pp. 146–50.

[79] Council Directive of 23 July 1990 on the common system of taxation applicable in the case of parent companies and subsidiaries of different Member States, Directive 90/435/EEC *OJ* 1990 L225/6. See further Farmer and Lyal *EC Tax Law*, *supra* note 76 at pp. 254–76; Williams *EC Tax Law*, *supra* note 76 at pp. 143–4.

[80] Council Directive of 23 July 1990 on the common system of taxation applicable to mergers, division, transfers of assets and exchanges of shares concerning companies of different Member States, Directive 90/434/EEC *OJ* 1990 L 225/1. See further Farmer and Lyal *EC Tax Law*, *supra* note 76 at pp. 277–92; Williams *EC Tax Law*, *supra* note 76 at pp. 144–6.

[81] F. Beveridge and C. A. Riley 'The Tax Goals of the EC' in G. G. Howells (ed.) *European Business Law* 1996, p. 137; Vanistandael 'The Limits', *supra* note 76.

and the principle of non-discrimination on the basis of nationality are cornerstones, are to be reconciled with the tax practices of states derived from well-established principles of international law, such as sovereignty and its attendant concepts of jurisdiction.

Though most of the cases with which the ECJ has dealt have been concerned with the free movement of workers or goods, it should be noted that the ECJ treats the issues arising under each of the separate free movements similarly and will apply principles developed in relation to one of the relevant treaty articles in a case concerning another. The cases discussed below therefore illustrate the approach of the Court to the general issues concerned and give strong indications about the likely approach of the Court faced with similar questions in relation to the rights of establishment and the right to provide services, the rights which principally affect foreign investment within the EC.

Article 90EC requires that taxes do not discriminate against goods imported from other Member States. The protection given by this provision is twofold – it protects imports from discrimination vis-à-vis like products and also against products with which they are in 'legitimate confrontation'.[82] This non-discrimination requirement has proved the source of a considerable volume of litigation and of resulting jurisprudence. Indeed, at some stages in the development of the Community, when the political will for fiscal reform seemed lacking, the ECJ was the driving force of fiscal progress. At an early stage, Article 90EC was determined to have direct effect,[83] the Court affirming that this did not depend on any prior harmonisation. Furthermore, harmonisation measures enacted under Article 93EC must comply with the basic non-discrimination requirement of Article 90EC.[84]

Article 90EC interacts with a number of other provisions of the Treaty relating to trade in goods. Taxes are unlawful under Article 90EC only to the extent that they are discriminatory, whereas customs charges are wholly unlawful under Article 25EC. The Court has thus had to draw a distinction between these two types of charge and there has been a considerable volume of literature on this point. In essence, a customs duty is one the imposition of which results from the importation itself,[85] and this should be distinguished from a charge which though applied consequent upon the importation of goods, is in fact part of a wider system of taxation which extends also to domestic products.[86]

[82] These provisions are complemented by Articles 28EC and 29EC, which prohibit quantitative restrictions and measures having equivalent effect.

[83] Case 57/65 *Lutticke* v. *Hauptzollamptm Saarlouis* [1966] ECR 205.

[84] Case 15/81 *Gaston Schul* v. *Inspecteur der Invoerrechten en Accijnzen* [1982] ECR 1409.

[85] Case 24/68 *Commission* v. *Italy* [1969] ECR 193.

[86] Case 193/85 *Cooperative Co.-Frutta Srl.* v. *Amministrazione delle Finanze dello Stato* [1987] ECR 2085.

More recently, the ECJ has had to grapple with the question of whether discrimination can ever be justified. The question is one which has major ramifications for the tax regimes of Member States, since these have been based historically on concepts such as residence, domicile and territorial presence which, as the cases have demonstrated, sit uneasily with the non-discrimination and free movement provisions of the Treaty.

Biehl

The case of *Biehl*[87] concerned a German national who had worked for some years in Luxembourg, but who in 1983 returned to Germany, part way through the Luxembourg tax year. The Luxemboug tax authorities, in accordance with national law, refused to repay deductions which had been taken from his salary during his part year of residence which were in excess of his total liability to taxation in that tax year. The ECJ ruled that income tax provisions could be caught by the non-discrimination provision of ex-Article 48(2)EC (now 39(2)), pointing out that the principle of equal treatment in respect of remuneration would be ineffective if it could be undermined by discriminatory tax provisions. Luxembourg offered anti-avoidance objectives as justification, pointing out that taxpayers could avoid higher rates of taxation by realising part of their overall income in different Member States and hence undermine the generally progressive tax regimes in the Member States. However, the Court pointed out that the provisions had a much wider effect, covering situations such as Biehl's or situations where the taxpayer ceased to have any income on moving. Accordingly they could not be justified and were found to be contrary to the EC Treaty. While *Biehl* concerned the free movement of workers, the residence criteria in tax provisions has been problematic in relation to establishment and services as well. In the *Avoir Fiscal Case*,[88] the ECJ ruled that foreign companies were entitled to equality of treatment in a Member State, regardless of whether there were other benefits which accrued to such companies from their non-national status. This was followed by the ruling in the *Commerzbank Case*,[89] which concerned the entitlement of a company to payment of interest on tax which had been collected in the UK, then refunded. The refund was due precisely because the company was non-resident and the UK government argued that the treatment of the non-resident company could not be said to be unfavourable as compared to a resident company, since a resident company would have been liable to tax on the relevant income, whereas the non-resident company was relieved of this liability. However, the Court

[87] Case C-175/88 *Biehl* v. *Administration des Contributions de Luxembourg* [1990] ECR I-1779.

[88] Case 270/83 *Commission* v. *France* [1986] ECR 401.

[89] Case C330/91 *R Inland Revenue Commissioners, ex parte Commerzbank AG* [1993] ECR I-4017.

rejected the comparison as inapt, pointing out that the payment in respect of interest was available generally, regardless of the reason for the overpayment, and found that to deny it to non-residents did constitute unlawful discrimination.

Bachmann

The Court came full square to the question of justification for discrimination in the case of *Bachmann.*[90] This involved a Commission action against Belgium over the treatment of resident workers from other Member States. At issue was the treatment under Belgian tax law of insurance premiums on certain types of policies. Where these were paid to a Belgian insurer, the amount could be deducted from gross salary and taxation was then calculated on the remaining salary, net of these payments. This allowance against taxable income was not made in respect of premiums paid to a non-Belgian insurer. The applicant was a German national who had concluded a voluntary sickness insurance contract, an invalidity insurance contract and a life assurance contract with German companies in 1971. From 1972 to 1976 he had resided and worked in Belgium and sought to take advantage of the allowance outlined above. His attempt was rejected and on appeal an Article 177 reference was made. Bachmann argued that the provision was indirectly discriminatory, as workers from other Member States were more likely to have concluded insurance contracts in another state, whereas Belgian workers who had always resided in Belgium were likely to have policies with Belgian companies. Indeed the provision encouraged this; hence it was argued that the case raised questions relating to the provision of services and the movement of capital, as well as to the free movement of workers such as Bachmann.

The justification for the difference in treatment offered by the Belgian government related to *fiscal supervision*. Taxpayers paying premiums to Belgian companies could choose whether to deduct the payments from taxable income, and then be taxed on any capital sum accruing from those policies, or whether to pay the premiums from their net income and become exempt from taxation on the capital sum. The provision which prevented the allowance of premiums paid to non-Belgian insurers thus removed this tax deferral option from those policy holders. The Belgian government claimed there was a public interest in preventing the deferral in such cases, because of the difficulty of monitoring the payment of capital sums by non-Belgian companies, especially if the taxpayer had by then also moved outside Belgium. Advocate-General Mischo pointed out that in the *Avior Fiscal Case*, the Court had not ruled out the possibility of justification for discriminatory

[90] Case C-204/90 *Bachmann* v. *Belgian State* [1992] ECR I-249. See also Case C-300/90 *Commission* v. *Belgium*, a Commission enforcement action concerning the same provision: [1992] ECR I-305.

treatment in the tax field and, moreover, that in *Cassis de Dijon*[91] 'the effectiveness of fiscal supervision' was one of the mandatory requirements identified by the Court. The acceptance of the possibility of 'objective justification' in the services field, as discussed in the *Insurance Cases*,[92] was also noted.

The Advocate-General proceeded to offer an analysis of the justifications offered in relation to the particular provisions at issue. The allowance of payments against taxable income could, he suggested, be made conditional on the fulfillment of requirements on the part of the insurance company, to ensure adequate fiscal supervision. For instance, the company could be obliged to provide certificates confirming that the payments had been received. He acknowledged, however, that there were greater problems in relation to the taxing of capital sums accruing from the policies. Whereas Belgian companies could be required to deduct taxation at source, or otherwise co-operate with the tax authorities:

> [i]f the capital fund is also realised abroad, as will certainly be the case where the worker concerned has left Belgium and returned to the country in which he concluded his insurance contract, it is highly doubtful that it will be possible to tax him in Belgium and that the Belgian State will thus be able to ensure that the deduction of the premiums is 'compensated' by the taxing of the capital fund.[93]

The Advocate-General concluded, though, that the problems were not insurmountable, and that ex-Articles 48EC (now 39) and 59EC (now 49) had therefore been breached.

The Court took a different view on this final point. While it found the provisions discriminatory,[94] and found that appropriate measures would be possible to obtain proof of payments in respect of premiums,[95] it accepted the argument that it would be difficult to assure that tax would be collected on capital payments arising from the policies, since even where undertakings were given by the insurance company in question, there was no guarantee that these would be enforceable before the Courts of another state. Thus in the absence of international conventions or EC co-ordination measures, the 'coherence' of the Belgian tax system could not be ensured by

[91] Case 120/78 *Rewe-Zentrale* v. *Bundesmonopolverwaltung fur Branntwein* [1979] ECR 649, para. 8.

[92] See, e.g. Case 205/84 *Commission* v. *Germany* [1986] ECR 3755.

[93] *Bachmann*, *supra* note 90, Opinion of the Advocate-General (Mischo) at para. 24. This observation arises presumably from the general position in domestic laws whereby the Courts of one state will not enforce tax judgements of another state. The rule derives from the doctrine of sovereign equality, but may be thought to sit ill at ease with the market integration ethos. See further S. Picciotto *International Business Taxation* 1992, pp. 299–301; D. W. Williams '*Asscher*: The European Court and the Power to Destroy' *6 EC Tax Review* (1997) 4.

[94] *Ibid.*, Judgment of the Court paras 11–13.

[95] *Ibid.*, paras 18–20.

measures less restrictive than those at issue. The measures could therefore be justified.[96]

The acceptance by the ECJ of the need to maintain 'fiscal coherence' as a ground of justification for discrimination represents a new application of the 'rule of reason' developed in *Cassis de Dijon* and its scope remains to be clarified in future case-law. It has been argued that the *Bachmann Case* indicates a willingness on the part of the ECJ to be flexible in the area of taxation 'given the sensitivity of the subject-matter in light of national sovereignty concerns and the weakness of Community powers'.[97]

In summary, foreign investors established in one Member State who seek to extend their operations into the territory of another, whether by way of multi-establishment, the creation of branches or the cross-border provision of services may find the ECJ's rulings on discriminatory tax provisions helpful, but only to a limited degree. Purely discriminatory and arbitrary tax provisions will be struck down, but Member States will be able to defend provisions by reference to 'mandatory requirements' or internal needs of the state, such as effective fiscal supervision or the coherence of the tax system, a concept which currently lacks clarity.

It also remains to be seen what the impact will be of Article 58EC (ex73d). This provision, inserted by the Treaty of Maastricht, provides that the freedoms of movement of capital and payments are without prejudice to the right of Member States to apply the relevant provisions of their tax law which distinguish between taxpayers who are not in the same situation with regard to their place of residence or the place where their capital is invested,[98] and to take all requisite measures to prevent infringements of national law, especially in relation to taxation.[99] However, such measures should not in either case constitute an arbitrary discrimination or a disguised restriction on the free movement of capital or payments.[100] Here again, it seems, Member States should be able to objectively justify resort to criteria which are discriminatory.

Two cases – *Schumacker* and *Wielockx* – are significant in that they challenge the traditional treatment under tax law of non-resident taxpayers in a Member State. The cases are significant both for frontier workers – of which Mr Schumacker was one – and more widely for the free movement provisions of the Treaty.

[96] *Ibid.*, paras 21–7.

[97] J. Wouters 'Fiscal Barriers to Companies' Cross-Border Establishment in the Case-Law of the EC Court of Justice' *14 YEL* (1994) 73 at p. 86. Wouters also describes the ECJ's application of the proportionality test in *Bachmann* as 'lenient': *ibid.*

[98] Art. 58(1)(a)EC.

[99] Art. 58(1)(b)EC.

[100] Art. 58(3).

Schumacker

The case of *Schumacker*[101] involved a Belgian national who was resident in Belgium, but worked in Germany. As a non-resident worker, he was liable under the German taxing statute for income tax on a 'limited' basis, that is he was liable to taxation only on that part of his income which arose in Germany. Schumacker was taxed under German law without regard at all to his personal circumstances, that is, without being granted any allowances against tax in respect of his circumstances. The result was that he was taxed more heavily than taxpayers resident in Germany with similar incomes and similar circumstances.

Advocate-General Leger explained that this state of affairs, besides being the international norm in such cases, was regarded as justified since a taxpayer such as Schumacker, who chose to live in one state but retain his/her principal residence in another state, had in effect created a personal link; 'by choosing to reside in a particular State, a person assumes the obligation to contribute to the costs of public administration and the public services made available to him by that State. It is therefore logical that that State should tax the entirety of his income, on a comprehensive basis. It is also that State, where the taxpayer has focused his family life, which will grant him allowances and reliefs'.[102]

This position was in accordance with normal international taxation practice and sanctioned in the OECD 1977 Model Tax Convention. It could also be said to be an important anti-avoidance provision since, as was also argued in the case of *Commission* v. *Luxembourg*,[103] a taxpayer who could spread his income around two or more states could use the non-discrimination argument to reduce his liability in each and avoid or mitigate the generally progressive nature of income tax regimes. This point was acknowledged by the Advocate-General in *Schumacker*.[104] However, in Mr Schumacker's case, almost all his income was derived in Germany; hence there was insufficient income taxed primarily in Belgium on which the reliefs otherwise available in Belgium could be granted. The usual justification therefore did not exist in the circumstances of the case and the overtaxation which occurred in such cases potentially affected many frontier workers.

[101] Case C-279/93 *Finanzamt Köln-Altstadt* v. *Roland Schumacker* [1995] ECR I-225.

[102] *Ibid.*, Opinion of the Advocate-General, para. 36.

[103] Case C-151/94 [1995] I-STC 1047.

[104] *Schumacker*, *supra* note 101, Opinion of the Advocate-General, para. 62: 'It is a cohesive system: if the Federal Republic of Germany took account of the personal circumstances of a taxpayer subject to limited taxation – which it could do only in respect of income earned there – those circumstances would be taken into account twice, by the State of employment and by the State of residence, leading to an unjustified tax benefit'.

The *Schumacker Case* thus raised the important question of whether such over-taxation was compatible with Article 39EC, and in particular the non-discrimination requirement, since non-nationals were likely to suffer disproportionately in most states. The immediate questions for the Court were therefore, first, whether Mr Schumacker was in fact discriminated against, and, in particular, by comparison with whom, and if so, then, second, whether his treatment might be justified. This second question would require the ECJ to consider whether and to what extent discriminatory treatment might be objectively justifiable under a doctrine of mandatory requirements or similar.[105]

The Advocate-General argued that, in general, resident and non-resident taxpayers could not be compared because they were in different situations, but asked whether those such as Schumacker with most of their income in one state were not in a different situation. Where an individual earned all his/her income in a state other than their state of residence there would, he argued, clearly be discrimination, since the resident and non-resident taxpayer were 'in the same specific situation from the tax point of view'.[106] Whether or not there was discrimination in a particular case should be determined, in the Advocate-General's view, by reference to the particular facts of the case rather than to some threshold percentage of income arising in the non-resident state.

The Advocate-General then turned to the question of justification and rejected each of the grounds put forward by Germany. The first was that only the state in which a taxpayer was resident was capable of ascertaining precisely the situation of the taxpayer. This had previously been rejected by the Court as unsustainable, given the existence of provisions for co-operation between tax administrations in different Member States. In any case, the availability of the benefit, here the right to have personal circumstances taken into account, could be made subject to the provision of full proof.

Germany also relied on the need to preserve the cohesion of the tax system, as recognised by the Court in *Bachmann*. However, Germany had already made special provisions to allow frontier workers from the Netherlands

[105] The doctrine of mandatory requirements, or objective justification, may be used in relation to discriminatory treatment of goods and in relation to establishment and services: see generally D. Chalmers 'Free Movement of Goods within the European Community: An Unhealthy Addiction to Scotch Whiskey?' *42 ICLQ* (1993) 269; D. Chalmers 'Repackaging the Internal Market – the Ramifications of the Keck Judgement' *19 EL Rev.* (1994) 385; J. Steiner 'Drawing the Line: Uses and Abuses of Article 30 EEC' *29 CMLR* (1992) 749; L. Gormley 'Reasoning Renounced? The Remarkable Judgement in Keck and Mithouard' *Euro Bus L Rev.* (1994) 63; S. Weatherill 'After *Keck:* Some Thoughts on how to Clarify the Clarification' *33 CMLR* (1996) 885. The taxation cases considered here are the first group of cases to raise the same question in relation to the free movement of persons, and may have consequences in the fields of workers, establishment and services.

[106] *Schumacker*, *supra* note 101, Opinion of the Advocate-General, para. 71.

to be treated in the same way as residents, where at least 90 per cent of their income arose in Germany, under Bilateral Treaty Arrangements with the Netherlands. It was therefore disingenious for Germany to argue that cohesion was at stake. The Advocate-General thus found in favour of Schumacker.

The ECJ began by affirming that, while direct taxation was not as such within the scope of Community law, Article 39EC did impose an obligation on Member States not to treat nationals of other Member States less favourably than their own nationals as regards the collection of direct taxes.[107] The granting of benefits on the basis of residence could constitute indirect discrimination.

In relation to direct taxes, though, the ECJ expressed the view that residents and non-residents are not normally in a comparable situation. The use of a residence criterion was therefore not necessarily unacceptable. However, in a case such as Schumacker's, where the non-resident earned all or almost all of his/her income in a state other than that in which she/he resided, there was 'no objective difference' between the non-resident and a resident engaged in comparable employment.[108] No grounds were found to justify the differential treatment of residents and non-residents in such circumstances.[109] Less favourable treatment at the procedural level was also found to fall foul of the non-discrimination requirement.[110]

The decision in this case thus indicated that the residence criterion, long established and widely used in transnational taxation provisions, was too blunt an instrument for Community law. Though not incompatible with the non-discrimination requirement in all circumstances, there were fact situations where use of residence as a basis for the availability of benefits would result in less favourable treatment of free movers, contrary to the provisions of the Treaty.

While *Schumacker* concerned the free movement of workers, and in particular frontier workers who typically earned all or almost all their income in a state other than that in which they resided, the decision could clearly have wider implications. It was not immediately clear to what extent the decision could extend to other freedoms and other 'benefits' contingent on residence: could non-natural legal persons benefit from this ruling? To what extent would it run through the other free movement provisions of the Treaty? Nor was it clear how deep into national tax provisions the Court might wish to go in seeking discrimination and/or justification. The facts of *Schumacker* presented an extreme case because there was no possibility of obtaining reliefs in the state of residence comparable to those denied in the state of employment. What would be the position of the ECJ when this was

[107] *Schumacker*, *supra* note 101, Judgment of the Court paras 20–4.
[108] *Ibid.*, para. 37.
[109] *Ibid.*, paras 40–6.
[110] *Ibid.*, paras 48–59.

more marginal? The field of establishment and services offers the potential to throw up yet more difficulties. At what point would the ECJ cease to regard the resident and non-resident business/service provider as objectively in the same circumstances for taxation purposes and recognise instead the 'coherence' issue which formed the basis of the decision in *Bachmann*. Finally, where residence and/or other business arrangements can be seen to be influenced by tax-avoidance motives, how far will the non-discrimination requirement be maintained?

Wielockx

Schumacker was followed by the case of *Wielockx*,[111] which concerned Article 43EC and the treatment of certain reserves of business profits for pensions under Dutch tax law. A voluntary pension-reserve tax scheme allowed the self-employed to reserve part of their business profits for a pension without removing them from the business. The moneys set aside in this way were treated very favourably for tax purposes, taxation effectively being deferred. This beneficial treatment was enjoyed, however, only by residents. Wielockx was a 'frontier worker', a partner in a physiotherapy practice, and received all his income in Holland though continuing to reside in Belgium. His situation was thus very similar to Schumacker's, though as a self-employed partner he fell under Article 43EC rather than Article 39EC.

The Advocate-General followed the decision in *Schumacker* on residence, recognising that while resident and non-resident taxpayers would not normally be comparable, this was not the case where the non-resident received all or almost all their income in the taxing state. Thus the Court concluded that the provision in question was discriminatory in *Wielockx's* case. In turning to whether the discrimination was justified, the Advocate-General noted that '[t]he question of justification and the possible applicability of the principle of fiscal cohesion as laid down by the Court in *Bachmann* and *Commission* v. *Belgium* is extremely difficult'.[112]

In the *Bachmann Case*, cohesion was based, the Advocate-General reasoned, on a principle of correlation between deductibility of contributions, whether for social or other reasons, and the (later) taxation of the fruits of those contributions (in *Wielockx*, the pension). However, the Advocate-General observed that Member States were not obliged to invoke this argument regarding cohesion and could, instead, decide to accord equal treatment to free movers. The proportionality test could be invoked to determine whether the invocation of cohesion was justified in a particular case. Here, there was a means of ensuring that taxation deferred through the

[111] Case C-80/94 *G H E J Wielockx* v. *Inspecteur der Directe Belastingen* [1995] ECR I-2493.

[112] *Ibid.*, Opinion of Advocate-General Leger, para. 30.

deductibility of contributions was later collected, since the pension funds in question were by definition located in the Netherlands. An alternative measure less damaging to the non-discrimination principle, and hence to the fundamental freedoms guaranteed in the EC Treaty could be used. Finally, the impact of the international conventions subsisting between the Member States in this case was considered. The Double Taxation Convention between the Netherlands and Belgium,[113] in line with the OECD Model Convention on Double Taxation,[114] stated that pensions should be taxed only in the state of residence of the beneficiary. However, the Advocate-General argued that an international convention could not serve as justification for discriminatory treatment under EC law. Thus he concluded that the discrimination was unjustified. The Court adopted the reasoning of the Advocate-General: 'Fiscal cohesion has not . . . been established in relation to one and the same person by a strict correlation between the deductibility of contributions and the taxation of pensions'.[115]

As Vanistandael demonstrates,[116] the implications of these decisions are potentially far reaching. If the ECJ was prepared to apply the *Schumacker–Wielockx* rule when the impossibility to benefit from tax reliefs available to resident taxpayers resulted not from factual impossibility (the absence of income in the jurisdiction), but from legal impossibility (rules which restrict such reliefs on foreign-sourced income) 'the Court would put the country of source in charge of providing tax relief, a taxing power which under conventional international tax rules belongs to the country of residence'.[117] Moreover, if the discrimination in the country of residence results from legal rather than factual impossibility, it would have to be asked whether there were circumstances in which this could be justified, for instance under *Bachmann*.[118] In both respects such a development would constitute a radical departure from established international double taxation rules which so far have been preserved and respected under EC law. However, the ECJ did recognise in *Schumacker* that the factual situation of Schumacker was exceptional and that generally residents and non-residents would not be regarded as comparable. In so doing, a much more fundamental challenge to international tax principles is avoided, 'the entire tax discrimination issue

[113] Double Taxation Convention of 19 October 1970 between the Kingdom of Belgium and the Kingdom of the Netherlands on Income and Capital and Certain Other Fiscal Matters.

[114] Model Double Taxation Convention on Income and on Capital, OECD 1977, Art. 18.

[115] *Wielockx*, *supra* note 111, Judgment of the Court para. 24.

[116] F. Vanistandael 'The Consequences of Schumacker and Wielockx: Two Steps Forward in the Tax Progression of Echternach' *33 CMLR* (1996) 255.

[117] *Ibid.*, pp. 262–3.

[118] *Ibid.*, pp. 264–5; P. J. Wattel 'The EC Court's Attempts to Reconcile the Treaty Freedoms with International Tax Law' *33 CMLR* (1996) 223 at p. 238 *et infra*.

is pre-empted, and the free movement of persons is deprived of meaning, except for those non-residents who earn their entire income in the source State'.[119] To have held otherwise would have produced 'chaos'.[120]

Asscher

Fiscal cohesion was again at issue in the case of *Asscher*.[121] Asscher was a Dutch national who had been resident in Belgium for a number of years and worked as a director of a Dutch company in Holland and as a director of a Belgian company in Belgium. Asscher paid tax and national insurance in Belgium on his income from the Belgian company; he was also subjected to taxation as a non-resident under Dutch law. Under the relevant provisions he was taxed at the (non-resident) rate of 25 per cent, whereas Dutch residents were taxed at a lower rate of 13 per cent. Asscher challenged the deduction of tax and the matter was eventually referred to the ECJ.[122]

The first question which arose was whether Asscher was a 'free mover' and thus protected by EC law, given that his complaint was against his own state of nationality. Distinguishing the situation of Asscher from that in the earlier case of *Werner*,[123] the ECJ found that Asscher had through his economic activities 'exercised the rights and liberties recognised by the Treaty'.[124] He was thus in relation to his state of origin in a situation 'equivalent to that of any other person relying as against the host Member State on the rights and liberties guaranteed by the Treaty';[125] a 'free mover'.

The Court then proceeded to deal with the substantive questions, effectively whether the discrimination suffered by Asscher was contrary to Article 52EC (now 43). The Court noted its previous jurisprudence, to the effect that discrimination based on residence tended to affect non-nationals more than nationals and thus will often constitute indirect discrimination.[126]

[119] Wattel, *ibid.*, p. 230.

[120] F. Vanistandael 'The Limits', *supra* note 76, at p. 311; Wattel, *ibid.*, pp. 231–2.

[121] Case C-107/94 *P. H. Asscher* v. *Staatssecretaris van Financien* [1996] ECR I-3089.

[122] Under Dutch tax laws, Asscher was classified as a worker and the Hoge Raad der Nederlanden referred a number of questions relating to the interpretation of ex-Article 48 (now 39). However the Advocate-General and the ECJ itself were in no doubt that, given Asscher's position as sole director and sole shareholder, the matter properly fell within the scope of ex-Article 52 (now 43), and proceeded on that basis.

[123] C-112/91 *Werner* v. *Finanzampt Aachen Innenstadt* Case [1993] ECR I-429. Werner was a German national who had qualified and established himself in Germany and merely resided in another Member State. The ECJ regarded his position as purely internal. A-G Darmon noted that the material facts arose prior to the adoption of Council Directive 90/364/EEC of 28 June 1990 on the right of residence (*OJ* 1990 L 180, p. 26).

[124] *Asscher*, *supra* note 121, Judgment at para. 33.

[125] *Ibid.*, para. 34.

[126] To fall into the category to which the lower rate of taxation was applied, individuals had to be resident in Holland and earn at least 90 per cent of their

Discriminatory treatment was prohibited by Article 52EC (now 43), whether it took the form of failure to take account of personal or family circumstances[127] or a higher rate of taxation.[128]

Attention thus focused on the question of whether there were objective differences between the two groups which would justify the differences in treatment in this case. The Dutch government argued that the higher rate of taxation was justified because non-residents did not pay national insurance contributions and thus suffered a lower overall tax burden, for which the higher rate compensated. They also invoked the *Bachmann* argument that the measure was necessary to ensure cohesion in the tax system, in particular to ensure the progressivity of taxation. However, the Court rejected both these points. Though noting that residents and non-residents are not generally comparable, there being objective differences between their situations,[129] these objective differences must justify the different treatment at issue. Therefore, though not explicitly endorsing the view of the Advocate-General, the Court seemed to accept his argument that the objective difference relied on must be '*fiscally relevant*, that is to say that it must be sufficiently closely linked to the field of taxation in issue'.[130]

Dealing with the issue of progressivity, the Court noted that under the applicable Double Taxation Agreement, the state of residence had the option to take into account income received in another state in order to apply the rule of progressivity, though such income was exempt from taxation by that state.[131] The Dutch government thus had no cause to treat the non-resident taxpayer differently from the resident taxpayer on this basis.

Turning to the link with national insurance contributions and the overall tax burden, the Court treated this as a payment for social security cover:

> either Mr Asscher is properly insured with the Belgian social security scheme alone and there can be no question of penalising him by means of a tax differential for not paying social security contributions in the Netherlands; or he should be insured either exclusively or additionally with the Netherlands social security scheme, which would enable the Netherlands to claim social security contributions from him and would thus take him out of the 'foreign' scale of tax rates.[132]

worldwide income there. The significance of this was that this would bring them within the Dutch national insurance scheme. The Dutch government argued *inter alia* that the higher rate of tax for non-residents compensated for the lower overall tax burden borne by them (since they did not pay into the national insurance scheme).

[127] *Schumacker*, *supra* note 101.

[128] As was the case here.

[129] Both with regard to the source of their income and the ability of the taxing state to take account of their personal and family circumstances: Judgment para. 41.

[130] Opinion of A-G Leger, para. 74.

[131] Judgment, para. 47.

[132] Judgment, para. 54.

Far from establishing coherence, the Dutch government, it seemed, had failed to establish any proper link between the discriminatory treatment and the situation of the taxpayer. The higher rate of taxation did not result in any social security protection in Holland. Moreover, Community law itself in the shape of Council Regulation 1408/71[133] provided that free movers would in principle have social insurance solely in their state of residence.[134]

Futura[135]

This was an Article 234EC reference from a Luxembourg Court regarding a dispute between the Luxembourg tax authorities and the French company Futura over the taxation of the company's Luxembourg branch, Singer. For tax purposes, the profits of the branch were calculated on an apportionment basis, calculated by reference to the turnover figures of each part of the company. Futura wished to offset certain losses against the profits for 1986 and calculated these also by apportionment. However, the relevant Luxembourg provisions restricted the offset of losses to losses which could be shown to be related to the income received in Luxembourg and shown in accounts kept in Luxembourg. Apportionment was not permitted.

The case thus raised two main questions. First, whether Luxembourg was justified in the substantive restriction in the relevant offsetting provisions to losses related to the activities carried on in its territory and, second, whether it was entitled to insist on accounts being maintained in Luxembourg as a condition for allowing the offsetting of losses. Unfortunately, the questions were put as one to the ECJ[136] and though both the Advocate-General and the Court itself addressed both questions raised, examination of the first was extremely cursory. Both were happy to accept without close examination the proposition that the requirement that there was an economic link between the losses and activities of the company in Luxembourg (the territorial principle of international tax law) was not contrary to Article 43EC. This is curious,

[133] Council Regulation (EEC) No. 1408/71 of 14 June 1971 on the application of social security schemes to employed persons and their families moving within the *Community* (*OJ*, English Spec. ED. 1971(II), p. 416).

[134] Judgment, paras 59–60.

[135] Case C-205/95 *Futura Participations SA and Singer* v. *Administration des Contributions* [1997] ECR-I 2471.

[136] The question referred was:

> Are Article 157 of the Law on Taxation of Revenue and, in so far as is necessary, Article 4 and the second subparagraph of Article 21(2) of the France–Luxembourg Convention on Double Taxation compatible with Article 52 of the EEC Treaty inasmuch as they make application to non-resident taxpayers having a permanent business in Luxembourg of provisions on the carrying forward of losses subject to the condition that the losses should be related to income received locally and that accounts should be duly kept and held within the country?

Opinion of the A-G, para. 15, Judgment para. 13.

since the resultant need to desegregate accounts for operations in each Member State where an enterprise has permanent establishment undoubtedly presents in many cases a 'double burden'. There is *prima facie* a case of discrimination, though it may well be objectively justifiable discrimination in the light of the need for effective fiscal supervision. Without entering discussion of this, the Advocate-General merely noted that neither the parties nor the Commission had questioned the compatibility of the international law principle with Article 43EC (ex 52). Likewise the Court, though noting the non-discrimination requirement of Article 43EC (ex 52) and its previous case-law, accepted without question the compatibility of the territorial principle.

Turning to the second question, however, the issue of the double burden carried paramount significance. Luxembourg argued that the keeping of separate accounts in Luxembourg was a necessary condition to guarantee effective fiscal supervision. The Advocate-General and the Court accepted that effective fiscal supervision was an overriding requirement of general interest, capable of justifying a restriction on the exercise of the fundamental freedoms guaranteed by the Treaty (following *Cassis de Dijon*[137]). But any such justification was subject to the requirement of proportionality and that requirement was not met here. Luxembourg was entitled to oblige the taxpayer wishing to offset losses to demonstrate 'clearly and precisely' that the losses in question related to activities carried on in Luxembourg. However, this did not justify the requirement that separate accounts be kept in Luxembourg. Siding with the European Commission and rejecting the arguments of the UK and Luxembourg, the Advocate-General and the Court distinguished between accurate figures and separate accounts. The former could be required and checked, if necessary utilising existing co-operation and mutual assistance arrangements;[138] the latter went beyond what was necessary and therefore constituted unjustifiable discrimination.[139]

Observations on the Court's jurisprudential approach

On the whole, the approach of the ECJ in the field of taxation is consistent with its general approach in relation to the free movement provisions of the EC Treaty. Direct taxation is within the competence of Member States, not of the Community, but in keeping with the doctrine of supremacy of EC law, Member States must exercise that competence consistently with Community law. In particular, the fundamental freedoms must be respected and

[137] Case 120/78 *REWE-Zentral etc*, *supra* note 91.

[138] Particular reference was made to Council Directive 77/799 of 19 December 1977 concerning mutual assistance by the competent authorities of the Member State in the field of direct taxation, *OJ* 1977, L 336/15: *Futura*, *supra* note 135, Judgment para. 41.

[139] *Ibid.*, para. 39.

the principle of non-discrimination on grounds of nationality observed in relation thereto. Indirect discrimination, often arising from the use of a residence criterion in tax provisions, has been found unlawful in a range of situations.[140] Throughout the series of cases outlined above the Court has recognised, however, that discrimination might occur by the application of *different* rules to comparable situations or the application of the *same* rule to different situations.[141] Thus it has ruled that differences in the treatment accorded to different taxpayers must relate to actual differences in their situations. This is in effect a requirement that the Member State objectively justify the difference in treatment between nationals and non-nationals once it is established *prima facie*.

Where discrimination is established, the question of objective justification arises again, to determine whether the doctrine of mandatory requirements is satisfied, i.e. to establish whether there is a genuine issue of effective fiscal supervision and, if so, whether the principle of proportionality has been satisfied.[142] The *Cassis de Dijon* doctrine of mandatory requirements has been presented to the Court and handled by the Court in exactly the same way, regardless of the freedoms at issue, and the Court has shown itself willing to subject the Member States' laws and practices to close scrutiny in order to satisfy itself as to the legitimacy of the discrimination.[143]

As in other fields, however, it is not for the Court to extend the protection of Community law beyond discrimination. Fundamentally, barriers to free movement arise from differences in both the rates of taxation and the method for establishment of the tax base. In the absence of harmonisation measures, the ECJ can do no more than to ensure that Member States observe the requirements of rationality and equality of treatment in the exercise of their powers, and only in so far as free movers are concerned.

Thus, as far as foreign investment is concerned, the matter of direct taxation of investments from third states is still governed exclusively by the Member States, and there has been no harmonisation of direct taxes between them. In dealing with foreign investment, they will each apply any double taxation agreements and may also use unilateral measures to address questions of double taxation, and the tax structure, the overall tax burden and procedural requirements may vary greatly between Member States. Membership of the EU has had little or no effect in this regard. In respect of intra-community investment, however, the free movement principles of the Treaty, together with the non-discrimination principle, can be relied on

[140] For example *Wielockx, Asscher, Futura*, as discussed, *supra*.

[141] *Wielockx*, *supra* note 111, Judgment para. 17.

[142] *Futura*, *supra* note 135.

[143] In this it has often been aided by the European Commission, which made submissions in all the major cases discussed above including *Bachmann, Schumacker, Wielockx, Asscher* and *Futura*.

by investors to tackle at least some aspects of discrimination and double taxation suffered by non-national enterprises. Thus the ECJ cannot ensure uniformity of treatment and in particular cannot tackle the double burden which arises from having to deal with more than one tax authority.

Despite its rigorous approach to the question of discrimination, the ECJ recognises limits to its ability to tackle the most entrenched forms of discrimination in the taxation field. These are the differences in treatment which flow from the existence of separate sovereign states. By contrast to its approach to other forms of restriction on free movement, the Court has not been able to introduce any principle of equivalence or mutual recognition. In *Futura* the basic problem for the free mover, a French company with a branch in Luxembourg, was that they had to submit to two separate tax authorities. Inevitably this meant that two sets of figures had to be prepared. But, in addition, the Court accepted that there was no requirement that the Luxembourg authorities rely on the figures already established by the French authorities,[144] as the Commission had suggested they could. 'No provision has yet been made for harmonising domestic rules relating to determination of the basis of assessment to direct taxes.'[145] Thus Luxembourg's objective of effective fiscal supervision could not be met without the imposition of an additional evidentiary requirement which branches of businesses established in Luxembourg would not face.

The frequency with which Member States intervene in cases before the ECJ is perhaps an indication that the Court's instincts are correct here; there is as yet insufficient harmonisation and co-operation to render an equivalence route politically acceptable. The sources of the barriers to free movement here are rules fundamental to the structure of international tax law, and lie in an area – taxation – where the notion of state sovereignty is highly prized. Hatzopoulos,[146] commenting on *Futura*, points to precedents in other fields, citing in particular the principles of international environmental law recognised in *Commission* v. *Belgium (Walloon Waste)*.[147]

In conclusion, the ECJ has been able to tackle fiscal provisions which indirectly discriminate against investors or service providers from other Member States, except to the extent that such provisions can be objectively justified as, for instance, necessary to ensure adequate fiscal supervision or

[144] This could be seen as comparable to the ruling in services cases, such as the *Insurance Cases*, that the authorities of one Member State accept authorisations and licences issued in an enterprise's home state as proof that the enterprise is satisfactory in relation to the matters addressed in that home state's authorisation and licensing process; this does not prevent the host state requiring proof of satisfactory standing in relation to additional matters addressed in its own authorisation of licensing processes; see further *Commission* v. *Germany*, *supra* note 17.

[145] *Futura*, *supra* note 135, judgment para. 33.

[146] Case note on *Futura* at *35 CMLR* (1998) 493 at 502.

[147] Case 2/90 [1992] ECR I-4431.

to maintain cohesion in the tax system. Finally, taxpayers facing double taxation can rely for assistance on the Arbitration Convention,[148] which obliges the two states involved in any alleged double taxation situation to seek a solution or accept arbitration to eliminate the double taxation.

6.2.2 *Taxation of foreign investment under NAFTA*

The market access and national treatment/MFN obligations of NAFTA are severely curtailed in relation to taxation.

As with GATT, taxation could, in the absence of further clarification, fall foul of NAFTA rules on trade in goods wherever a tax measure constituted unjustifiable discrimination or, more generally, where such measures had the effect of nullifying or impairing any benefit reasonably expected to accrue directly or indirectly from NAFTA.[149] In relation to foreign investment, taxation is not addressed directly in Chapter Eleven but clearly, in the absence of further clarification, could be implicated where a tax measure was in contravention of the national treatment and/or MFN standards established therein or amounted to a prohibited performance requirement.[150]

However, Article 2103 contains a general exception stating simply and categorically '[e]xcept as set out in this Article, nothing in this agreement shall apply to taxation measures'.[151]

Moreover, Article 2103(2) addresses double taxation agreements and similar tax conventions and makes clear that in the event of any inconsistency between the provisions of such agreements and NAFTA, the former will prevail. Thus in general terms tax matters are excluded from the ambit of NAFTA.

A limited number of exceptions to this general approach of exclusion are then laid out. In relation to trade in goods a GATT-based approach is endorsed, whereby taxation measures which would amount to a breach of GATT Article III[152] are to be treated similarly under NAFTA. In relation to the cross-border provision of services and financial services, certain discriminatory forms of taxation are outlawed in principle, but existing discriminatory provisions are protected and 'grandfathered' and discrimination flowing from MFN clauses in existing tax treaties is also tolerated.[153] Article 2103(4)(g) clarifies that taxation measures introduced to improve the administration and/or collection of taxes will not be unlawful, provided that such

[148] Convention of 23 July on the Elimination of Double Taxation in Connection with the Adjustment of Profits of Associated Enterprises: *OJ* 1990 L225/10.

[149] See further Section 4.2.1 above.

[150] See further Section 6.1.2 above.

[151] NAFTA Art. 2103(1).

[152] See further Section 4.2.1 above.

[153] NAFTA Art. 2103(4).

measures do not constitute arbitrary discrimination or arbitrary nullification or impairment of any benefit arising from NAFTA.

By contrast, it is clearly stated that taxation measures will fall foul of NAFTA where they constitute performance requirements prohibited under Chapter Eleven.[154] Similarly, it is clear that, where a taxation measure amounts to an expropriation, it will fall foul of the provisions of Chapter Eleven on expropriation.[155] However, an exceptional procedure is established for the resolution of any such dispute whereby the 'Competent Authorities' may make a determination that a disputed measure does not amount to expropriation;[156] only where such a decision has not been taken after six months can the aggrieved party resort to the dispute resolution procedures established in Chapter Eleven.[157] Given that the 'Competent Authorities' are government representatives, there is clearly room for political accommodation and negotiation in relation to tax matters, even where they clearly operate contrary to the prevailing free trade ideology which underpins NAFTA.

From this brief outline, it can be concluded that the NAFTA Parties are not yet ready to bring the free trade agenda to bear on the historic patterns of taxation of foreign investors, traders and service providers. Both the general policy of excluding tax matters from the scope of NAFTA, and the cautious approach to exceptions to this policy, indicate the persisting political sensitivity of states to tax matters. This is very clearly illustrated by the provision of a political route for dispute resolution exclusively in relation to expropriation and taxation.

6.3 Dispute resolution in the EU and NAFTA – some issues

Dispute resolution within the EC pillar of the EU is judicial in nature and public, with the judgments of the ECJ being published. Where an action is brought against a state alleged to have breached an obligation arising from the EC Treaty itself, the European Commission will attempt to resolve the matter without going to court. Such actions are, however, relatively rare; the bulk of the case-load of the ECJ is actions instigated by individuals or other legal persons (such as companies), with the majority reaching the Court by referral from a national court, as laid down in Article 234EC. In such cases, and in other instances where cases are instigated by individuals, no provision is made for a period of notice, or for a process of consultation

[154] NAFTA Art. 2103(5). On performance requirements, see further Section 6.1.2 above.

[155] NAFTA Art. 1110.

[156] The 'Competent Authorities' are in each case a deputy finance or treasury minister of the governments (one from each): NAFTA Annex 2104.6.

[157] These are discussed below at Section 6.3.2.

or conciliation, as is common in many other areas of international law. This formal, legalistic and rule-based approach to disputes characterises the legal regime which operates within the EC pillar of the EU and serves to distinguish this regime from other regional and global trade regimes.

The legal system of the EC broke new ground in cases such as *Van Gend en Loos*[158] in recognising that private parties who were the beneficiaries of the rights created in the Treaty of Rome and measures of EC law (Regulations and Directives) could rely on these rights in the national courts of their Member States. Furthermore, the Article 234EC system of referring cases to the ECJ for rulings on the correct interpretation of European Economic Community (EEC) law went some way towards ensuring that the law was given a uniform and consistent effect throughout the Member States, and that disguised restrictions on trade can be dismantled.[159] In more recent years, the ECJ has been concerned to ensure that parties can be fully compensated for injury resulting from breach of the free movement provisions of the Treaty.[160] While the sight of private individuals, corporate entities and trade associations pleading the free movement principles of EC law against their own or other Member States has become commonplace, it is still a relatively scarce phenomenon from a global perspective that the beneficiaries of international treaties are given direct litigation rights in courts to enforce obligations arising from those treaties or secondary measures taken under their provisions.

Under NAFTA, provision is made for disputes between foreign investors and host states[161] to be settled by a process which is referred to as arbitration, but which displays some features more characteristic of an adjudicative process. Under Article 1118, the disputing parties should first seek to settle their disputes through consultation or negotiation; where they wish to proceed to arbitration, ninety days notice must be given. Arbitration may then be sought under the ICSID Convention or the Additional Facility Rules of ICSID as appropriate,[162] or may be arranged under the UN Commission on International Trade Law (UNCITRAL) Arbitration Rules. NAFTA itself constitutes the agreement of the State Parties to all of these and the investor

[158] *Supra* note 10.

[159] See, for instance, cases such as *Van Binsbergen*, *Commission* v. *Germany (Re Insurance Services)*, and *Alpine Investments*, discussed above at Section 6.1.1.

[160] Case C-48/93 *R* v. *Secretary of State for Transport, ex parte Factortame Ltd and Others (Factortame III)* [1996] ECR-I-1029.

[161] A dispute, essentially, must constitute a claim that one of the investment provisions outlined above has been breached by a state Party and that an investor has suffered loss or damage as a result. Claims must be brought within three years of when the investor first acquired, or should have acquired, knowledge of the alleged breach and knowledge that the investor has incurred loss or damage: NAFTA Art. 1116.

[162] This depends on whether both the state of the investor and the state Party alleged to have breached NAFTA provisions are Parties to the ICSID Convention.

can choose which to utilise. The investor's submission of the dispute for arbitration is deemed to constitute consent on its part.

The arbitral tribunal will consist of three arbitrators, one appointed by each disputant and the third (presiding) arbitrator by agreement between them;[163] failing this, the Secretary-General of ICSID will serve as appointing authority.[164] The applicable rules are those of NAFTA and of international law.[165] Tribunals are empowered to order interim measures of protection;[166] final awards may consist of monetary damages and interest thereon or restitution.[167] Where the latter is awarded, the disputing state Party may opt to pay damages in lieu of restitution.[168] Punitive damages are not permitted.[169]

The Investor–State dispute provisions thus provide a dispute settlement mechanism which, though voluntary on the side of the investor, are compulsory on the side of the state Party. Though the state Party may choose one arbitrator and participate in the selection of another, there is, as is common in international arbitration agreements, a default mechanism, allowing an independent party to fill the breach if the disputants fail to appoint or cannot reach agreement. In addition, the choice of law is predetermined and the outcome is binding on the Parties. Failure by a state Party to comply can lead to further action (by the state whose investor was a party to the dispute) before a NAFTA panel.[170]

This dispute resolution procedure is potentially an important tool in enhancing compliance with NAFTA obligations. The same consideration applies here as in relation to the EU: that the injured investor is the party with the greatest interest in enforcement and the mechanism created is less heavily politicised than would be a State–State mechanism. However, unlike the EU, the NAFTA 'arbitration' remains confidential thus denying the opportunity to allow uncertainties over the meaning of the rather novel provisions of NAFTA to be resolved.[171] Whereas the provisions of EC law allowing for adjudication can be said to promote clarity and uniformity between the laws and policies of the Member States, increasing both investor

[163] NAFTA Art. 1123.
[164] NAFTA Art. 1124.
[165] NAFTA Art. 1130.
[166] NAFTA Art. 1133.
[167] NAFTA Art. 1134(1).
[168] *Ibid.*
[169] NAFTA Art. 1134(3).
[170] NAFTA Art. 1135(6).
[171] Note that, formally, any award made under the investment provisions of NAFTA is binding only on the disputing parties: Art. 1135(1). While this equates with the formal position under EC law, NAFTA adopts an 'arbitral' approach of confidentiality, whereas the ECJ's proceedings are judicial and public in nature, and the ECJ operates a *de facto* system of precedent in citing and following its own previous decisions.

and Member State confidence about their rights, the NAFTA provisions offer no such opportunities.

Investors who are not the subject of any NAFTA obligations remain subject only to the domestic laws of the Parties, leading some anti-NAFTA activists to claim that the provisions lack balance. Environmental activists in particular have expressed concern that the NAFTA mechanism permits companies to bring actions against governments while doing nothing directly to enhance the accountability of companies, either to government or to communities. Moreover, the provisions are castigated for giving companies an additional weapon – the threat of litigation – which can be used to dissuade the government from taking even legitimate action. The relationship between the rights of investors under NAFTA and legitimate environmental regulation is addressed directly within NAFTA. Article 1114 states:

> (1) Nothing in this Chapter shall be construed to prevent a Party from adopting, maintaining, or enforcing any measure, otherwise inconsistent with this Chapter, that it considers appropriate to ensure that investment activity in its territory is undertaken in a manner sensitive to environmental concerns.
>
> (2) The Parties recognise that it is inappropriate to encourage investment by relaxing domestic health, safety or environmental measures. Accordingly, a Party should not waive or otherwise derogate from, or offer to waive or otherwise derogate from, such measures as an encouragement for the establishment, acquisition, expansion, or retention in its territory of an investment of an investor.[172]

The following cases have served to highlight these concerns.

Metalclad Corporation v. Government of Mexico

In January 1997 Metalclad, a US-based waste disposal company, brought an Investor–State action against Mexico before ICSID. It alleged breaches of NAFTA, flowing from the refusal of the government of San Luis Potosi state to allow the reopening of a waste disposal plant on environmental grounds. The Governor subsequently declared the ecologically sensitive site part of an ecological zone. Metalclad claimed that these actions amounted to *de facto* expropriation and claimed $90 million in damages, including loss of future profits. The action thus demonstrates how the property focus of the investment protection provisions of NAFTA and of other investment protection provisions plays into the hands of the 'takings' movement, or 'property rights' activists who have argued from a property rights basis for the compensation of landowners adversely affected by environmental regulations.

Environmental campaigners also argued that this case demonstrated how a national government could rely on its international obligations as a way of

[172] NAFTA Art. 1114. Consultations may be sought where one Party believes another Party to have acted in breach of Art. 1114(2).

defeating local opposition; 'Metalclad claims the Mexican federal government is (unofficially) encouraging the company's NAFTA lawsuit so that it can deflect the political fall-out of forcing the state to open the facility . . . this case raises the disturbing possibility that investors can use their rights to collude with governments to force unwanted, or even dangerous investments on unwilling populations'.[173]

Ethyl Corporation v. Government of Canada

In April 1988, the Canadian government banned the import and interprovincial transportation of the gasoline additive MMT. MMT is a manganese-based compound added to gasoline as a lead substitute to enhance octane and reduce engine 'knocking'. The Canadian legislature was concerned that MMT emissions pose a significant risk to public health but was unable, apparently due to the lack of adequate data on health risks, to impose an outright ban under the terms of the Canadian Environmental Protection Act.[174] MMT is used only in Canada and Ethyl Corporation, a US-based company, is its only manufacturer.

Ethyl Corporation commenced an action against the Canadian government under the investment chapter of NAFTA, seeking compensation of $US 251 million for the expropriation of its MMT production plant and its 'good reputation'. The amount requested is reported to be higher than that requested in any ICSID Investor–State dispute to date.[175]

As required under NAFTA, Ethyl submitted notice of their intention to bring an action six months before doing so; in fact, this was done six months prior to the MMT ban being passed. They then claimed that the legislative debate itself constituted an expropriation, since the company was criticised and suffered damage to its reputation during that period. In 1998, Canada settled with Ethyl, agreeing to pay $13 million in respect of damages and legal costs. Canada also undertook to repeal the ban on MMT and to issue a public declaration that MMT is safe. Such a declaration would contradict the opinion reached previously by the Canadian Environmental Protection Agency.

The *Ethyl Case* has disturbed environmentalists for a number of reasons. The protection of investors offered under NAFTA rules clearly should be balanced against the demands of public health and environmental protection. Under the Investor–State dispute settlement mechanism of NAFTA, the task of balancing competing claims is shifted from politicians to the arbitrators

[173] *Our Future Under the Multilateral Agreement on Investment* Public Citizen: Global Trade Watch 1988, http://www.citizen.org/pctrade/nafta/metalcla.htm.

[174] Briefing Paper *Ethyl Corporation vs. Government of Canada: Now Investors Can Use NAFTA to Challenge Environmental Safeguards* Public Citizen: Global Trade Watch 1988, http://www.citizen.org/pctrade/nafta/Ethylbri.htm.

[175] Briefing Paper, *ibid.*

or judges. While this may at times prove beneficial from an environmentalist standpoint, it is clearly a risky strategy and one which has been regarded by some as anti-democratic. Of particular concern has been the fact that only one side in the environmental protection battle – the investor – can avail itself of this enforcement tool, as there is no provision for a 'public interest' action by environmental campaigners or others, nor any mechanism by which they can intervene in such actions. Moreover, unlike the EC, there are no institutions within NAFTA which can participate in such proceedings or actively seek to displace a court ruling regarded as unhelpful with legislation. The 'depoliticisation' of disputes much vaunted in the investment protection debate is precisely what environmentalists challenge.

The *Ethyl Case* also aroused concern because the intention of the company to take action was announced during the passage of the national legislation. Though this had the effect of restoring to the legislature responsibility for deciding how competing concerns should be balanced, the threat of legal action was interpreted by environmentalists as an attempt to intimidate the Canadian legislature, that is, as a SLAPP suit; 'While Ethyl failed in this instance, the ability of investors to use their private legal standing to credibly threaten major suits could lead to successful efforts in the future to derail the democratic decision-making process and alter the outcome of legislative debate'.[176]

This, of course, is precisely the intention of such measures. If a state party to an international treaty purporting to protect foreign investors from particular types of regulatory or expropriatory action was undeterred by these treaty obligations and the possibility of enforcement action, the treaty would be judged a failure. Thus 'US government negotiators have actually argued that the ability of investors to use legal threats to influence legislative debates is a healthy innovation that will prevent governments from passing laws that violate international agreements'.[177]

S. D. Myers Inc. v. Government of Canada

The Ottowa Federal government banned the export of PCB contaminated waste in 1995, but revoked the ban in 1997 when a number of US firms threatened to take action under NAFTA. Myers launched an action in August 1998 seeking $6.3 million from the Canadian government for loss of profits, estimated at $15 million, during the period of the ban, despite the fact that the US had since banned the import of PCBs, thus eclipsing the trade in any case. The company argued that the ban was tantamount to a direct or indirect expropriation.

[176] Briefing Paper, *ibid.*

[177] *Ibid.*, citing US Department of Treasury, Briefing to the Senate Committee on Banking, Housing and Urban Affairs on the MAI and Financial Services Agreement, 21 April 1997.

Loewen Group, Inc. v. United States

This case, involving the funeral conglomerate, Loewen, was the first Investor–State case brought against the US. The basis for the action was a breach of contract case in the state of Mississippi, in which damages had been awarded against Loewen for breach of an agreement giving another company exclusive rights to provide funeral insurance services. The case involved allegations of anti-competitive and predatory practices on the part of Loewen and the jury awarded compensatory damages of $100 million along with punitive damages of $400 million. Loewan wished to appeal, but under Mississippi law was required to post a bond of 125 per cent of the damages owed before doing so. The Mississippi Supreme Court refused to set aside this requirement, stating that it served to prevent defendants using the lengthy appeals process to hide assets or otherwise evade liability.

Loewen launched an action against the US under Chapter Eleven of NAFTA, claiming that the requirement for a 125 per cent bond effectively expropriated its assets without compensation and violated the company's right to fair and equal and non-disriminatory treatment. It also claimed that the conduct of the trial judge, the size of the jury award, the courtroom strategy of the plaintiff's attorneys and the rulings of the Supreme Court constituted a 'denial of justice'. Loewen chose the ICSID route for this case.

This case was regarded by critics as an attack on fundamental aspects of the US civil justice system, in particular of the system for punitive damages and of administrative tools such as the requirement for the lodging of a surety before commencing an action.[178]

These cases became the focus for Non-Governmental Organisation (NGO) unease about the Investor–State dispute settlement provisions of NAFTA and took on greater political significance when the NAFTA provisions were used as the model for the MAI dispute settlement provisions.[179]

The dispute resolution systems of the EU and NAFTA have some common important features. One is that they establish a means whereby the duties of host and home states vis-à-vis investors (rather than each other) can be explored and developed. This occurs particularly in the EU where a *de facto* system of precedent operates and where the process is public in nature. Another has been the enhancement of the enforcement of the obligations established in the relevant treaties and secondary legislation. The creation of rights of action for the individuals and companies who are the victims of violations of the duties established between states frees those victims from the vagaries of the system of diplomatic protection, discussed in Chapter 5, and has shown itself to be a very effective enforcement tool. In

[178] *Canadian Corporation Found Liable in Mississipi Courts Uses NAFTA to Claim Legal System Violated Its Rights* Public Citizen: Global Trade Watch at http://www.citizen.org/pctrade/nafta/cases/Loewen.htm.

[179] See Section 7.5 below.

each case, the dispute settlement mechanism provided achieves the 'internationalisation' of the dispute vaunted in earlier foreign investment arbitrations, placing the state party and the investor on the same level before a tribunal whose findings will be binding.

However, opposition to the NAFTA cases brought to date has been strong and vocal, particularly from environmentalists. Political activists opposed to actions of the sort illustrated by the cases discussed above have drawn attention to some of the consequences of such a system. In the first place, providing that the delicate task of balancing the competing claims of, for instance, economic actors and environmentalists should be resolved by a judicial or arbitral process has the effect of presenting the claims of the two sides as if they are morally equivalent. Under a legal discourse, the concept of rule of law and its attendant concept of equality before the law appear to treat the claims of one private party (the investor) as equivalent to the claims of the public body, the state party. The additional 'public interest' element of the government's case is lost. Moreover, neither EC law nor NAFTA allows public interest groups to make representations to the tribunal hearing the case. Indeed, under the NAFTA system, public interest groups have no right of access to documents detailing the claim and any counterclaims or defence, since the arbitration procedures utilised are confidential to the Parties.[180]

Resort to judicial or arbitral processes also places great faith in the legal rules in these free trade areas – the NAFTA Treaty or the *acquis communitaire* of the EC. Even very creative tribunals such as the ECJ can only work with the rules given to them. Two observations follow from this. One is that the real complaint of opponents of the NAFTA dispute resolution provisions is that NAFTA itself does not give adequate recognition to environmental concerns, but instead tips the balance of interests too far towards the market. The second is that in both the EU and in NAFTA, it is open to the state Parties to change the rules if they are shown by litigation to be unsatisfactory. Again the real complaint would seem to be not about the dispute resolution processes as such, but about the responsiveness of the political actors, in NAFTA the state Parties, to environmental concerns. These concerns raised by the above NAFTA disputes are, however, serious and legitimate and should be addressed before attempts are made to reproduce the NAFTA solution at a global level.[181]

[180] NAFTA does however, provide that a public register be maintained of all requests for arbitration: NAFTA Art 1125(12).

[181] See further Section 7.5 below.

7

The treatment of foreign investment: towards a new paradigm

New international standards – introduction

This chapter examines a number of legal developments which, it is argued, have shaped current approaches to the treatment of foreign investment. As has already been seen, the free trade and market integration goals of the EU and NAFTA provided within those respective spheres an important impetus for the development of new approaches to foreign investment issues and for the development of new legal norms, concepts and dispute settlement techniques. These developments have also been instrumental in shaping the international agenda relating to foreign investment and have strongly influenced recent multilateral initiatives. This chapter examines first the *Foreign Investment Review Act (FIRA) Case*, a pre-Uruguay Round GATT dispute between Canada and the US, which throws into sharp relief the ideological debate over the role of the state in the regulation of foreign investment and the relationship between foreign investment regulation and trade disciplines. It then looks at the foreign investment implications of the Uruguay Round Agreements, in particular TRIMs which clarifies the relationship between GATT and the regulation of foreign investment, GATS, which concerns market access for and treatment of service providers, and the Trade Policy Review Mechanism (TPRM), the WTO mechanism whereby the trade policies of Members are subject to regular scrutiny by other WTO Members. Finally, this chapter examines in some depth the draft MAI, the text which emerged from a failed attempt by the OECD to negotiate a comprehensive multilateral treaty for the liberalisation of foreign investment regulation and the protection of foreign investors. This text, together with the history of the negotiating process, forms an extremely valuable source of evidence about the current state of the debate over the regulation of foreign investment and about its likely future direction.

7.1 The treatment of foreign investment under GATT – the *FIRA Case*

GATT is concerned essentially with trade rather than investment *per se*, but the effective liberalisation of trade under free market principles requires factor mobility, including the ability of investors to locate in areas offering low economic rents and/or other 'market' advantages. Measures which impede factor mobility may indirectly impede trade, and it is this which provided the key to bring foreign investment issues into the Uruguay Round of Multilateral Trade Negotiations. However, although promotion of an open operating climate for foreign investment had long been recognised in the West as an important objective, and although 'trade-related investment measures'[1] had been specifically identified as a hurdle to investment (and the focus of US policy) by the beginning of the 1980s, the 1982 Ministerial Declaration did not specifically identify TRIMs as an agenda item.[2] The relationship between existing GATT obligations (national treatment and MFN obligations, in particular) and domestic rules on the treatment of foreign investment was as yet unclear. The GATT Panel Report on Canada's Administration of the Foreign Investment Review Act, adopted in February 1984, did much to clarify the issues.

In 1982, the US commenced GATT proceedings against Canada in respect of the provisions of the Canadian Foreign Investment Review Act (FIRA) of 1973. FIRA contained a number of provisions under which performance and export requirements could be imposed on foreign investors. Section 2(1) of FIRA provided that the acquisition or establishment of individual businesses by foreign nationals would be permitted only where a determination was made that their operations would be of 'significant benefit' to Canada. Under section 2(2), five factors were to be considered in making this determination:

1 the effect of the acquisition or establishment on the level and nature of economic activity in Canada, including its effect on employment, resource processing, utilisation of domestically produced parts, components and services and on exports from Canada;
2 the degree and significance of participation by Canadians in the business enterprise or new business and in any industry or industries in Canada, of which the business enterprise or new business forms or would form a part;
3 the effect of the acquisition or establishment on productivity, industrial efficiency, technological development, product innovation and product variety in Canada;

[1] That is, investment regulation measures which have a trade-distorting effect.
[2] See T. P. Stewart (ed.) *The GATT Uruguay Round: A Negotiating History (1986–1992)* Volume II, 1993 pp. 2062–3.

4 the effect of the acquisition or establishment on competition within any industry or industries in Canada; and
5 the compatibility of the acquisition or establishment with national industrial and economic policies, including those of the provincial governments.

FIRA provided further that foreign investors could submit written undertakings (voluntary performance requirements) on such matters, which would bind them if the investment proceeded.

The US argued that the administration of FIRA fell foul of GATT Articles III.4 and 5,[3] XI[4] and XVII.1(c),[5] because of its impact on goods produced elsewhere. In particular, they objected to agreements based on requirements that goods be purchased in Canada, and/or on export performance requirements. When negotiations between the Parties failed to reach a satisfactory conclusion, a Panel was convened to deal with the complaint.

The GATT Panel found, in part, in favour of the US. Having examined the provisions of FIRA and statistics on its operation,[6] the Panel found that 'undertakings to purchase *goods of Canadian origin* without any qualification exclude the possibility of purchasing available imported products so that the latter are clearly treated less favourably than domestic products . . . such requirements are therefore not consistent with Article III:4'.[7] Similarly, requirements to buy from Canadian suppliers indirectly disadvantaged imported products and also breached Article III:4.[8]

Thus the GATT Panel Report recognised that some measures designed to regulate foreign investment would be caught by GATT provisions, clearing the way for efforts to identify and catalogue this group of 'Trade-Related Investment Measures'. At the same time the GATT Panel Report provided impetus for US efforts to bring this issue into a new negotiating Round under GATT.[9]

[3] Art. III imposes the national treatment standard on trade in goods. Art. III(4) provides that the products of one contracting state imported into another shall be treated no less favourably than domestic products. Art. III(5) prohibits the use of quantitative restrictions on the mixing, processing or use of products which amounts to a domestic sourcing requirement, or which protects domestic products.

[4] Art. XI prohibits quantitative restrictions.

[5] Art. XVII.1 deals with state trading enterprises, requiring non-discrimination between such enterprises and private traders.

[6] Report of the Panel, Section 2.8.

[7] *Ibid.*, Section 5.8.

[8] *Ibid.*, Section 5.10. Undertakings to purchase a proportion of supplies would also be caught by Art. III:4 so that it was unnecessary to consider potential breaches of Art. III.5. *Ibid.*, Section 5.13. Since purchasing requirements did not prevent importation as such, the Panel found that there was no breach of Art. XI:1. *Ibid.*, Sections 5.14, 6.1. The Panel did not find it necessary to consider Art. XVII:1(c) separately. *Ibid.*, Sections 5.15, 5.16.

[9] T. S. Shenkin '"Trade-Related Investment Measures" in Bilateral Investment Treaties and the GATT. Moving Toward a Multilateral Investment Treaty' *55 U. Pitt. L. Rev.* (1994) 541 at p. 563.

7.2 Clarifying the relationship between GATT and investment regulation

Throughout the Uruguay Round negotiations on TRIMs, it remained difficult to draw the line between investment regulation measures which were acceptable and those which were unacceptable. In 1994, MacDougall and Cameron[10] compiled a list of practices which had at one time or another been described as TRIMs and which included, broadly speaking, any measure affecting the establishment or operation of foreign investment which had the potential to affect trade between the state of establishment and other states. It included:

- local content requirements;
- export performance requirements;
- trade balancing requirements (imports);
- technology transfer requirements;
- production mandates;
- foreign exchange restrictions;
- remittance restrictions;
- prohibition and/or limitation on foreign investment and ownership (generally or sectorally);
- requirements to employ host nationals;
- domestic manufacturing requirements;
- domestic sales requirements;
- manufacturing limitations;
- local equity requirements; and
- licensing requirements.[11]

This wide list includes many strategies commonly employed by both developed and developing host countries at times to enhance the beneficial effects of foreign investment for the host country or to eliminate or reduce its detrimental impacts. Many of them affect foreign trade only indirectly, if at all. The GATT Panel Report on the *FIRA Case*, by contrast, was concerned only with breaches of GATT and accordingly focused solely on measures which were found to be trade distorting and hence contrary to established GATT principles. Moreover, the Panel took arguably a narrow view of this issue when it found that purchasing requirements did not breach Article X1:1, because they did not actually prohibit importation of the goods. Indeed the Panel expressed sympathy 'with the desire of the Canadian authorities to ensure that Canadian goods and suppliers would be given a fair chance to compete with imported products'[12] and merely felt that the

[10] D. MacDougall and P. Cameron 'Trade in Energy and Natural Resources' *28(3) JWT* (1994) 171 at p. 172.

[11] *Ibid.*

[12] Report of the Panel, Section 6.3.

measures taken 'tipped the balance' too far.[13] The contrast between the list and the restricted approach of the GATT Panel demonstrates clearly that the issue of TRIMs lacked clarity. What types of measures were to be included, and how was the element of illegality to be identified?

The agenda could have been restricted to dealing with cases where distortions to trade could be shown to have occurred but was capable of being extended, whether within GATT or elsewhere, to involve a wide-ranging review of government policies and practices running contrary to 'free trade' ideals, specifically the maintenance of a 'level playing field' for foreign investment.[14] The latter approach would represent a major departure from the traditional approach in international law to the treatment of foreign investment, outlined above, and would be interpreted by developing countries, and possibly by some developed countries, as an unwarranted intrusion on state sovereignty. It transpired that this lack of clarity needed to be addressed *before* agreement could be secured to include this subject in the Uruguay Round Multilateral Trade Negotiations.

Negotiations on a TRIMs agenda for GATT revealed crucial differences in policy between different Parties.[15] Both the US and Japan wished to outlaw completely a range of practices considered to be contrary to specific GATT Articles. The EC did not want the scope of GATT broadened to address foreign investment generally, but felt that certain practices directly related to trade in goods could be tackled. Developing countries approved this approach and argued that measures such as local equity requirements and investment incentives should not be included.[16] In addition, they argued that the inclusion of measures relating to TRIMs should be linked to the future negotiation of a code on Restrictive Business Practices.[17] Though no

[13] Suggestions as to how to bring the Canadian practice into conformity with GATT were offered which fell short of abandoning the practice of obtaining undertakings. *Ibid.*, Section 6.7.

[14] The approach of the EC to state aids could be said to be an example of this sort of approach. See, e.g. D. Lasok 'State Aids and Remedies Under the EEC Treaty' *ECLR* [1986] 53; F. Cowrie 'State Aids in the Eighties' *EL Rev.* (1986) 247; V. Rose (ed.) Bellamy and Child, *Common Market Law of Competition* (4th edn, 1993); D. Schina *State Aids Under the EEC Treaty* 1987; I. Harden (ed.) *State Aid: Community Law and Policy* 1993.

[15] See E. M. A. Knaw '"Trade Related Investment Measures" in the Uruguay Round: Towards a GATT For Investment?' *16 NCJ Int'l L. and Com. Reg.* 309 at pp. 325–7; Shenkin 'Trade-Related Investment Measures', *supra* note 9 at pp. 563–4; Stewart *A Negotiating History*, *supra* note 2 at pp. 2068–71.

[16] The representative from India, for instance, expressed the view that 'investment issues were not within the competence of GATT, and therefore that investment regimes could not be a subject for negotiations within the GATT': GATT Doc. No. PREP.COM(89)SR/4 p. 40, quoted in Stewart *A Negotiating History*, *supra* note 2 at p. 2069; note 270.

[17] Shenkin 'Trade-Related Investment Measures', *supra* note 9 at p. 565.

commitment to such a code was secured, the mandate that finally emerged in the Punta Del Este Declaration of 1986[18] was restricted to trade-distorting measures, and hence acted as an important limitation during the negotiations which followed.

Despite the limits on the mandate, though, the importance of securing a formal commitment to examine GATT-related foreign investment measures should not be overlooked. The 'New Agenda' for foreign investment was now well developed, though no binding commitments had yet emerged. Government measures designed to capture certain 'benefits' deriving from foreign investment or to minimise perceived detrimental impacts of foreign investment were now confirmed to be potentially trade distorting and within the proper province of GATT. Thus, in the context of the wide-ranging Uruguay Round of Multilateral Trade Negotiations, 'Trade Related Investment Measures' became a legitimate concern and an area for negotiation. This commitment to examine trade-distorting practices in relation to trade in goods was supplemented by the commitment to examine trade in services, with a view to establishing multilateral rules in that field, previously beyond the scope of multilateral trade rules.

7.3 **Foreign investment under the WTO Code**

7.3.1 *The Agreement on Trade-Related Investment Measures (TRIMs)*

In the event, the substance of the Agreement on TRIMs is modest. The Parties ('Members' in WTO terminology) undertake not to apply in the field of trade in goods any TRIM that is inconsistent with either Articles III (on national treatment) or Article XI (on quantitative restrictions) and an Illustrative List of TRIMs contrary to each of the two Articles is attached to the Agreement on TRIMs. This Illustrative List in the event is narrow in its scope, dealing only with the effect of these measures on Trade in Goods[19] and within this category, only those where a clear conflict can be detected between GATT Articles and the measures identified.[20] Compliance is to be achieved in two years by developed countries, in five years by

[18] GATT – Ministerial Declaration on the Uruguay Round of Multilateral Trade Negotiations (1986) 20 September 1986, reproduced at *25 ILM* (1986) 1623.

[19] For an account of the relevant features relating to services see P. Sauvé 'A First Look at Investment in the Final Act of the Uruguay Round' *28 JWT* (1994) 5.

[20] Included are local content requirements, where particular levels of local sourcing are required; and trade-balancing requirements, where the volume of imports which an enterprise can buy or use is tied to the volume or value of products it exports, or where levels of imports are tied to the level of foreign exchange inflow attributable to the enterprise; and export restrictions, whether specified by volume or value or as a proportion of volume or value produced.

developing countries and in seven years by least-developed countries, and a Committee, the Committee on TRIMs, is to monitor the operation and implementation of the Agreement and report annually to the Council for Trade in Goods. The Council for Trade in Goods itself is to review the operation of the Agreement and propose amendments. In particular, this body is to consider whether the Agreement should be 'complemented' with provisions on investment policy and competition policy.

The adoption of the Agreement on TRIMs represents a major shift in focus in international law relating to foreign investment. In terms of process, there has been a shift from the non-intrusive approach of traditional international law, represented by the expropriation debate, towards acceptance of external scrutiny of the policies of governments towards foreign investors. This shift has become established and institutionalised within the Agreement on TRIMs and is further reinforced by the development of the TPRM.[21]

The substantive obligations on host states have also undergone reorientation. Measures which impinge on foreign investment are now judged not solely on whether they amount, *de jure* or *de facto*, to expropriation but are now judged according to their impact on 'free trade'. So long as the new legal obligations contained in the Agreement on TRIMs are centred firmly on existing GATT provisions, this may be of limited practical consequence for host governments, which are already subject to many other influences encouraging them to adopt 'free market' policies. But under the TRIMs Agenda as it emerged through the 1980s, the 'managed trade' paradigm which underlay efforts to produce Codes of Conduct for multinationals was replaced by a 'free trade' paradigm.

Under this new paradigm all measures, domestic or international, which sought to regulate the conduct of foreign investment are implicitly open to criticism as potentially 'trade distorting'. Such measures require justification under this paradigm, and on some basis other than the political preference of a sovereign state. Some types of measure were deemed to fall foul of existing legal provisions (see Illustrative List), while the remainder seemed to have been set up as legitimate targets of scrutiny in the future. Overall, a shift can be seen from the traditional rules founded on the 'disjunctive' principles of sovereign equality, mutual respect and reciprocity towards a prescriptive agenda involving substantive obligations derived from a particular economic and political standpoint.

It remains a moot point whether this represents a new consensus in the international community or whether the ascendancy of the GATT regime, and its 'capture' of issues such as foreign investment, reflect a revival of US hegemony in the international arena. The impact of TRIMs in North–South

[21] See Section 7.3.3 below.

trade, or in South–South trade is unclear.[22] Nor is it clear that the policies designed to ensure a level playing field as between developed countries should be automatically transplanted into the developing world.[23]

7.3.2 *The General Agreement on Trade in Services (GATS)*[24]

GATT 1994 was supplemented by GATS, an agreement on the liberalisation of trade in services, which establishes a set of general and state-specific commitments to liberalisation and establishes a basis for future negotiations to extend these commitments further.

Trade in services is defined widely. Article 1 lists four modes of supply which are covered by GATS:

1 services supplied from the territory of one Member into the territory of another;
2 services supplied in the territory of one Member to the consumers of another (i.e. consumption abroad);
3 services supplied via a 'commercial presence' in the territory of another state; and

[22] UNCTAD *The Impact of Trade Related Investment Measures on Trade and Development* UN Doc. ST/CTC/120 (1991); T. H. Moran and C. S. Pearson 'Do TRIMs Trip Up Foreign Investment? An International Business Diplomacy Perspective' in C. D. Wallace (ed.) *Foreign Direct Investment in the 1990s: A New Climate in the Third World* 1990, at p. 28; D. Greenaway 'Trade Related Investment Measures and Development Strategies' *45 Kyklos* (1992) 139; O. Morrissey and Y. Rai 'The GATT Agreement on Trade Related Investment Measures: Implications for Developing Countries and Their Relationship With Transnational Corporations' *31 Journal of Development Studies* (1995) 702.

[23] It is noted in the UNCTAD survey (see note 22 above) that the 'reassessment' of trade policy which led to the focus of attention on TRIMs has generally been limited to the effects within developed countries: 'the area in which North–South tensions about what constitutes legitimate public action is most keenly felt, namely, the debate about employing TRIMs to support developmental or commercial goals, remains untouched by the subtlety of this reassessment. In the TRIMs debate, a certain dogmatism prevails, to the effect that public sector intervention is by definition distortionary and deserving of peremptory condemnation by responsible policy makers', *ibid.*, at p. 63.

[24] M. C. E. J. Bronckers and P. Larouche 'Telecommunications Services and the World Trade Organization' *31(3) JWT* (1997) 5; A. Mattoo 'National Treatment in the GATS – Corner-Stone or Pandora's Box?' *31(1) JWT* (1997) 107; N. Mukherjee 'GATS and the Millennium Round of Multilateral Negotiations – Selected Issues from the Perspective of the Developing Countries' *33(4) JWT* (1999) 87; A. Sapir 'The GATS From 1994 to the Year 2000' *33(1) JWT* (1995) 51; P. Sauvé 'Assessing the GATS – Half-Full or Half-Empty?' *29(4) JWT* (1995) 125; Yi Wang 'Most-Favoured-Nation Treatment Under the GATS – And Its Application in Financial Services' *30(1) JWT* (1996) 91; F. Weiss 'The General Agreement on Trade in Services' *32 CMLR* (1995) 1197.

4 services supplied by nationals of one Member state in the territory of another.

Thus trade in services is defined under GATS to include investment. 'Commercial presence' in (3) above is defined as 'any type of business or professional establishment, including through (i) the constitution, acquisition or maintenance of a juridical person, or (ii) the creation or maintenance of a branch or a representative office, within the territory of a Member for the purpose of supplying a service'.[25]

This definition therefore captures foreign investment in a similar way to the concept of establishment in the EU, though the parameters are not drawn in precisely the same way.[26] And, whereas GATT is concerned only with measures affecting the products covered, GATS is concerned both with measures affecting the services themselves and with measures affecting service suppliers.

GATS recognises the right of Members to regulate the supply of services within their territory. Two general principles, however, are established to regulate this right. The first is the *most-favoured nation* principle, requiring that Members 'accord immediately and unconditionally to services and service suppliers of any other Member treatment no less favourable than that it accords to like services and service suppliers of any other country'.[27] Despite the language used in this provision, the MFN principle of GATS is subject to numerous exceptions. First, a large number of exemptions (country-specific exceptions), negotiated and agreed with other Members, are listed in the Annex on Article II Exemptions. These are intended to be temporary and will become subject to review in due course.[28] Second, certain permanent derogations or exceptions are permitted, for instance for economic integration[29] or labour market integration[30] agreements, or for government procurement.[31]

The second general principle is that of transparency, requiring Members to publish promptly all relevant measures affecting trade in services,[32] report at least annually any significant changes to the Council for Trade in Services[33]

[25] GATS, Art. I(2).

[26] See Section 6.1, *supra*.

[27] GATS, Art. II.

[28] In some instances these exceptions have been used to introduce an element of reciprocity into Members' undertakings. As Yi Wang points out there is a risk that this could undermine the unconditional most-favoured nation principle: 'Most-Favoured Nation Treatment Under the GATS' *supra* note 24 at p. 107.

[29] GATS, Art. V.

[30] GATS, Art. V bis.

[31] GATS, Art. XIII.

[32] GATS, Art. III.

[33] GATS, Art. III:3.

and answer enquiries from other Members and furnish them with pertinent information.[34]

These general obligations are then supplemented by specific commitments made by each state on market access and national treatment. As Mattoo explains, '[a] Member's specific commitments can be seen as the outcome of a two-step decision. Each Member first decides which service sectors will be subject to the GATS market access and national treatment disciplines. It then decides what measures will be kept in place for that sector which violate market access and/or national treatment respectively'.[35] Thus, in a sector under which a Member has agreed to be 'bound', that Member is prohibited from maintaining or adopting measures which restrict market access, except to the extent agreed with other Members and laid down in its Schedule. This covers measures:

1 limiting the number of permitted service suppliers;
2 limiting the total value of supply transactions or assets permitted;
3 limiting the number of permitted services operations or the total quantity of services output;
4 limiting the number of natural persons who may be employed in a particular sector;
5 stipulating specific types of legal entity through which services can be supplied; or
6 restricting foreign equity participation.[36]

In relation to sectors where the Member has agreed to become 'bound', it is required to accord to services and service suppliers of any other Member State treatment no less favourable (that is national treatment) than that it accords to its own like services and service suppliers, in respect of all measures affecting the supply of services.[37] National treatment covers both *de jure* and *de facto* discrimination. Though it is not specifically provided for in the GATS itself, in practice states specify their commitments and the exceptions to those commitments in terms of the modes of supply outlined above. Thus within a particular sector, a Member might for example permit the provision of a particular service through a commercial presence in its territory but prohibit the provision of the same service from the territory of another state. To determine the level of market access granted in a particular Member's schedule, it is necessary to look first at the range of activities covered in each sector and then at the limitations on market access and national treatment specified for different modes of supply. Finally, it is necessary to examine that Member's MFN exemptions, to identify where preferential or discriminatory treatment is given to one or more trading partner.

[34] GATS, Art. III:4.
[35] Mattoo 'National Treatment', *supra* note 24 at p. 111.
[36] GATS, Art. XVI.
[37] GATS, Art. XVII.

This fragmentation of commitments has been criticised by some commentators, who argue that the approach undermines the whole agreement. Sauvé, for instance, argues that some of the obligations applying only to scheduled commitments could be applied across the board, where they could perform a useful 'policy-signalling' role.[38] Mattoo examines the fragmentation which follows from the approach of scheduling commitments according to mode of supply and the problems which this poses for interpretation and application of the national treatment obligation: 'If "likeness" of a service were defined independently of the mode of supply, then there would be built-in protection within the Agreement for foreign suppliers of services through all modes against national subsidisation. . . . On the other hand, if likeness were held to depend on the mode of supply (as the structure of the Schedules suggests), then foreign suppliers through a particular mode may not be protected against national subsidisation'.[39] This, he argues, needs to be addressed to prevent erosion of the agreement through the fragmentation of Member commitments.

Sauvé argues that the design of the scheduling process also impedes the proper functioning of the transparency provisions of the agreement, since one consequence is that no information is generated in the Schedules of National Commitments about sectors, subsectors and activities where no liberalisation commitments have been made.[40]

However, the consequences of the adoption of this approach in relation to foreign investment have been interesting. According to Sauvé, the bulk of commitments made by states, particularly those made by developing countries, relate to the 'commercial presence' (i.e. foreign investment) mode of supply:

> While such an outcome is hardly surprising when viewed against the establishment-related nature of much 'trade' in services, the decision to schedule commitments by mode of supply clearly resulted in fewer commitments on the cross-border movement of services and service suppliers. This is because it provided Members with what could be called an architectural incentive to impose TRIM-like requirements (even when cross-border trade may be feasible or preferable from a business viewpoint) on foreign services and service suppliers, to establish a commercial presence as a pre-requisite for supplying services in their territories.[41]

[38] Sauvé 'Assessing the GATS', *supra* note 24 at p. 132.

[39] Mattoo 'National Treatment', *supra* note 24 at p. 120.

[40] Sauvé 'Assessing the GATS', *supra* note 24 at p. 138. 'The across-the board adoption of a top-down, "list it or lose it", negative list approach, such as that used for services and investment in the NAFTA, would have both significantly enhanced transparency and been more inherently liberalizing by automatically covering (and binding at "free") all new service activities.' *Ibid.*

[41] *Ibid.*, p. 138. Sauvé points out the inherent tension between this and Article XVI; see text at note 40 above.

The focus in GATS on the entry and operating parts of the lifecycle of foreign investment follows the general trend towards liberalisation of international economic activity[42] and the trends established in free trade areas such as the EU, NAFTA and others.[43] GATS, however, represents a significant new development in a number of regards.

First, its near-global coverage, together with the unconditional MFN principle, is far beyond than that achieved in any other context. While these general features have to be understood alongside the country-specific schedules of commitments in the way described above, the conclusion of the agreement is of symbolic importance in bringing the services field under the WTO umbrella.

Second, its location within the WTO's institutional structure, making it subject to the WTO dispute settlement processes[44] and to the TPRM,[45] seems likely to ensure that states will have to deliver on the commitments they have made and move forward to adopt further commitments in due course. Situating the GATS agreement within the WTO institutional framework produces links between investment issues and trade issues. This arises in relation to negotiation of specific commitments, development of the respective normative frameworks and resolution of disputes; one important feature of the WTO dispute resolution system is the possibility which it allows for cross-retaliation between the different agreements in certain circumstances.

A third contribution made by the conclusion of the GATS is the establishment of a framework for future negotiations. Its role here has already been demonstrated by the conclusion in 1997 of WTO agreements on basic telecommunications services and on financial services and future additional agreements are likely, for instance on maritime transport services.

A fourth observation is that the coverage of GATS concepts is very wide; the lack of any distinction between entry and operating restrictions is one

[42] See, for instance, the OECD National Treatment Instrument, *supra*, Chapter Two, dealing with post-entry treatment, and the OECD's Code on the Liberalization of Capital Movements, *ibid.*

[43] Examples include the Australia–New Zealand Closer Economic Regulations Trade Agreement (ANZCERTA), the Common Market of the Southern Cone (Mercosur), the Caribbean Economic Community (CARICOM), the Arab Maghreb Union (AMU) and the Economic Community of West African States (ECOWAS).

[44] Governed by the Understanding on Rules and Procedures Governing the Settlement of Disputes in GATT in GATT *The Results of the Uruguay Round of Multilateral Trade Negotiations* 1994. For an account, see e.g. P. T. B. Kohona 'Dispute Resolution Under The World Trade Organisation: An Overview' *28(2) JWT* (1994) 5; E. U. Petersmann *The GATT/WTO Dispute Settlement System: International Law, International Organisation and Dispute Settlement* 1996; A. H. Qureshi *The World Trade Organisation – Implementing International Trade Norms* 1996; D. P. Steger and S. M. Hainsworth 'World Trade Organisation Dispute Settlement: The First Three Years' *1(2) JIEL* (1998) 199.

[45] See below, Section 7.3.3.

facet of this, the covering of both services and service suppliers is another. In addition, unlike more traditional approaches to foreign investment, no distinction is drawn between direct and indirect investments. Instead the focus is on the service and its supplier, whatever the legal forms of business actually adopted.[46] Thus, the property rights focus of traditional international law approaches to foreign investment[47] is replaced by a focus on the service, and hence on the market and the consumer. As Mattoo notes, '[t]he logic of the national treatment discipline would suggest beginning with the presumption that suppliers of like services are like suppliers'.[48] If followed to its logical conclusion this would significantly erode the distinction between domestic and foreign investment, as well as that between direct and indirect investment. However, GATS does not go as far as this, in two important respects. First, it inherently recognises the right of states to regulate foreign investment, through the provision of both general and specific grounds of exception. Second, by allowing the Members to schedule their commitments in accordance with modes of supply, the distinction between these modes is reinforced. A contrast can be drawn with the EU where, arguably, the distinction between foreign direct investment and the provision of services from outside the territory of a Member State is increasingly blurred.[49]

7.3.3 *The Trade Policy Review Mechanism*[50]

The adoption of TRIMs and GATS embodies a shift in relation to foreign investment from the traditionally non-intrusive, territory-centred approach, outlined in Chapters 1 and 2, towards a more regulatory and intrusive approach under which host state policies with respect to foreign investment are regularly subjected to scrutiny by other Member States and by organs of the WTO. This shift is reinforced by the TPRM, which establishes a system of 'state-reporting' on WTO obligations. All WTO Members are required to undergo a periodic review of their trade policies.[51] The review examines the impact of a state's trade policies and practices on the WTO-based trading

[46] This can be compared, for example, with the concepts used in EC law of establishment (permanent presence) and supply of services (which is temporary). See further Section 6.1, *supra*.

[47] See Section 5.1, *supra*.

[48] Mattoo 'National Treatment', *supra* note 24 at p. 133.

[49] See further Section 6.1, supra.

[50] Final Act Embodying the Results of the Uruguay Round of Multilateral Trade Negotiations, Annex 3 – Trade Policy Review Mechanism in GATT *The Results of the Uruguay Round of Multilateral Trade Negotiations – The Legal Texts* 1994 at p. 434. See generally Qureshi, *The World Trade Organisation*, *supra* note 44, Chapter Six.

[51] The four major players determined by share in world trade will undergo review every two years, the next largest every four years and all others every six years. Longer review periods may be fixed for least developed Members.

order and Members are required to submit a Country Report, in a prescribed form, outlining their trade policies, the domestic regime under which policy is formulated and reviewed, the actual trade policy measures in use and prospective changes.[52] Information is also given about the relevant economic background, both internal and external, against which the trade policy operates. The Country Report is supplemented by a WTO Report, compiled by the WTO secretariat, which consists of an account of the Member's trade policies and practices. The Trade Policy Review Body then conducts its review on the basis of these two reports. Two discussants are appointed in consultation with the Member under review, to introduce the discussion. Following the review meeting, the two reports and a summary record of proceedings at the review meeting are published and forwarded to the Ministerial Conference to be noted.

The TPRM, in common with many similarly constituted state-reporting mechanisms in the human rights field, is not explicitly censorious, and no sanctions can result from the operation of this process. The Agreement establishing the TPRM explicitly states that its function is to 'contribute to improved adherence', and hence to the 'smoother functioning' of the multilateral trade system, by improving adherence and understanding. It is stated that it is not intended to 'serve as the basis of the enforcement of specific obligations, or for dispute settlement procedures, or to impose new policy commitments'. Some countries preface their reports with such denials.[53] This has led to some dispute as to the character of the process, in particular over whether it serves any enforcement purpose. As Abbott has noted, if states had thought they were creating some kind of enforcement tribunal, the TPRM would probably never have been established.[54]

However, it seems undeniable that the TPRM plays an important enforcement role in respect of WTO obligations.[55] As Qureshi argues, '[i]t can be conceived from an enforcement perspective in two respects. First, it has enforcement characteristics itself. Secondly, it facilitates enforcement'.[56]

The enforcement characteristics lie in the fact that the TPRM is compulsory, and in the fact that the process comprises approbation and disapprobation, expressed in terms of a (pre-existing) normative framework; 'conformity with the WTO code of country trade policies and practices is

[52] For a detailed account, see A. H. Qureshi *International Economic Law* 1999, pp. 313–32.

[53] *Ibid.*, at p. 318.

[54] R. Abbott 'GATT and the Trade Policy Review Mechanism: Further Reflections on Earlier Reflections' *27(3) JWT* (1993) 116 at p.118.

[55] This is convincingly argued by Qureshi: 'Some Lessons from Developing Countries' Trade Policy Reviews in the GATT Framework: An Enforcement Perspective' *18 World Economy* (1995) 489 at pp. 494–5; *International Economic Law*, *supra* note 52, pp. 318–22.

[56] Qureshi *International Economic Law*, *supra* note 52 at p. 319.

a concern of the TPRM, and is stated as such in the agreement establishing it'.[57] Thus the TPRM, though non-adjudicatory, is 'corrective' and 'conditioning' of Member State behaviour. The conditioning:

> stems particularly from the probing of policy, policy formulation and the objectives of policies . . . invitations to describe the objectives of national trade policy, the process of policy formulation, the domestic trade legislation and international agreements and their respective objectives, existing programmes for trade liberalisation and prospective changes in trade policies, cannot be mere objective descriptions without more – they are in fact descriptions made to the WTO through a mould already cast . . . the process of description is not a mere contribution to transparency but rather its very proffering has the added consequence of having the potential to engender a degree of sensitivity on the part of the member to the ethos of the WTO code.[58]

The TPRM can also be presumed to facilitate enforcement and closer adherence to the WTO Code by exposing areas of trade policy where a Member is in breach of WTO obligations, or where closer adherence, better monitoring or greater transparency could be achieved. The Member State under review may choose to address this by giving a unilateral undertaking; alternatively it is conceivable that the information gathered from Trade Policy Reviews may inform the WTO and its Members in future reviews of WTO disciplines. Finally, it is possible that an individual Member may launch enforcement proceedings based on evidence revealed in the course of a review of another Member's policies and practices. In conclusion, it is a reasonable presumption that the TPRM will contribute to enforcement of WTO disciplines, both in the short and long term.[59]

It remains to be asked what impact the TPRM has in relation to foreign investment law. It has already been noted in relation to both TRIMS and the GATS that the focus of investment obligations under the WTO Code has shifted from expropriation (at the end of the life cycle of an investment), to entry and treatment of foreign investment. This, it was noted, involved a measure of acceptance of external scrutiny of the policies of governments towards foreign investors. In common with NAFTA and the EC, the WTO framework establishes a means by which enforcement action may be brought against a Member which breaches its commitments in relation to the access for and treatment of foreign investors, though the focus is on state–state actions rather than investor–state actions.[60] Although the early indications are that the DSU is working well, is well supported by Member States and

[57] *Ibid.*, p. 319.

[58] *Ibid.*, pp. 319–20.

[59] This will of course depend to an extent on the quality of the reporting process. For an interesting discussion of the criteria used in the review see further Qureshi, *ibid.*, pp. 322–8.

[60] See Section 6.3, *supra*.

will be resorted to often, adjudication between states even under these conditions is costly in both financial and political terms and is time consuming. Against this background it seems clear that the TPRM can play an important additional function, enhancing the responsiveness of states to their WTO commitments and edging them towards greater transparency and compliance. It has the capacity to slowly but steadily erode the notion that as sovereign states Members have the right to treat foreign investment and investors much as they will, and to replace it with the notion that states are obliged to treat foreign investment and foreign investors fairly, and to allow them access to the economy on terms equal to that available to domestic industries. While the specific commitments of individual Members may at present be somewhat piecemeal and fragmented, there can be no doubt about what 'good behaviour' entails. The TPRM therefore promotes 'good behaviour' in respect of foreign investment, constituted in terms of the free market and liberalisation objectives of the WTO Code.

7.4 The Multilateral Agreement on Investment – a model for the future?

Despite an apparent modest success in introducing investment concerns into the multilateral trade negotiations, developed countries wasted no time in opening the issue again, this time under the auspices of the OECD.[61] In May 1995, the OECD launched formal discussions on an MAI[62] and in May 1998 released a draft negotiating text.[63]

A key aim of the negotiations on an MAI was 'to establish a broad multilateral framework for international investment with high standards for the liberalisation of investment regimes and investment protection and with effective dispute settlement procedures'.[64] This was based on a recognition of the limitations of the bilateral approach, the limited geographic coverage of regional agreements such as NAFTA, and absence of binding force or

[61] The OECD was discussed at Section 5.2, *supra*.

[62] The OECD was involved in this area prior to that date. See Section 2.2, *supra*, and T. L. Brewer and S. Young *The Multilateral Investment System and Multinational Enterprises* 1998, pp. 93–6.

[63] OECD: Directorate for Financial, Fiscal and Enterprise Affairs *The Multilateral Agreement on Investment Negotiating Text* (as of 24 April 1998) (hereinafter the MAI Text). A previous version of the Negotiating Text was leaked in February 1997 and widely circulated on the internet. The 24 April 1998 Text does not give consecutive numbering for its Articles which are broadly organised under numbered chapters (upper-case Roman numerals), Articles (identified by numbers in some areas, subject headings in others) and numbered paragraphs (Arabic numbers, e.g. Paragraph 1).

[64] MAI Text: Preamble. While there was a broad consensus for some parts of this negotiating text, many key issues were unresolved, a state of affairs reflected in the alternative formulations within the negotiating text.

effective dispute resolution procedures from previous OECD instruments.[65] The economic situation demanded such a response, '[g]lobalisation is increasing every day. It calls for enhanced international co-operation for the world economy to be better organised and the efficiency and equity of the markets to be protected. The usefulness of the GATT is now generally recognised. The time has come for a multilateral agreement on investment'.[66]

Though the negotiations ultimately failed (see below), the MAI Text provides valuable insight into the current issues surrounding investment protection. Moreover, the history of this negotiation, which was effectively thrown off-track by well-organised elements of civil society, highlights areas of great controversy concerning globalisation, deregulation and foreign investment. It also raises important questions about the ways in which new 'economic' law is developed within the international legal system.

The key provisions of the MAI Text concern the treatment accorded to foreign investment before, during and after cessation of operations in the host state and thus the MAI immediately departs from the approach of BITs which are generally concerned only with the treatment of investors after the investment has been made. The MAI can be seen to build on, and carry forward, many of the new approaches developed in NAFTA and the WTO Agreements, including TRIMs.

Scope and application

The terms 'investor' and 'investment' are given very wide meanings,[67] leading to the description of the MAI as a 'top–down' agreement (that is, covering anything which is not specifically excluded).[68] It was anticipated that Contracting Parties would then lodge country-specific exceptions so that a schedule would be maintained for each Contracting Party, GATT-style, listing all its current exceptions. The formal definitions of investor and investment are wide enough to catch non-profit-making associations and personal assets. However, it is anticipated that an interpretative note would be added to indicate that to qualify under the MAI, an asset 'must have the characteristics of an investment, such as the commitment of capital or other resources, the expectation of gain or profit, or the assumption of risk'.[69] Thus, an economic test will be added. Beyond this there are further areas which are recognised as requiring clarification. Though indirect investment, intellectual property rights, concessions, public debt and real estate are all recognised in principle as assets which can constitute an

[65] OECD 'The Multilateral Agreement on Investment' Policy Brief No. 2–1997.
[66] *Ibid.*
[67] MAI Text, Chapter II, Article on Definitions, Paras 1 and 2.
[68] See e.g. Canadian Labour Congress 'The Multilateral Agreement on Investment – A Preliminary, Critical Analysis' undated.
[69] MAI Text, Chapter II, Article on Definitions, footnote 2.

investment,[70] it is also recognised that some clarification may be required as to the appropriate treatment of each of these categories.[71]

The extension of protection to indirect investments, for instance, raises the possibility of shareholders who are nationals of MAI Contracting Parties seeking to rely on the MAI to protect assets held or directly controlled by companies based in non-MAI states. This could occur notwithstanding the lack of reciprocity between the host and home states and the absence of any real relationship, least not any effective governance mechanisms, between the shareholder states and the 'offshore' companies. The extension of protection to shareholders also has implications for the operation of the dispute resolution processes (see below).

Clarification is also required of the circumstances in which intellectual property rights, contract rights and debts will be protected and how these relate to normal and legitimate governmental regulatory action which might adversely affect such rights. Some critics have raised fears that, for instance, changes to patent acts could be challenged as expropriations or that damages could be claimed from governments if a change in government policy were to result in a contract with a foreign buyer not being fulfilled.[72]

Non-discrimination – the national treatment and Most-Favoured Nation principles

The MAI Text requires observation of both the national treatment[73] and MFN[74] principles.

The national treatment principle requires that Contracting Parties treat foreign investors and their investments 'no less favourably' than its own nationals in relation to the 'establishment, acquisition, operation, management, use, enjoyment and sale or other disposition of investments'. This is potentially a very significant provision, because many states, both developed and developing have used at some time in their history, barriers to entry which are based on nationality requirements. Such barriers may take the form of total or sectoral exclusion or a review process which might result in the imposition of conditions on foreign investors.[75] One major use has been in relation to 'key sectors': '[t]hese areas generally encompass industries relevant to national security and defence, for example shipbuilding or aerospace, culturally significant industries, such as film or broadcasting, and public utilities . . . they

[70] *Ibid.*, Para. 2. The list is also cast as non-exhaustive: 'Investment means . . . every kind of asset . . . including . . .' *Ibid.*

[71] *Ibid.*, footnote 1.

[72] Canadian Labour Congress, *supra* note 68.

[73] MAI Text, Chapter III, Article on National Treatment and Most Favoured Nation Treatment, Para. 1.

[74] *Ibid.*, Para. 2.

[75] P. T. Muchlinski *Multinational Enterprises and the Law* 1995, Chapter One at p. 172 *et infra.*

pose few problems for states . . . representing a recognised "reserved domain" for national ownership and control'.[76] However such exclusionary policies have become unfashionable in the current pro-liberalisation climate and have been tackled to an extent in the EC and NAFTA,[77] while the Energy Charter Treaty has made major inroads into nationality-based discrimination on investment in the utilities sector. The exclusions proposed in relation to national treatment under the MAI continue to reflect concerns in relation to national security, but not in relation to cultural industries or utilities[78] which could only be protected through inclusion in the lists of country-specific exceptions. Critics argue that this reflects the interests of developed states and ignores the different needs of developing states (see below).[79] The failure to grant any explicit exclusion for utilities, and the failure to recognise any general right for developing states to protect 'infant industries' from foreign competition are indicative of the general underlying philosophy of the MAI, which promotes foreign investment as an instrument of growth, modernisation and development, and follow the orthodoxy of the World Bank Group on the role of foreign investment in reconstruction and development. The issue of development is examined in greater detail below. For the present, it can be noted that these provisions signal the end of the concept of a 'reserved domain' in all but the narrowest of 'national security' areas and would have the effect of denying to many less developed states a range of policies used historically to protect the national interest, including joint venture laws, indigenisation laws, laws restricting foreign shareholdings and screening laws.[80] There will inevitably be many country-specific exceptions proposed precisely to mitigate these effects.

The MFN clause requires that Contracting Parties treat foreign investors and their investments no less favourably than those of any other state. This raises two specific problems; first, the problem of free trade areas and, second, the problem of sanctions imposed against another state for 'legitimate' public purposes.

Free trade areas such as the EC and NAFTA, which have extended liberalisation beyond the movements of goods into movements of capital and liberalisation of investments, may already permit investment from their free

[76] *Ibid.*, at p. 175.

[77] See Section 6.1.1 and 6.1.2, *supra.*

[78] The MAI Text, Chapter VI, Article on General Exceptions, Para. 2, excludes the armaments industries from the scope of the MAI and allows states to take action in relation to non-proliferation programmes which would otherwise be in breach of MAI rules. Departure from any MAI obligation is permitted, except the expropriation provisions where specific provision is made for non-discrimination in compensation processes following war, internal strife, etc.

[79] See e.g. Oxfam UK and Ireland Briefing Paper 'The OECD Multilateral Agreement on Investment (MAI)' October 1997.

[80] See generally Muchlinski *Multinational Enterprises, supra* note 75.

trade partners on terms far more favourable than those offered to investors of third states. For instance, discrimination in state aids or procurement policies may have been substantially reduced or eliminated in respect of nationals of free trade partners, but not in relation to nationals of third states. The MFN clause in the MAI Text would extend the non-discrimination principle into areas hitherto outside the scope of existing GATT disciplines, where the MFN principle already applies. Therefore the question arises whether better treatment will be permitted vis-à-vis the nationals of free trade area partners. As was noted above, the GATS makes an exception for free trade areas[81] and the EC argued that an MAI should do likewise.

Sanctions – privileging of UN

Under the General Exceptions Article, an exception to the MFN principle would be permitted to allow a Contracting Party to fulfil its obligations under the UN Charter, for example to implement mandatory sanctions.[82] Sanctions from other possible sources (such as regional sanctions) are not acknowledged as the basis of an exception in this way. Nor is it recognised as legitimate for individual countries to depart on a unilateral basis from the MFN principle on ethical or foreign policy grounds (except in relation to armaments, as noted above). It is doubtful whether this moral privileging of UN sanctions can be justified by reference to the record of the UN Security Council on issues such as human rights abuses, which is widely recognised to lack consistency. However, there is an important pragmatic question to be addressed if sanctions imposed by individual states or regional political associations are to be placed on an equal footing to those of the UN: how to prevent states from using issues such as human rights abuses or other foreign policy concerns as an excuse for arbitrary and unjustifiable discrimination.

By contrast, a public order exception can be invoked to justify departure from either the national treatment or the MFN principles. This public order exception[83] follows very closely the EU law model. Action taken must not constitute arbitrary or unjustifiable discrimination or a disguised restriction on investment.[84] Moreover, action cannot be taken solely for economic reasons and must be proportionate.[85] Though not stated, it would seem that this provision anticipates a threat to the public order of the Contracting Party wishing to invoke the exception, not that of any other.

[81] See Section 7.3.2 above.

[82] MAI Text, Chapter VI, Article on General Exceptions, Para. 2(c).

[83] *Ibid.*, Para. 3.

[84] *Ibid.*

[85] *Ibid.*, Para. 5. These latter two requirements attach to all the General Exceptions clauses. In addition there is a reporting requirement (*ibid.*, Para. 4). Parties suspecting abuse may request consultations (*ibid.*).

The national treatment and MFN provisions are supplemented by a requirement of transparency, for instance in privatisation programmes,[86] and a requirement of non-discriminatory practice in relation to for example, the treatment of monopolies and state enterprises.[87]

Performance requirements and investment incentives

Certain performance requirements, including employment requirements, are prohibited.[88] In general the aim of the provision is to enact a prohibition on trade-related performance requirements. However the MAI Text goes well beyond the existing NAFTA, TRIPs and Energy Charter Treaty provisions on such matters. There has been great concern in many quarters that the resulting provisions are likely, without further clarification, to have many unintended consequences in areas where legitimate social, economic and environmental policies have incidental or unintended, possibly even unforeseen, impacts on foreign investment or investors. It seems likely that any future agreement modelled on the MAI Draft would have to clarify these issues.[89]

Essentially the MAI Text proposes that certain types of conditions imposed on foreign investors linked to their establishment, operation, expansion, etc., or to the granting of an advantage or incentive be outlawed. Since the objective is to tackle market distortion, these conditions would be outlawed in relation to investors of both Contracting and Non-Contracting Parties, and regardless of whether they were imposed through law or voluntarily undertaken. Moreover, the prohibition goes beyond the non-discrimination focus of the national treatment principle into prescriptive territory. The MAI provisions are modelled on NAFTA but contain a longer list of prohibitions. They are also wider in scope than the TRIPs/WTO disciplines, both in terms of the list of prohibited practices and the sectoral coverage (they will be of greater impact than WTO rules, particularly in the services sector).

The conditions outlawed are as follows (existence of similar provisions in NAFTA or TRIPs indicated in brackets):

- export requirements (NAFTA, TRIPs);
- domestic content requirements (NAFTA, TRIPs);
- domestic sourcing requirements (for goods or services) (NAFTA, TRIPs);
- import/export matching requirements (NAFTA, TRIPs);
- trade related domestic sales restrictions (NAFTA).

[86] MAI Text, Chapter III, Article on Transparency, Paras 1–3; Chapter III, Article on Privatisation, Para. 4.

[87] *Ibid.*, Article on Monopolies/State Enterprises/Concessions. There are many unresolved issues in these areas.

[88] *Ibid.*, Article on Performance Requirements.

[89] See further below.

The following conditions are outlawed in relation to establishment, expansion, etc., though not in relation to the granting of an advantage:

- technology transfer requirements (NAFTA);
- headquarters location requirements (new);
- a requirement to supply goods or services to a region or globally from the Contracting State (NAFTA);
- research and development location requirements (new);
- requirements regarding the hiring of nationals (new);
- a joint venture requirement (new); or
- domestic equity requirements (new).

As noted above, there has been concern that these provisions would restrict the legitimate pursuit by governments of environmental and social policies. Like NAFTA there is no general exception in the MAI Draft along the lines of GATT Article XX, allowing measures designed to protect living or non-living resources or human, animal or plant life or health. There seems to be general acceptance among the negotiating parties to the MAI that none is needed; that legitimate measures would not be affected by these provisions. However it would seem, in view of the sensitivity of this issue, that this could be clearly and securely established in an exceptions clause, or at least in an Interpretative Note. Similarly, it could be made clear that employment policy programmes designed to assist underdeveloped regions or disadvantaged groups or persons would be unaffected. The environmental and development issues relating to performance requirements are considered in greater detail below.

The issue of performance requirements is closely related to the issue of investment incentives, and, while some delegations to the MAI negotiations wished these two to be addressed in separate provisions, others did not see any need for this. The draft text which exists[90] spells out that the national treatment, MFN and transparency provisions of the agreement would be applicable to investment incentives. Thus it clarifies that the dispute settlement provisions of the agreement could be used by investors or their home states to challenge the use of investment incentives in ways which were discriminatory. However, there are underlying differences of opinion as to whether all investment incentives should be regarded as bad.[91] Some negotiating parties would like to develop an approach whereby the distorting effects of investment incentives on investment decisions and capital flows could be balanced against their possible benefits in furthering, for example, states' regional, structural, social, environmental or R&D policies.[92] One

[90] MAI Text, Chapter III, Article on Investment Incentives.
[91] *Ibid.*, Footnote 97.
[92] *Ibid.*, Para. 3.

suggestion was to return to this subject-matter after the conclusion of these negotiations with a view to concluding a separate instrument.

A further area of dispute concerns the effects of non-discriminatory investment incentives. These, it is recognised, can have a distorting effect on the (transnational) flow of capital and on investment decisions. Some delegations proposed that Contracting Parties who considered that their investors or their investments were adversely affected by such measures should be able to seek consultations and possibly to refer the matter to the Parties Group.[93]

Expropriation and compensation

The most significant contribution of the MAI negotiations to the development of new disciplines for foreign investment undoubtedly lie in the liberalisation provisions outlined hitherto. However, no MAI would be complete without provisions on the long-established concerns of expropriation and compensation.[94] The MAI Draft follows very much the model established in BITs, first establishing a general obligation to treat foreign investments fairly and equitably and to accord them protection, defined here as 'full and constant protection and security'.[95] The international law standard (of protection of foreign nationals) is incorporated as a benchmark, a reference which is regarded as critical.[96] Though the wording may seem ambiguous, it is assumed that this does not impose any higher standard than exists under customary international law rules on state responsibility, so that some fault on the part of a Contracting State would be required before liability for failure to protect could be established.[97] A more specific obligation requires Contracting States not to take measures which impair the operation, management, maintenance, use, enjoyment or disposal of foreign investments. Such measures are unlawful where they are unreasonable and/or discriminatory, it being undecided whether these requirements should be applied separately or conjunctively.[98] It is questionable whether these general provisions would in practice add anything to the national treatment and MFN obligations outlined above, but the general provisions are included because they represent an absolute obligation rather than the relative obligation established by these other non-discrimination

[93] *Ibid.*, para. 2 and footnote 98. The Parties Group is discussed further below.

[94] MAI Text, Chapter IV, Article 2: Expropriation and Compensation.

[95] *Ibid.*, Article 1: General Treatment.

[96] OECD Multilateral Agreement on Investment, Commentary to the MAI Negotiating Text (as of 24 April 1998) (hereinafter MAI Commentary), Commentary on Chapter IV.

[97] See generally Harris *Cases and Materials on International Law* 5th edn, 1998, Chapter Eight; see also the *Hostages Case: US Diplomatic and Consular Staff in Tehran, ICJ Reps.* (1980) 3.

[98] MAI Text, Chapter IV, Article 1: General Treatment, para. 1.2.

principles.[99] The inclusion of the general provisions in a multilateral treaty could also of course help to strengthen customary international law in this area.

The expropriation and compensation provisions focus, as do BITs, on the conditions which have to be satisfied before an expropriation or nationalisation can be regarded as legitimate and make no explicit reference to the sovereign right to nationalise. Expropriation and nationalisation, whether direct or indirect, and measures having equivalent effect (creeping expropriation) are prohibited except:

- for a purpose which is in the public interest;
- on a non-discriminatory basis;
- in accordance with due process of law;
- accompanied by payment of prompt, adequate and effective compensation.[100]

It is noteworthy that these formulations of the international law requirements are drawn largely from existing investment protection instruments. The formulation in (a) is a compromise between the 'public interest' and 'public purpose' requirements of different groups of legal systems and is drawn from the Energy Charter Treaty;[101] the formulations in (b) and (c) replicate or closely follow those of NAFTA.[102]

Some considerable effort has gone in to refining the compensation requirement in (d) (the Hull formula) and additional requirements specify that compensation should be paid without delay,[103] that it should represent the 'fair market value' of the expropriated investment (excluding any change in value which had occurred because the impending expropriation had become publicly known)[104] and that compensation should be fully realisable and freely transferable.[105] Some negotiating parties favoured including a separate provision requiring interest on compensation at a commercial rate.[106] Efforts were made to go further by providing one or more formula(e) to calculate compensation; these formulae addressed the problems of currency fluctuation and interest (also addressed in NAFTA).[107] However, it became clear that a majority favoured making no explicit provision of this sort, though an Interpretative Note was seen as appropriate;[108] this could perhaps

[99] MAI Commentary, Commentary on Chapter IV.

[100] MAI Text, Chapter IV, Article 2: Expropriation and Compensation, para. 2.1.

[101] ECT Art. 13(1)(a); MAI Commentary, Commentary on Chapter IV.

[102] NAFTA Art. 1110.

[103] MAI Text, Chapter IV, Article 2: Expropriation and Compensation, para. 2.2.

[104] *Ibid.*, para. 2.3.

[105] *Ibid.*, para. 2.4.

[106] *Ibid.*, para. 2.5.

[107] MAI Commentary, Commentary on Chapter IV (see also NAFTA Art. 1110(4) and (5).

[108] MAI Text, Chapter IV, Article 2: Expropriation and Compensation, Footnote 2.

be seen as an indication that there is still no generally accepted method for calculating compensation.[109]

Dispute resolution
The dispute resolution provisions in the MAI Draft draw on the developments established in NAFTA and in the Energy Charter Treaty, providing for both State–State dispute resolution[110] and for Investor–State 'arbitration'.[111]

State–State procedure
The State–State procedure anticipated is an *ad hoc* arbitral tribunal. Resort can be had to the procedures established for arbitration by any Contracting Party alleging that another Contracting Party has acted in breach of the Agreement.[112] It is left open (consciously) whether a dispute can be regarded as ripe for arbitration where a legislative measure has been adopted but not yet applied to any concrete case.[113] Exhaustion of local remedies is not required before the MAI dispute resolution processes can be invoked.[114] However, it was agreed that this should be recorded in the Commentary 'rather than include in the articles of the MAI a provision which might cast doubt on the dispute settlement provisions of other investment agreements which had the same intent and were silent on the matter'.[115]

Referral of a dispute to arbitration would occur only after a period of consultation,[116] which might include consideration of the matter by the Parties Group.[117] Good offices, mediation or conciliation could also be utilised.[118] All such procedures, including the consultation phase, would be subject to confidentiality and without prejudice.[119]

[109] For a full discussion of the issues see M. Sornarajah *The International Law on Foreign Investment* 1994, Chapter 9.

[110] MAI Text, Chapter V, Articles A–C: State–State Procedures.

[111] *Ibid.*, Article D: Investor–State Procedures.

[112] *Ibid.*, Article C(1)(a).

[113] MAI Commentary, Commentary on Chapter V. The question is left open for an arbitral tribunal to decide 'in light of all the relevant circumstances and the jurisprudence' (*ibid*).

[114] Cf. the *ELSI Case Elettronica Sicala* (US v. Italy) 1989 *ICJ Rep*. 15.

[115] MAI Commentary, Commentary on Chapter V, Article C(1)(a).

[116] MAI Text, Chapter V, Article B(1). Requests for consultation must be in writing and provide sufficient information for the other party to understand the basis of the request. The Parties Group must also be furnished with a copy of the request. The requested party must respond within thirty days, and arbitral proceedings cannot be commenced within sixty days from the date of receipt of the request.

[117] MAI Text, Chapter V, Article B(2). The disputing parties must request this by agreement. The Parties Group must conclude its deliberations within sixty days of receipt of the request and can make recommendations to the disputing parties.

[118] *Ibid.*, Article B(3).

[119] *Ibid.*, Article B(4). See also the general provision on confidentiality: *Ibid.*, Article A(2).

The arbitral tribunal would be composed of members appointed from a roster of highly qualified, willing individuals to be maintained by the Parties Group.[120] Normally the members would be proposed by the Secretary-General of ICSID and normally there would be three, though either party or side could elect to have two additional members, one appointed by each party or side.[121] If the parties fail to appoint members to the panel, the Secretary-General of ICSID can be requested to make the appointments.[122] As with the WTO dispute resolution procedures, time-limits are set for each stage of the procedures from start to finish, though these may be extended where appropriate.

The procedure for arbitration allows for intervention by third parties[123] and for the request by the tribunal of scientific, technical or other expert reports.[124] The tribunal may indicate provisional measures.[125] The tribunal should, in its award, set out its findings of law and fact and give reasons, and may award by way of relief:

1 a declaration of illegality;
2 a recommendation that a Party brings its actions into conformity with its MAI obligations;
3 pecuniary compensation for loss or damage suffered by the requesting Party's investor or investment; and
4 any other form of relief to which the Party against which the award is made consents, including restitution in kind to an investor.[126]

The requirement of consent to restitution in kind in (4) is noteworthy, given the uncertainty which surrounds this type of remedy in international law;[127] however, the provision can be explained by reference to the arbitral nature of the proceedings. Costs incurred will be borne by the parties themselves and the cost of the tribunal divided equally unless the tribunal indicates otherwise.[128]

The award will normally be rendered within 180 days from the date of formation of a tribunal and will be issued in the first place to the parties who may, within 30 days, submit comments which will then be considered

[120] *Ibid.*, Article C(2)(f). Article C(2)(c) provides that an individual with special expertise from outside the Panel may be appointed where such expertise is required and not available within the roster.

[121] *Ibid.*, Article C(2)(a). The Panel should be appointed within thirty days of receipt of the request for arbitration.

[122] *Ibid.*, Article C(2)(b). This should be done within thirty days of receipt of a request from either party to do so.

[123] *Ibid.*, Article C(4).

[124] *Ibid.*, Article C(5).

[125] *Ibid.*, Article C(6)(b).

[126] *Ibid.*, Article C(6)(c).

[127] C. Gray *Judicial Remedies in International Law* 1987, pp. 12–16 and 95–6.

[128] MAI Text, Chapter V, Article C(6)(g).

by the tribunal. The final award will then be issued within 15 days after the closure of the comment period.[129] A copy will be sent to the Parties Group, which will make it publicly available.[130] Automatic publication at this stage serves two purposes. First, though the award is binding only between the parties to the dispute, it maximises the impact of awards as a source of clarification of the obligations of the MAI. Second, and more pragmatically, it maintains pressure on the parties to settle the dispute by agreement right up to the end of arbitral proceedings by adding the threat of public defeat to the measures available to the tribunal by way of relief.

A process for appeal before a new tribunal is provided for where it is claimed by one of the Parties to the dispute that the original arbitration was flawed. That is, that:

- the tribunal was not properly constituted;
- the tribunal manifestly exceeded its powers;
- there was corruption on the part of a member of the tribunal or a person providing decisive expertise or evidence;
- there was a serious departure from a fundamental rule or procedure; or
- the award failed to state the reasons on which it was based.

Thus there is a clear break from the WTO dispute settlement provisions where any 'issues of law covered in the panel report and legal interpretations developed by the panel' may form the subject of an appeal.[131] This underlines the essentially arbitral nature of the MAI proceedings, as opposed to the more judicial nature of the WTO proceedings.

The final area of note in relation to State–State proceedings is the question of countermeasures in the event of non-compliance, where there are significant outstanding issues.[132] Generally, it was agreed that countermeasures would be appropriate after a period of consultations[133] and provided they were proportionate.[134] There was a difference of opinion, however, on whether counter-measures should be limited to suspension of benefits under the MAI itself (excluding certain obligations such as those on expropriation and denial of treatment in accordance with international law), or whether a broad approach should be permitted allowing any responsive measure permitted under customary international law.[135]

[129] *Ibid.*, Article C(6)(d).

[130] *Ibid.*, Article C(6)(e).

[131] WTO Agreement, Annex 3: Understanding on Rules and Procedures Governing the Settlement of Disputes, Article 17:3.

[132] MAI Text, Chapter V, Article C(9).

[133] *Ibid.*, Article C(9)(a).

[134] *Ibid.*, Article C(9)(b).

[135] MAI Text, Chapter V, Article C(9)(a) and MAI Commentary, Commentary on Chapter V. In the Commentary it is argued that these two positions would not be

It was agreed that the intention to take counter-measures should be notified to the other party and to the Parties Group,[136] but the role of the Parties Group was another area of dispute. While it was agreed that a party to the dispute could request that the Parties Group consider the matter, some delegations proposed that the party proposing the counter-measures should refrain for a period of twenty days while the Parties Group consider its response.[137] It was agreed also that the Parties Group should be able to make recommendations and to suspend the non-complying party from the Parties Group. However, there was disagreement over whether the Parties Group should have the power to decide that some of the proposed counter-measures should not be taken.[138]

Investor–State procedure

The Investor–State dispute settlement procedures developed in the MAI negotiations are very heavily influenced by NAFTA arrangements in many key aspects.[139] As with the State–State procedure, consultation and/or negotiation is preferred in the first instance.[140] Resort may not be had to arbitration until the expiry of sixty days notice, subject only to a five-year longstop.[141] Resort may be had to any competent court or tribunal of the State Party to the dispute or to any agreed procedure or to arbitration in accordance with:

- the ICSID Convention;
- the ICSID Additional Facility (if available);
- the UNCITRAL rules; or
- the ICC rules.[142]

The MAI itself provides the consent of the State Party to any of these forms of arbitration; the agreement in writing of the investor is required.[143]

---

as far apart as might be assumed, provided the MAI neither expressly provided for retaliatory suspensions under WTO agreements, nor waived the parties' rights of action under the WTO dispute resolution procedures, since the risk of action under the WTO DSU would effectively curtail many responses otherwise permissible under customary international law. MAI Commentary, *ibid.*

[136] MAI Text, Chapter V, Article C(9)(a).

[137] *Ibid.*, Article C(9)(c).

[138] *Ibid.*

[139] NAFTA Articles 1115–36 and Annexes.

[140] MAI Text, Chapter V, Article D(2).

[141] *Ibid.*, Article D(4). NAFTA, by contrast, requires that at least six months has lapsed since the events giving rise to the dispute (NAFTA Art. 1120) and that ninety days notice has been given (NAFTA Art. 1119).

[142] *Ibid.*, Article D(2). Under NAFTA the first three of these are available: NAFTA Art. 1120.

[143] *Ibid.*, Articles D(3) and (5).

Time limits and default procedures are established for the appointment of arbitrators.[144] Two types of dispute may be submitted to arbitration. First, disputes concerning an alleged breach of the MAI obligations of the host state;[145] here the applicable law is the MAI itself, interpreted and applied in accordance with international law rules.[146] Second, disputes concerning alleged breaches of any other obligation entered into by the host state in respect of a specific investment of the investor through an investment authorisation or written agreement, on which the investor has relied in establishing, acquiring or expanding an investment;[147] here the applicable law is stated to be as agreed by the parties or failing that, the law of the host state, the law governing the authorisation or agreement and such rules of international law as may be applicable.[148] Interim relief may be awarded to preserve the rights of the disputing parties or preserve the Tribunal's jurisdiction.[149] The final award will set out its findings in law and in fact and give reasons, and may include:

- a declaration of breach of obligation;
- pecuniary compensation, which will include interest;
- restitution in kind where appropriate, provided that the Contracting Party may pay pecuniary compensation in lieu *where restitution is not practicable*;[150]
- any other form of relief agreed to by the parties.[151]

Awards are binding on the parties to the dispute and are made public, subject to confidentiality safeguards.[152]

The dispute settlement provisions of the MAI Draft have given rise to much critical comment, particularly for the apparent one-sidedness of the arrangement: '[t]he MAI would be the first multilateral agreement to give

[144] *Ibid.*, Article D(7).

[145] *Ibid.*, Article D(1)(a).

[146] *Ibid.*, Article D(14)(a).

[147] *Ibid.*, Article D(1)(b). Under NAFTA, decisions made by Canada pursuant to the Investment Canada Act, and decisions made by the Mexican National Commission on Foreign Investment, on whether to permit an acquisition are exempt from the dispute settlement provisions: NAFTA Annex 1137.2.

[148] MAI Text, Chapter V, Article D(14)(b).

[149] *Ibid.*, Article D(15).

[150] It is not clear what this means. No such restriction is placed on the right of state parties to pay damages in lieu of restitution under NAFTA: NAFTA Art. 1134(1)(b).

[151] MAI Text, Chapter V, Article D(16)(a). NAFTA makes provision only for monetary damages (with interest) and/or restitution (possibly substituted by damages): NAFTA Art. 1134(1).

[152] *Ibid.*, Article D(16)(c),(16)(d) and (17). There is no requirement under NAFTA that awards must be made public, though a public register is maintained of requests for arbitration: NAFTA Art. 1125(12).

multinationals the right to sue national and local governments in an international tribunal . . . Meanwhile there are no corresponding requirements for companies to act responsibly'.[153] Many NGOs, particularly environmental NGOs, have warned of the potential 'chilling effect' of threatened legal challenges to governments in respect of legitimate forms of regulation of enterprises.[154] The dispute settlement provisions are thus seen as extremely sinister, 'a far-reaching move to bring international law into the service of the powerful and economically strong, while entirely neglecting the interests of the poor and economically weak'[155] and an attack on the democratic powers of both national and local governments.[156]

Many of these criticisms are of course compound criticisms regarding the alleged unfairness or one-sidedness of the *substantive* provisions of the MAI, rather than of the dispute settlement provisions *per se*. The Canadian House of Commons Sub-Committee on International Trade, Trade Disputes and Investment considered that there was little new in these provisions:

> the proposed investor-state mechanism in the MAI is similar to that found not only in NAFTA but in the bilateral investment treaties of Canada and other countries, as well as in 'a long established series of agreements that have been negotiated under the auspices of the New York Convention, the International Centre for the Settlement of Investment Disputes, on to the PanAmerican Convention.' A similar approach is used by the Multilateral Investment Guarentee Agency of the World Bank.[157]

This Committee contented itself with noting that the confidentiality of this type of proceeding, though a classic feature of arbitration, was neither transparent nor open to third parties and recommended that Canada 'continue to press for open, accessible and transparent procedures for dispute resolution.'[158]

In reality, the truth lies somewhere between these two positions. While all the developments identified in the Canadian House of Commons report have taken place and are similar in type, the MAI seeks to establish a pattern of dispute resolution which would be much more comprehensive in

[153] World Development Movement briefing paper 'The MAI – A Dangerous Leap into the Dark' 1997, available at http://www.gn.apc.org/negreens/mai-leap.htm.

[154] See further the discussion of MAI and the environment, below.

[155] Oxfam UK and Ireland, *supra* note 79.

[156] World Development Movement 'A Dangerous Leap', *supra* note 153; Oxfam UK and Ireland *The MAI*, *supra* note 79; M. Sforza-Roderick, S. Nova and M. Weisbro 'Writing the Constitution of a Single Global Economy' Preamble Collaborative, 1998, available at http://www.islandnet.com/~ncfs/maisite/analysis.htm.

[157] House of Commons Sub-Committee on International Trade, Trade Disputes and Investment, Report No. 01 1998, available at http://www.islandnet.com/~ncfs/maisite/report.htm.

[158] *Ibid.*, Recommendation No. 11.

terms of both the investments covered and its geographic scope. The element of consent, another classical feature of arbitration and one which underlies most of the developments referred to in the Canadian report, is present in the MAI only in a formal sense, since the State Parties, by acceding to the MAI, would give a broad consent to all future actions concerning MAI obligations. It is a key feature of most of the other developments referred to (including NAFTA) that the right to resort to arbitration arises from a specific Investor–State agreement or under a system where investment screening procedures or controls are maintained (such as by Canada and Mexico in the context of NAFTA). Thus there is an interrelationship between the substantive obligations of the parties and their consent to arbitration which should not be overlooked. The MAI proposes to establish as the default procedure a type of dispute settlement which, though increasingly common, has hitherto been the exception and one founded on the specific agreement of the parties. A more apt comparison would be to the dispute settlement procedures of the WTO which, despite their steady judicialisation and increasingly rule-oriented form, remain firmly State–State in their operation.[159]

The charge is therefore properly laid that the MAI seeks to hold governments to account, while doing little or nothing to address the accountability of multinationals and it is disingenuous to attempt to analyse the dispute settlement provisions without reference to the substantive provisions of the MAI.

Some of the specific issues raised in the MAI Draft are considered in greater detail below. In general terms it can be said that the MAI Text explicitly pursues the liberalisation agenda and carries it much further than was possible in the Uruguay Round of Multilateral Trade Negotiations. Besides being tougher on performance requirements, the MAI Text seeks to adopt a wide definition of investment, broad enough to afford protection to indirect or portfolio investments as well as direct investments.[160] And freed from the trade focus of GATT,[161] the MAI text covers the whole lifecycle of investments, bringing together like NAFTA the issues of barriers to investment, trade-distortion in the treatment of investment, and treatment after expropriation. The ambitious scope of the MAI was, however, to contribute to its downfall.

Like NAFTA and the Agreement on TRIMs, the MAI Text is concerned with the regulation of host states, not the regulation of the investors themselves, though it is intended that the OECD Guidelines on Multinational

[159] Sforza-Roderick *et al.* 'Writing the Constitution', *supra* note 156.

[160] Some safeguards are included and many of the provisions are still subject to negotiation.

[161] It was noted above that the Mandate negotiated for the Uruguay Round only permitted consideration of trade distorting performance requirements.

Enterprises[162] be attached (as non-binding guidelines).[163] The one-sidedness of this 'free trade' approach to the regulation of foreign investment, together with the choice of the OECD as a forum for negotiation, has attracted a wealth of criticism, and indeed has served to politicise the issue of foreign investment regulation as never before (see further below). In particular, the NGO community has raised concerns from both environmental and development perspectives.

7.5 The MAI and the environment

Environmentalists have argued that the MAI would prohibit or inhibit environmental regulatory activity on the part of national or local government. In particular they have singled out the restrictions on performance requirements and the provisions on investment protection. The restrictions on performance requirements, it is argued, could be used to prevent governments imposing conditions, for example regarding the use of recycled materials wherever possible or to outlaw preferences in the award of public contracts for environmentally responsible firms.[164] The provisions permitting Investor-State claims could be used as seen in the *Ethyl Corporation*[165] and *Metalclad*[166] *Cases* under NAFTA to challenge national or local environmental regulation.[167] Moreover, they could be coupled with an expropriation claim for 'lost profits' making the threat of any such action a serious issue, particularly for poorer governments. Thus laws banning the production or sale of dangerous products (as in *Ethyl*) or restricting land use or conserving natural resources for environmental reasons (as in *Metalclad*) could be pursued

[162] OECD Guidelines on Multinational Enterprises and the Third Revised Decision of the Council on National Treatment, discussed at Section 2.2, *supra*.

[163] MAI Text, Chapter X, Article on the OECD Guidelines for Multinational Enterprises. The MAI Text states (para. 1(1)): 'The Contracting Parties at the invitation of the (OECD) are encouraged to participate in the Guidelines work of the Organisation in order to promote co-operation on the application, clarification, interpretation and revision of the Guidelines and to facilitate the maintenance of consensus among the Contracting Parties and the Members of the Organisation on the matters addressed in the Guidelines'. The Declaration on International Investment and Multinational Enterprises and Guidelines which form part thereof were to be attached to the MAI as an Annex, either in the Agreement itself or in the Final Act. The Contracting Parties would have been required or encouraged (undecided) to set up National Contact Points for dealings and discussions relating to the Guidelines.

[164] Sforza-Roderfick *et al.* 'Writing the Constitution', *supra* note 156.

[165] See Section 6.3, *supra*.

[166] *Ibid.*

[167] Sforza-Roderick *et al.* 'Writing the Constitution', *supra* note 156; World Development Movement 'A Dangerous Leap', *supra* note 153.

as 'property' claims by foreign investors with vested interests. Alternatively they could perhaps be pursued by home state governments through the State–State dispute settlement provisions as discriminatory or as a breach of the performance requirements provisions (as in the *FIRA Case*). The MAI was thus portrayed as an initiative which would promote free trade at the expense of environmental protection: 'The MAI is the latest in a network of international agreements being used to undermine local, national, provincial and international initiatives for various public policy goals, through the creation of a legal regime of deregulated trade and deregulated investment. The goal is achieved by regulating national governments, through the agreements, preventing them from exercising powers available to them in their national constitutions'.[168]

Efforts were made in the later stages of the MAI negotiations to address some of these concerns. In the MAI Text of 24 April 1998, an Annex of 'Chairman's Proposals' is included which seeks to clarify a number of questions regarding the relationship between the MAI proposals and 'other important areas of public policy . . . and to avoid unintended consequences on normal regulatory practices'.[169] This represents a partial victory for the anti-MAI lobby, which had succeeded in persuading the OECD Parties to the negotiation that these issues were of great importance and had to be addressed. The Chairman's statement was said to have the support of a 'large majority', believing it to be a basis for future work.[170] However, it is clear that in relation to the environment no radical change of direction was regarded as necessary; the Chairman's Proposals essentially seek to assure concerned parties that necessary safeguards were in place to prevent the realisation of fears expressed by anti-MAI campaigners. Specifically highlighted are the Preamble, the right of Contracting Parties to regulate in a non-discriminatory manner, the 'not lowering measures' provision, the expropriation provisions and the exceptions to the performance requirements disciplines. The Chairman's Proposals also explicitly endorse the annexation of the OECD Guidelines for Multinational Enterprises to the Text of the MAI. These are now examined in turn.

The Preamble

Although it is generally agreed that there will be a recognition of environmental issues in the Preamble, there is little agreed about its form and content; many delegations wish to restrict this part of the Preamble to one

[168] Canadian Environmental Law Association 'The Multilateral Agreement on Investment and the Environment: Context and Concerns' prepared for the House of Commons Sub-Committee on International Trade, Trade Disputes and Investment, 24 November 1997, available at www.web.net/cela/maibrief.htm.

[169] MAI Text, Annex 2, Chairman's Proposals on Environment and Related Matters and on Labour, para. 1.

[170] *Ibid.*, footnote 1.

short paragraph, while others are of the view that a much fuller detailing of the relationship between investment and the environment is required. Though 'sustainable development' is recognised as a goal in each alternative formulation, with a general reference to the Rio Declaration on Environment and Development and Agenda 21, there are differences regarding the strength of the commitment to this goal. Additionally, it is not agreed whether a general reference to the Rio Declaration and Agenda 21 is sufficient, or whether specific elements of environmental law, such as the polluter pays principle and the precautionary approach, should be explicitly endorsed.[171]

The right to regulate in a non-discriminatory manner

The Chairman's Proposals suggest that the phrase 'in like circumstances' should be incorporated into the non-discrimination clauses of the MAI Text and an Interpretative Note should be attached, in which it is made clear that non-discriminatory regulation remains permissible. The proposed text for this note emphasises the relative nature of the national treatment and most favoured nation standards of treatment and states: 'Governments may have legitimate policy reasons to accord differential treatment as between domestic and foreign investors and their investments in certain circumstances . . . the fact that a measure applied by a government has a different effect on an investment or investor of another Party would not in itself render the measure inconsistent with national treatment and most favoured nation treatment.'[172]

In addition, the Chairman's Proposals suggests the inclusion of a new Article specifically affirming that 'normal' non-discriminatory regulatory activity in the environmental field is not inhibited; a proposal for this is included and an alternative general exception clause, along the lines of GATT Article XX also suggested.

The 'not lowering measures' provision

As noted earlier, the MAI Draft Text includes a proposal that prevents governments from lowering their health, safety, environmental or labour measures to encourage foreign investment, though there is little consensus on its precise content. The Chairman's Proposals seek to clarify that this is limited to the lowering of domestic requirements for particular investors and is not meant to inhibit normal regulatory activity. It is suggested that an Interpretative Note should be attached to the relevant Article, recognising that governments retain 'flexibility to adjust their overall health, safety, environmental or labour standards over time'.[173]

[171] See MAI Text, I General Provisions, Preamble and notes thereon and compare MAI Text, Annex 2 (Chairman's Proposals, *supra* note 169) and the Annex thereto.
[172] MAI Text, Annex 2, Annex, para. 2.
[173] *Ibid.*

Expropriation and compensation

There was concern amongst some anti-MAI campaigners that the reference to *de facto* expropriation, 'measures having equivalent effect', could be exploited by 'takings' or 'property-rights' activists to undermine legitimate environmental regulation. Such fears were hardly to be dispelled by the second paragraph on this issue in the MAI Draft which read as: '1.2 A Contracting Party shall not impair by [unreasonable or discriminatory] [unreasonable and discriminatory] measures the operation, management, maintenance, use, enjoyment or disposal of investments in its territory by investors of another Contracting Party'.[174] The failure to amplify on the meaning of 'unreasonable' or to incorporate in the provision the common 'except for a public purpose' type of formulation could serve only to cause alarm, particularly in the wake of cases such as *Ethyl*. The Chairman's Proposals, reflecting the views of the parties, seek to clarify that normal regulatory activity which is non-discriminatory will not be inhibited (whether it impinges on the use, etc., of investments or amounts to a taking, provided that the international law rules on expropriation and compensation are respected). It is suggested that this could be achieved by adding an Interpretative Note clarifying that the 'de facto' expropriation clause is intended only to reflect international law on takings where title is not actually assumed and 'does not establish a new requirement that Parties pay compensation for losses which an investor or investment may incur through regulation, revenue raising and other normal activity in the public interest undertaken by governments'.[175]

It remains to be seen whether critics will be satisfied with this formulation. It is noticeable that there is no suggestion in the Chairman's Proposals that the principles of state sovereignty and permanent sovereignty over natural resources or the right to expropriate should be reflected either in the text or in the Interpretative Note; the rights of states in this field are all cast, under the MAI, in the negative: 'A contracting State shall not expropriate . . . except'.

Exceptions to the performance requirements disciplines

Fears about the inhibiting effects of the performance requirements provisions on environmental regulation were noted above, and there had been considerable discussion during the negotiations as to how this should be addressed (and not only in relation to the performance requirements disciplines). Some proposed a clarificatory provision specific to the environment, along the lines of NAFTA Article 1114(1),[176] though there were concerns

[174] MAI Text, Chapter IV, Investment Protection, Article 1 (General Treatment), Para. 1.2.

[175] MAI Text, Annex 2, Annex, para. 5.

[176] See Section 6.1.2, *supra*.

about the self-executing character of the NAFTA provision and its precise formulation. This approach was perceived as one which would tilt the balance in favour of the environment by establishing a presumption that environmental regulation does not breach the investment protection provisions.[177] Another approach considered was the general exception approach of GATT Article XX, also used in the Energy Charter Treaty, though it was recognised that the GATT jurisprudence on environmental matters was 'problematic'.[178] The Chairman's Proposals take as a starting point the argument that, because the performance requirements proposals go beyond non-discrimination, an exceptions article is required to clarify the scope remaining to governments to impose requirements on foreign investment in areas such as the environment. The proposed exception reads as follows:

> Provided that such measures are not applied in an arbitrary or unjustifiable manner, or do not constitute a disguised restriction on investment, nothing in (the performance requirements Articles) shall be construed to prevent any Contracting Party from adopting or maintaining measures, including environmental measures:
> (a) necessary to secure compliance with measures that are not inconsistent with the provisions of this Agreement;
> (b) necessary to protect human, animal or plant life or health; or
> (c) necessary for the conservation of living or non-living exhaustible natural resources.

This proposal leaves a lot of questions unanswered. The reference to measures applied in an 'arbitrary or unjustifiable' manner could be taken as a reference to the non-discrimination requirements of the MAI (in which case the language of non-discrimination could be used) or it could be taken to refer to the public purpose and standard of evidence on which such measures should be based (the 'objective justification' requirement of EC law). If the latter, then the provision runs into the same criticisms as GATT Article XX. First, it could be said that it lacks certainty; there is no guidance as to how the environment is to be weighted in the assessment of 'unjustifiable'. This is compounded by the lack of agreement over the references to the environment in the Preamble, which would be used in the event of a dispute to aid with the interpretation of these provisions. Second, there is no explicit endorsement within this provision of the precautionary principle of international environmental law, making it unclear whether this could be used as the basis for an environmental measure which also had the effect of restricting investment. Of the sub-paragraphs, it can be noted that the word 'necessary' also raises problems regarding the precautionary principle. Sub-paragraph (a) is tautologous, though its utility would be assisted by the negotiation of an adequate Preamble. Sub-paragraphs (b) and (c) would

[177] See MAI Text, Proposed Additional Article on Labour and Environment.
[178] *Ibid.* See Section 8.1, below.

seem merely to extend the problems experienced by GATT Panels in balancing trade and environmental concerns to the investment or capital movement field.[179]

This part of the proposal in particular raises questions about the suitability of dispute panels to examine and decide these issues, one of the points raised by the *Sea Turtles Case*. The Chairman points out that individuals with individual expertise may be appointed to panels and that panels may avail themselves of expertise in labour or environmental matters.[180]

The annexation of the OECD Guidelines for Multinational Enterprises
The Chairman's Proposal endorses the view that the OECD Guidelines should be annexed to the MAI itself, rather than referred to in the Final Act. It is not clear whether this has more than political significance. From a legal point of view, if the provisions were annexed, there would be no doubt that they could be referred to in questions of interpretation, though there would still be doubt as to the weight to be placed on them, due to their continuing non-binding nature. But they could probably be referred to in a dispute even if they were only incorporated in the Final Act. Of greater significance may be the fact that a revision of the environment, employment and industrial relations chapters of the Guidelines was anticipated, which it may have been hoped would deflect concern from the MAI itself.

'Think global, act local'?
It is unlikely that anti-MAI environmental campaigners will be satisfied by the Chairman's Proposals, or by any revised Draft MAI in which they are reflected. While there has undoubtedly been an element of 'scaremongering', misinformation or exaggeration in the claims of some anti-MAI campaigners, there remain many grey areas in the provisions themselves, and the 'trust us!' tone of much of the Chairman's proposals is anathema to many of the MAI's opponents. Leaving it to international dispute settlement panels to balance the interests of the environment and the capital-exporting states and/or multinationals is precisely what environmentalists fear, and with the antecedents of GATT environmental disputes, and the Investor–State actions commenced under NAFTA, it is little wonder there is great hostility.

One of the greatest inspirations of the environmental lobby, reflected in Agenda 21, has been the 'Think global, act local' slogan, which focuses attention on community level preferences and community-based action. The globalisation/deregulation agenda of the MAI often appears diametrically opposed to this school of thought: individualised, localised negotiations

[179] Cases include the *Tuna/Dolphin Case*, the *Sea Turtles Case* and the *Beef Hormones Case*. These are examined further in Chapter 8.
[180] MAI Text, Annex 2, footnote 2.

with investors to secure environmental planning gains, for instance, seem to fall foul of the non-discrimination requirements, while general measures imposed at the state, regional or local, rather than the national level, also seem doomed. While the US has reputedly proposed a country-specific exemption for all US state and local government measures from the MAI,[181] not all countries will be inclined to seek a similar arrangement or in a position to negotiate one.[182]

7.6 The MAI and social concerns

Social concerns have been addressed in much the same way as environmental concerns in the MAI negotiating process. Originally pretty well ignored in the negotiations, concern over the impact of the MAI on social issues was raised by the NGO community: 'This (Agreement) represents a far-reaching move to bring international law into the service of the powerful and economically strong, while entirely neglecting the interests of the poor and the economically weak. As such it fails to balance the granting of rights with any acknowledgement of responsibilities for social improvement, human rights or the protection of the natural resource base on which the poor depend'.[183]

On labour standards it is argued that increased capital mobility and hence increased competition to attract investments leads to a lowering of labour standards. The unbalanced nature of the MAI, imposing obligations on states without any corresponding obligations on companies, is regarded as an exacerbating factor.

7.7 The MAI and development

Since the *raison d'être* of the MAI is to promote 'high standards for the liberalisation of investment regimes',[184] it should come as no surprise that it has its critics among those who do not subscribe to a neo-liberal view of development economics. Both in its rhetoric and its substance the MAI projects liberalisation as suitable for all, whatever their level of development and thus rejects the 'different and more favourable treatment' agenda of the New International Economic Order. While the MAI Draft was negotiated at the OECD and thus by representatives of only the richest states, it is

[181] World Development Movement 'A Dangerous Leap', *supra* note 153.

[182] Non-OECD countries invited to join at a later date will negotiate individually their terms of accession: see further the MAI and development below.

[183] Oxfam UK and Ireland 'The MAI', *supra* note 79, Executive Summary.

[184] MAI Text, Preamble.

intended that it is opened to accession by non-members, with their accession depending 'not so much on their level of economic development as such, but rather on their readiness and capacity to enter into high standard and legally binding commitments'.[185] It is not clear what threshold eligibility standards might be established for developing countries wishing to accede to a future MAI, nor which obligations would be regarded as 'core' (that is, unable to be the subject of country-specific exceptions). In theory, at least, 'the scope for creating special conditions for developing countries is not yet defined'.[186]

Yet the absence of developing countries from the negotiations, and the uncertainty about the terms on which they would be invited to accede to the MAI, have opened the OECD up to fierce criticism. There have been trenchant economic and political critiques of the potential impacts of the MAI on developing countries.

Development NGOs have broadly raised two strands of argument against the MAI; the first, an economic argument, denounces the liberalisation orthodoxy, arguing from an economic nationalism perspective that this does not serve the interests of poorer states or address the gap between rich and poor states. The MAI, they argue, would prevent developing countries from using policies which were commonly adopted by both OECD states and the 'tiger' economies during their development to restrict certain types of foreign investment, restrict investment to certain sectors, and to enhance the benefits flowing to the local economy. There is great anxiety, shared by developing states, that legitimate concerns over the economic impact of the operations of foreign investors within the host state are not given sufficient recognition; in short, that the agreement is unbalanced in promoting the interests of capital, while doing nothing to enhance the regulatory control of host states.

A second strand of criticism focuses more on the political implications of the MAI obligations for poorer, weaker states; in relation to the environment there is great concern that weaker states will have no choice but to accede to the MAI, will be in a weak bargaining position in relation to the terms of access and will, under the MAI rules, lose much of their sovereign regulatory rights where these impinge on the rights of foreign investors.

Yet, as Fitzgerald *et al.* point out 'international capital flows are a central characteristic of the global economy of which developing countries increasingly form a part' and in the last fifteen years developing countries, as well as developed countries, have liberalised their investment regimes to an unprecedented degree.[187] Thus, they argue, '[t]he MAI cannot be judged

[185] E. V. K. Fitzgerald, R. Cubero-Brealey and A. Lehmann *The Development Implications of the Multilateral Agreement on Investment* 1998 (report commissioned by the Department for International Development (DfID), UK) at p. 6.

[186] *Ibid.*

[187] *Ibid.*, pp. 13, 14.

from the standpoint of whether foreign investment is "a good thing" as such, but rather from that of whether such an arrangement enables the relationship between foreign investment and sustainable development to be strengthened'.[188] These authors proceed to analyse the development implications of the MAI from both a national and international perspective, and from the perspective of the poorer developing states (middle- and low-income), thereby making the important point that the effects will not be the same for all developing countries.

7.8 The future of the MAI

The MAI text has attracted great criticism, especially from the NGO community, for its failure to address concerns regarding social, labour and environmental issues; it is feared that on the contrary the Agreement would precipitate a 'race-to-the-bottom', whereby states desperate to attract foreign investment would lower their standards in such areas to reduce rents.[189] The stark contrast even on the face of the provisions between the binding obligations on host States in relation to the treatment of investors, and the non-binding Code on the behaviour of multinationals, have done little to dispel fears. And though there is some recognition of the possible benefits to be gained from the use of investment incentives, this important area of state policy is not satisfactorily addressed; under the MAI Text, investors' rights stand to be enhanced with scant attention being paid to protection of the legitimate concerns and policy choices of (sovereign) states and citizens.

The OECD negotiations were begun behind closed doors. Five non-OECD states – Slovakia, Argentina, Chile, Hong Kong and Brazil – were granted observer status, but otherwise negotiations were closed. With the voices of less developed states totally absent, the OECD proceeded to negotiate a draft Agreement to which it is intended less developed countries will be invited to accede. The release of a draft negotiating text in February 1997 served to fuel the concerns of groups which felt they had been left out of the negotiating process and which felt their concerns were not reflected in that text. Following an OECD–NGO consultation in October 1997, a coalition of 565 NGOs was formed to oppose the adoption of the MAI.[190] A well-organised and successful lobbying campaign ensued,[191] during which time

[188] *Ibid.*, p. 14.

[189] For a discussion, see, e.g. M. Daly 'Investment Incentives and the Multilateral Agreement on Investment' *32(2) JWT* (1988) 5 at pp. 5–6.

[190] See NGO/OECD Consultation on the MAI *Joint NGO Statement on the Multilateral Agreement on Investment (MAI)* Paris 27 October 1997, available at: http://www.corpwatch.org/trac/feature/planet/mai_ngo.html.

[191] Guy de Jonquieres 'Network Guerillas' *Financial Times* London, 30 April 1998.

many governments came under fire domestically for their stance towards the negotiating process and the draft text.[192] Though negotiations continued through until the summer of 1998, there was considerable slippage in the timetable for adoption of a final text, originally planned for May 1997. Finally, in October 1998 France announced its withdrawal from the talks, which were consequently suspended.

It remains to be seen what will emerge from the MAI negotiation. While some commentators were quick to declare that the MAI was 'clinically' dead, this was clearly not so; following a meeting between US and EU representatives on 19 October 1998, the US announced that they wanted talks at the OECD to continue, while the EU Commissioner on Trade, Sir Leon Brittan, in an address to the European Parliament,[193] supported the relocation of talks to the WTO.[194] The agreement of a mandate to negotiate new provisions relating to investment was one of the contested issues of the WTO Ministerial summmit in Seattle in November 1999.[195] Whatever the outcome, it is now clearer than ever that a genuine international consensus on the treatment of foreign investment is absent. While developed states may have succeeded in shifting the focus of attention away from expropriation on to issues connected to earlier stages in the lifecycle of investments, they have failed so far to produce a text which reconciles the issues of investment protection and host state regulation. The outcome of these and future negotiations remain to be seen.

[192] In the UK see Early Day Motion 833 of 25 February 1998; Early Day Motion 1466 of 24 June 1998. In July 1997 Ambassador Victor Marrero, US Representative to ECOSOC acknowledged the role of civil society as 'an increasingly important actor in policymaking and implementation', a role which must be supported domestically and in the UN '[b]oth from the standpoint of effectiveness and representation': Speech delivered to ECOSOC Conference, Geneva, 3 July 1997.

[193] 20 October 1998. The UK government appears to support this position: 'the Government – together with our EU partners – remains commited in the longer term to promoting negotiations on investment through the WTO': Minister for Trade Brian Wilson, Department of Trade and Industry, Press Notice P/98/799 21 October 1998. In another forum, the same Minister commented: 'I think this is an opportunity to start again with a blank piece of paper, to define our objectives afresh and then seek to pursue them on an open and consensual basis': Minister for Trade Brian Wilson addressing a Royal Institute for International Affairs seminar, 29 October 1998, text available at http://www.gn.apc.org/negreens/mai-dti1.htm.

[194] The WTO established a working group to examine the relationship between trade and investment at the December 1996 Ministerial Conference in Singapore.

[195] See further Section 8.4, below.

8

Towards international disciplines – some conclusions

Introduction

The early chapters in this volume outlined the historic approach to the questions of treatment and taxation of foreign investment, whereby the promotion of state interests has been pursued in accordance with the legal concept of state sovereignty and its concomitant principles of jurisdiction. The legal obligations between states were determined on the whole through a network of unilateral and bilateral provisions, and gave scant concern to the needs of investors themselves. Though some legal principles, particularly in relation to expropriation, had undoubtedly acquired the status of customary international law, there remained great uncertainty about the precise content of many aspects of the rules. Moreover, customary international law did not address many issues of concern to investors and states alike concerning other stages of the investment cycle, including access to markets and discrimination in the operating conditions imposed on foreign investors. On the contrary, international law recognised regulation of the access and operation of foreign investment as a legitimate sovereign function. Host states, both developed and developing, employed an array of techniques to exclude, regulate and control foreign investment in order to minimise the negative impacts which it was recognised foreign investment could have, and to maximise the benefits which foreign investment could bring. Such regulation was regarded as a purely internal economic matter for the host state concerned, provided that it did not tip over into indirect expropriation or into arbitrary race discrimination, though challenges on either of these grounds were rare in practice.

In relation to taxation, the OECD took an effective initiative in standardising the pattern of treatment of the capital and earnings accruing to foreign investors through the development of a Model Double Taxation Agreement. Besides providing an influential normative model for the tax treatment of foreign investment, this approach also reinforced the bilateral inter-state approach to the taxation of foreign investment, and this persists in the taxation field to the present day.

In relation to the treatment of foreign investment more generally, however, the 1980s and 1990s have seen immense changes in the approach of the international community. These changes relate both to the substance and the institutional aspects of foreign investment law. As discussed in Chapter 7, foreign investment has been addressed from the free trade perspective which has dominated international economic law discourses during these two decades. From this perspective, restrictions on foreign investment and/or the failure to provide adequate protection for foreign investment are trade distorting and have negative connotations. Though some restrictions may be permissible in deference to the sovereign rights of states or to national political preferences, the emphasis is on the removal and circumscription of restrictions. In relation to both the substance and the institutional aspects of foreign investment law, there is a clear trend towards the integration of foreign investment law into other international economic law disciplines. The conclusion of TRIPs within the framework of the WTO serves to underline the development of linkage, both formal and ideological, between the two fields, while the influence of both regional and WTO disciplines on the substance and focus of the MAI Draft is irrefutable.

It is hard to argue, though, on the basis of the MAI negotiations, that there has been any genuine effort to integrate the concerns of capital-importing states regarding the behaviour of multinationals with the regulation of foreign investment, though the connection is conceded by the attachment of the (non-binding) OECD Guidelines. Nor have legitimate concerns regarding the impact of foreign investors on the environment or on social concerns been adequately addressed. In this final chapter, some of these important issues are reviewed, and the suitability of the WTO as a forum for the development of future disciplines on foreign investment law is considered.

8.1 Addressing environmental concerns in WTO disciplines – the record[1]

It is an irrefutable and long-standing criticism of GATT that it lacks the capacity to address in a satisfactory way the legitimate concerns of states and communities concerning trade and the environment. Originally drafted in the post-war period when environmental concerns were not of interest to the international community, GATT contains no explicit provision on

[1] For a general discussion of applicable GATT law see, e.g. D. C. Esty *Greening the GATT: Trade Environment and the Future* 1984; E. U. Petersmann 'International Trade Law and International Environmental Law' *27 JWTL* (1993) 46; T. J. Schoenbaum 'International Trade and Protection of the Environment: The Continuing Search for Reconciliation' *91 AJIL* (1997) 268.

environmental protection. Measures of environmental protection taken by states have therefore had to be based on the rather more limited Article XX, which provides for exceptions to the trade rules contained in the remaining provisions of the document, on the grounds *inter alia* of protecting human, animal or plant life or health (Article XX(b)) or for the conservation of exhaustible natural resources (Article XX(g)). In either case the measures must not be applied in a manner which would constitute arbitrary or unjustified discrimination between countries where the same conditions prevail, or a disguised restriction on trade.[2]

GATT cases involving elements of environmental protection have already illustrated some of the difficulties in taking account of non-economic concerns within the free trade rules. Steinberg summarises GATT law as follows:[3]

> each country may maintain regulations necessary to protect life and health, and conserve exhaustible natural resources, and may determine for itself the level of risk it deems appropriate to embody in its product standards. In general, the products not meeting those standards may be prohibited . . . product standards that limit imports must be applied on a most-favoured nation (MFN) basis, must be subject to national treatment disciplines, must not 'arbitrarily or unjustifiably discriminate' against imports, and must not be 'more trade restrictive than necessary' to achieve the chosen level of environmental protection.[4]

The history of the application of Article XX has raised problems, however, relating to the territorial application of these provisions, the standard of evidence required to refute a charge of arbitrariness, and the process to be followed by a GATT/WTO panel in assessing the claims of parties to a dispute. The *Tuna/Dolphin Cases*,[5] in particular *Tuna II*, highlighted the territorial jurisdiction problem when the Panel ruled that measures taken by a state under Article XX(b) or (g) must be concerned respectively with the protection of human, animal or plant life or health within the territorial jurisdiction of that state or with the conservation of exhaustible natural resources within that state: 'GATT has not been interpreted to permit a green country to restrict imports of goods produced or obtained in the global commons or foreign countries by persons or vessels of a different nationality when that country considers the ways those goods were produced or obtained environmentally unsound'.[6] Products which differ materially only in respect of the way in which they were obtained or made are 'like

[2] See further Schoenbaum, *ibid.*, pp. 273–80 and references cited therein.

[3] R. H. Steinberg 'Trade-Environment Negotiations in the EU, NAFTA, and WTO: Regional Trajectories of Rule Development' *91 AJIL* (1997) 231.

[4] *Ibid.*, at p. 237.

[5] *United States – Prohibition on Imports of Tuna, 30 ILM* (1992) 1598 (*Tuna I*); *United States – Prohibition on Imports of Tuna, 33 ILM* (1994) 839 (*Tuna II*).

[6] Steinberg 'Trade-Environment Negotiations', *supra* note 3 at p. 238.

products' under Article III, and cannot be discriminated against on the basis of such a difference.[7]

The issue of the standard of evidence required to support a unilateral trade-restricting measure was central to the *Beef Hormones Case*.[8] The Appellate Body ruled that the EU ban on imports of meat derived from cattle treated with certain growth-promoting hormones was based neither on existing international standards nor on a proper risk assessment. Though the dispute concerned the Sanitary and Phytosanitary Agreement (SPS)[9] which specifically requires that trade-restricting measures are based on scientific principles, the case is of general importance for the interpretation of GATT Article XX on which that Agreement is based. A great deal of attention has focused on the Appellate Body's approach to the burden of proof and to the precautionary principle of international law, which provides that where there is a threat of serious harm, lack of full scientific certainty shall not inhibit states from taking effective preventive measures.[10] Article 5.1 SPS requires that measures be based on an assessment of the risks to human, animal or plant life or health. This was interpreted strictly by the Panel, who found that the defending state must show that at the time the contended measure was introduced it was justified by a risk assessment, that the risk assessment was a 'scientific' process rather than a policy exercise involving social value judgements by politicians, and that the contested measures conform to the conclusions of the risk assessment.[11] Thus '[t]he Panel understands "risk assessment" as being a strict scientific evaluation to be distinguished from a "risk management" as a social value judgement on whether the Member can accept the risks assessed'.[12] The Appellate Body, however, took a wider view of 'risk assessment', requiring only that there be

[7] Schoenbaum 'International Trade', *supra* note 1 at pp. 289–90.

[8] *EC – Measures Concerning Meat and Meat Products* (*Hormones Case*) Report of the Appellate Body, WT/DS26/AB/R, WT/DS48/AB/R. The earlier Panel Reports on the complaints brought against the EC by Canada and the US are published as WT/DS48/R/CAN and WT/DC26/R/USA, respectively. All are available on the WTO website www.wto.org. For an extensive account of the dispute and the proceedings, see D. E. McNiel 'The First Case Under the WTO's Sanitary and Phytosanitary Agreement: The European Union's Hormone Ban' *39 VJIL* (1998) 89; for critical discussion of the Appellate Body's ruling, see McNiel, *ibid.*; R. Quick and A. Bluthner 'Has the Appellate Body Erred? An Appraisal and Criticism of the Ruling in the WTO *Hormones Case*' *2(4) JIEL* (1999) 641.

[9] Agreement on Sanitary and Phytosanitary Measures, 1994 in GATT *The Results of the Uruguay Round of Multilateral Trade Negotiations: The Legal Texts* 1994, p. 69.

[10] See generally D. A. Freestone 'The Precautionary Principle, International Law and Global Climate Change' in R. R. Churchill (ed.) and D. A. Freestone (eds) *International Law and Global Climate Change* 1991 at p. 21.

[11] Panel Reports, *supra* note 8, para. 8. See further Quick and Bluthner 'Has the Appellate Body Erred?', *supra* note 8 at pp. 615–16.

[12] Quick and Bluthner, *ibid.* at p. 616.

reasonable support in its findings for the contested measure, which may come from minority scientific views and which may include consideration of control factors.[13] Thus the Appellate Body's findings:

> seem to contain some reflections of a precautionary approach, contrary to the rather rigorous rulings of the Panel . . . its broad interpretation of risk assessment provides the WTO Members with an opportunity to choose their level of health protection in a 'virtually' precautionary way. However the AB stops short of giving the precautionary approach an over-riding effect over substantive provisions.[14]

As well as stopping short of an actual endorsement of the precautionary principle, the Appellate Body gave no clear indication about whether risk assessment must be confined to scientific evidence, albeit broadly construed, or whether wider societal or consumer concerns can also be considered: '[t]he role of "sound science" in governing SPS measures must await the next case'.[15] The Appellate Body ruled that the EC ban was not based on a risk assessment and hence was inconsistent with *inter alia* Article 5.1 SPS. In the interests of 'judicial economy' the Appellate Body then declined to reach a conclusion on the question of whether there was sufficient evidence to justify the ban.

Though WTO disciplines generally militate against reference to protectionist national political preferences, all the WTO disciplines leave WTO Members with an element of discretion to protect their own vital interests including, for example, national security, plant, animal and human life and health and natural resources (GATT Article XX) subject to an element of WTO control. Thus as with the EU's 'hard cases'[16] there is within WTO disciplines an open question as to how the balance is to be struck between the 'free trade' objectives of the WTO Agreements and the regulatory objectives of WTO Members. It is a question which ultimately can only be addressed on a case-by-case basis, and one which is inherently subject to differing political views. In the *Beef Hormones Case*, for instance, it was left unresolved whether democratic considerations such as consumer concerns could legitimately inform the 'risk assessment' which was to be undertaken, or whether such matters were to be dismissed as mere protectionism where they lacked any demonstrable scientific basis.

Unlike EC law, however, GATT disciplines contain a closed list of grounds to which Members may have resort to justify their regulatory activities. The GATT Article XX exceptions, unamended since 1947, therefore contain no specific reference to issues which have come to dominate modern political

[13] Appellate Body Report, *supra* note 8 at para. 192 *et seq.* Quick and Bluthner, *ibid.*, at p. 617.

[14] Quick and Bluthner, *ibid.*, at pp. 625–6.

[15] McNiel 'The First Case', *supra* note 8 at p. 134.

[16] See the *Cineteque, Danish Bottles* and *Sunday Trading Cases*, cited at Section 6.1.1, *supra.*

debate, such as environmental protection and consumer protection and/or choice. In the *Shrimp/Turtle Case*,[17] the WTO Dispute Settlement Body (DSB) was faced with an environmental question, the protection of an endangered species, which did not seem to fit readily into any of the permitted grounds on which exceptions could be based. While some environmental protection measures could fall under the banner of 'human, animal or plant health or welfare',[18] the use of this ground and its application to extra-territorial situations had previously been restricted in the *Tuna Cases*.[19] An additional difficulty was that environmental protection measures aimed at the preservation of biodiversity, preservation of natural beauty, reduction of atmospheric pollution or the prevention of climate change had no explicit basis in Article XX and could only be justified if they could be 'squeezed in' to one of the grounds enumerated in Article XX. The *Shrimp/Turtle Case* provides an excellent illustration. The case concerned trade-restricting measures adopted by the US aimed at the conservation of several endangered species of turtle which were at risk, it was argued, from shrimp-catching operations, unless these operations were carried out in a way laid down in the relevant US legislation.[20] The case thus raised the same issue as the *Tuna Cases* concerning the conservation of natural resources outside the jurisdiction of the state, when the method of harvesting did not result in objective differences between the actual products. The Appellate Body in the *Shrimp/Turtle Case*, adopting an 'evolutionary' approach to treaty interpretation[21] and one which surprised many, accepted the US argument that such resources could be regarded as falling within Article XX(g) as an 'exhaustible natural resource': 'One lesson that modern biological sciences teach us is that living species, though in principle, capable of reproduction and, in that sense, "renewable", are in certain circumstances indeed susceptible of depletion, exhaustion and extinction, frequently because of human activities. Living resources are just as finite as petroleum, iron ore and other non-living resources'.[22] The willingness of the Appellate Body to read Article XX(g) 'in the light of contemporary concerns',[23] and in so doing to depart from previous GATT Panel practice in relation to the protection of animal life, had the important consequence in the case before it of reducing the

[17] *United States – Import Prohibition of Certain Shrimp and Shrimp Products, Panel Report*, WT/DS58/R, 15 May 1998 and *Report of the Appellate Body*, WT/DS58/AB/R, 12 October 1998.

[18] GATT Art. XX(b).

[19] *Supra*, text at note 5.

[20] *Panel Report*, *supra* note 17 at paras 2.1–2.16; *Report of the Appellate Body*, *supra* note 17 at paras 3–7.

[21] A. E. Appleton '*Shrimp/Turtle*: Untangling the Nets' *2(3) JIEL* (1999) 477 at pp. 481–3.

[22] *Report of the Appellate Body*, *supra* note 17, para. 135.

[23] *Ibid.*, para. 136.

severity of the test to which such measures would be subjected. Article XX(b) provides an exception for certain trade measures '*necessary* to protect human, animal or plant life or health', whereas Article XX(g) provides an exception for certain trade measures '*relating to* the conservation of exhaustible natural resources if such measures are made effective in conjunction with restrictions on domestic production or consumption'.[24]

Notwithstanding the merits of this approach, it is far from clear that all aspects of environmental protection could be approached by this route. As noted above, many elements of the natural environment would not readily fit in to Article XX(b) or (g), something which it would appear could be addressed only by amending or supplementing the grounds contained therein. In addition, the difficulties concerning the protection of resources located outside a state's jurisdiction, as seen in the *Tuna Cases*, were not resolved in the *Shrimp/Turtle Case*. In a single paragraph of its Report, the Appellate Body notes the highly migratory nature of sea turtles and notes that all the species to which the disputed measure referred were known to occur in waters within US jurisdiction.[25] Thus it found that there was sufficient nexus in the specific circumstances of this case between the endangered species involved and the US. However, the Appellate Body declined to rule on the important general question of 'whether there is an implied jurisdictional limitation in Article XX(g), and if so, the nature or extent of that limitation'.[26] Thus the Appellate Body chose to ignore an ideal opportunity to overhaul the extra-territoriality restriction attached to earlier applications of GATT Article XX(b) in cases such as *Tuna II*.[27] In this respect too, it seems clear that nothing short of a renegotiation of Article XX could satisfy the concerns of environmentalists.

Despite its partially helpful approach to the interpretation of Article XX(g), the Appellate Body found that the disputed US measures did not satisfy the requirements of the Chapeau of Article XX that they be applied in a manner which did not constitute 'a means of arbitrary or unjustifiable discrimination between countries where the same conditions prevail, or a disguised restriction on international trade'.[28]

The Appellate Body went to some length (unnecessarily, it has been argued[29]) to consider whether the contested US measures met these requirements

[24] Emphases added.

[25] Report of the *Appellate Body*, *supra* note 17 at para. 141: The Appellate Body relies in making this finding on the Panel Report, para. 2.6.

[26] *Ibid.*, para. 141.

[27] There is no doctrine of binding precedent in relation to GATT or WTO DSB Panel Reports, but in practice Panels are often heavily influenced by previous reports and place increasing value on consistency.

[28] GATT Art. XX, Chapeau.

[29] Appleton 'Shrimp/Turtle', *supra* note 21, argues that the Appellate Body should have contented itself with finding one basis for dismissal of the appeal and left the

and hence did much to clarify the question of how the balance is to be struck between the 'free trade' objectives of the WTO disciplines and the regulatory objectives of the Members. Members resorting to unilateral regulatory measures now know that they must pursue their regulatory objectives with due respect for the conditions prevailing in a particular country which will be affected by the measure, and to apply their policy flexibly and in a spirit of co-operation.[30] They know too, that in the spirit of co-operation they should seek first to negotiate an international agreement on the issue in question,[31] and that their approach to such negotiations must be serious. They know also that in the application of trade-restricting regulatory measures they must respect due process, administering their laws in a 'uniform, impartial and reasonable' manner, taking cognisance of the need for transparency and predictability and the possibility of judicial review, where appropriate.[32] Finally, the Appellate Body stated that a balance had to be struck between the rights of the Member adopting trade-restricting measures and the treaty rights of other Members;[33] as Appleton notes, the Appellate Body 'appears to be moving ever closer to adopting some type of proportionality enquiry'.[34]

The *Shrimp/Turtle Case* can thus be seen to have made a significant contribution to the development of WTO jurisprudence on GATT Article XX in relation to environmental protection. However, it does so only selectively, leaving unresolved issues such as the protection of extra-territorial resources. But above all, it is inescapable that any Panel or Appellate Body is ultimately constrained by the wording of Article XX, and by the absence of any specific recognition of environmental protection as a basis for exception to the GATT and other WTO disciplines. With issues such as the presence of genetically modified ingredients and derivatives in foods high on political agendas both in Europe and in North America, these questions will surely return to the DSB within a short time. In the meantime, further concerns about the suitability of the WTO as an institution, and of the DSB, have grown.

8.2 The WTO and social concerns

The continuing debate over the handling of environmental concerns under WTO disciplines is paralleled in debates regarding unilateral measures

other questions unanswered: '[h]aving already found one rationale for striking down the US measure, the Appellate Body, without need or explanation, developed at least six additional grounds to support its decision. Judicial economy was forgotten'. *Ibid.*, at p. 481.

[30] *Report of the Appellate Body*, *supra* note 17 at paras 169–73.

[31] *Ibid.*, paras 174–80. This point arose also in *Tuna II*, *supra* note 5.

[32] *Ibid.*, paras 181–3; 185–91.

[33] *Ibid.*, paras 164–7.

[34] Appleton 'Shrimp/Turtle', *supra* note 21 at p. 492.

adopted by states in pursuit of social concerns, such as labour standards generally[35] or the elimination of child labour,[36] or human rights.[37] Though recourse to the WTO DSB has been less common in relation to these areas,[38] the link between trade and social issues is clear and the subject of growing public awareness.

8.3 Non-governmental organisations

The experience of the OECD in its attempt to negotiate an MAI gives an important indication that foreign investment and trade disciplines will in future be influenced not only by state parties and capital but also by civil society. NGOs with interests in development and environmental issues proved themselves able to organise effectively and to mobilise support both outside and within governments with spectacular success in relation to the MAI. Though it might be argued that the OECD scored a number of 'own goals' in respect of the limited participation in the negotiations and in the lack of openness which characterised the negotiations, there are clear messages to be drawn from the whole episode both in relation to the substance and the procedure for future negotiations. On matters of substance, there is a clear need to integrate fully development, environmental and social concerns into international trade negotiations. While the merits of an integrated approach are clear, it has not often been regarded as practicable, politically expedient

[35] See, e.g. B. A. Langille 'Eight Ways to Think About International Labour Standards' *31 JWT* (1997) 27; G. van Liempt 'Minimum International Labour Standards and International Trade: Would a Social Clause Work?' *128 International Labour Review* (1998) 433; P. Waer 'Social Clauses in International Trade: The Debate in the European Union' *30 JWT* (1996) 25; H. Ward 'Common But Differentiated Debates: Environment, Labour and the World Trade Organisation' *45 ICLQ* (1986) 592.

[36] See, e.g. H. Cullen 'The Limits of International Trade Mechanisms in Enforcing Human Rights: The Case of Child Labour' *7 Int'l J. of Children's Rights* (1999) 1; J. M. Diller and D. A. Levy 'Child Labour, Trade and Investment: Towards the Harmonization of International Law' *91 AJIL* (1997) 663.

[37] See, e.g. essays in L. A. Compa and S. F. Diamond (eds) *Human Rights, Labor Rights and International Trade* 1996; also S. Charnovitz 'The Moral Exception in Trade Policy' *38 VJIL* (1998) 689; C. McCrudden 'International Economic Law and the Pursuit of Human Rights: A Framework for Discussion of the Legality of "Selective Purchasing" Laws under the WTO Government Procurement Agreement' 2 *JIEL* (1998) 3.

[38] See, however, *United States – Measure Affecting Government Procurement, Complaint by the European Communities*, WT/DS88/1; and *United States – Measure Affecting Government Procurement, Complaint by Japan*, WT/DS95/1, complaining about the effects of the Massachusetts Myanmar (Burma) procurement laws. For an analysis of this 'selective purchasing' law and its compatibility with GATT disciplines see McCrudden '"Selective Purchasing" Laws', *supra* note 37.

or convenient to attempt such integration, as witnessed by the scant attention paid to environmental matters in the Uruguay Round. In terms of procedure there is an urgent need to develop new mechanisms to ensure that such interests are represented in international negotiations.

The arrival in the trade arena of well-organised, vocal and influential NGOs may well mean that such issues can no longer be sidelined. Although the existence of such groups was acknowledged in the Final Act of the Uruguay Round,[39] a fierce debate has since been conducted about the roles which NGOs might play in WTO activities and about the ways in which their participation, where appropriate, should be secured. This is not of course a new theme and has been vented fully in relation to environmental issues. But the OECD and the WTO have come to this issue rather more recently and, as was graphically demonstrated in Seattle in late November 1999, have been overtaken by the demands of more radical NGOs.

Among the proponents of enhanced NGO participation, Charnowitz and Esty have argued that NGO participation at the WTO should be welcomed both as a valuable source of opinion and analysis regarding trade policy, and as a means of enhancing the WTO's legitimacy as a key player in international economic governance.[40] Arguing that NGOs should be formally incorporated in international economic policy-making structures, Esty argues:

> NGOs offer the promise of serving as 'connective tissue' that will help to bridge the gap between WTO decision-makers and the distant constituents which they are meant to serve, thereby ensuring that the WTO's actions are perceived as responsive and fair. Non-governmental organisations also can act as 'competition' to governments in international trade debates. In doing so, they could broaden the base of information and thinking upon which decisions are made, and thus improve the quality, authoritativeness, and perceived fairness of the policy choices and judgements emanating from the WTO.[41]

Esty identifies four areas in which NGOs might contribute to the work of the WTO, and in which he argues that their involvement is required if the WTO is to meet the challenges which it faces.[42] First, he points to the knowledge and expertise possessed by specialised NGOs, particularly in

[39] Final Act Embodying the Results of the Uruguay Round of Trade Negotiations, Art. 5(2): the Article allows for 'consultation and co-operation with non-governmental organisations'.

[40] S. Charnovitz 'Participation of Non-governmental Organisations in the World Trade Organisation' *17 University of Pennsylvania Journal of International Economic Law* (1996) 331; D. C. Esty 'Non-Governmental Organisations at the World Trade Organisation: Cooperation, Competition or Exclusion' *1 JIEL* (1988) 123.

[41] Esty, *ibid.*, at pp. 125–6. See also Charnovitz, *ibid.*, at p. 340.

[42] See also the review of the 'benefits and pitfalls' of WTO interaction with civil society by J. A. Scholte, R. O'Brien and M. Williams 'The WTO and Civil Society' *33(1) JWT* (1999) 107 at pp. 111–12.

relation to areas at the intersection of trade law and other policy areas, for instance the environment. This expertise is needed by the WTO, he argues, to help the WTO, particularly dispute settlement panels, to reach the 'right' decision, and thereby enhance the authoritativeness of the WTO: 'the WTO often lacks ready access to the necessary expertise for making well-regarded and broadly accepted decisions. Beyond the limited depth of the WTO's knowledge base, the organisation's dispute settlement mechanisms lack credibility and legitimacy outside the realm of trade issues'.[43]

This issue has since arisen in the course of a dispute under the DSU: the *Shrimp/Turtle Case*,[44] where a number of environmental NGOs attempted to submit *amicus curiae* briefs. Such briefs were both presented to the Panel directly and annexed to the US submissions to the Panel. Though 'third parties' can make representations in Panel proceedings, this extends only to WTO Members (that is, states). It was then argued before the Appellate Body that the Panel had erred in accepting the briefs in each case. *Amicus curiae* briefs were also submitted, directly and as annexes to a Party's submissions, to the Appellate Body itself, so that it had to decide separately as a preliminary issue whether it could accept such briefs and whether, in either case, it was obliged to consider their contents. The Appellate Body ruled in favour of the admissibility of the briefs in each instance. In relation to briefs submitted to a Panel directly, this was found to fall within the right of a Panel to 'seek information and technical advice' from any source.[45] It fell to a particular Panel to decide on the acceptability, relevance or weight of any information or advice received.[46] In relation to briefs attached to Members' submissions, the Appellate Body ruled that the Panel was entitled to take these into account.[47] In relation to briefs submitted to the Appellate Body itself, the ruling is less clear. In a preliminary ruling the Appellate Body indicated that it would accept such briefs, both directly and appended to the Parties' submissions, and that it would explain its reasoning in its Report. The Report, however, makes no reference to the brief submitted directly. In addition, the briefs appended to the US submission were apparently accepted but, since the US itself had qualified its concurrence with the contents of those briefs, they were effectively ignored in the proceedings. Thus, while *amicus curiae* briefs could be utilised to meet the concerns outlined above regarding the knowledge base of the DSB, the ruling of the Appellate Body in the *Shrimp/Turtle Case* leaves it far from certain that such submissions will form an important part of proceedings in the future.

The second role identified by Esty for NGOs relates to procedural fairness, in the context of both policy-making and dispute resolution:

[43] *Ibid.*, at p. 127.
[44] *Panel Report*, *Supra* note 17.
[45] DSU, Art. 13.
[46] *Report of the Appellate Body*, *supra* note 17 at para. 108.
[47] *Ibid.*, para. 113.

'[p]rocedurally, those who believe that they have an interest in the outcome of decisions must have an opportunity to be part of the process, with opportunities to submit views and to observe how a particular outcome is reached'.[48]

This point is closely related to the wider debate about openness in international fora. As was noted in Chapter 7, one of the mistakes made by the OECD in its handling of the MAI negotiation was its failure even to inform, never mind involve or consult, interested non-governmental parties. The apparent secrecy in which the MAI negotiation was conducted, though denied by the OECD, became an effective political weapon in the campaign mounted by NGOs against the MAI. The WTO's own record on openness and transparency may also be open to criticism; though much more information about the organisation and its activities is published than previously,[49] many documents remain confidential and the central structures and decision-making processes remain closed to public scrutiny.[50] Under current rules, future rounds of trade negotiations would similarly be conducted largely in privacy. It is seriously open to question whether there is any justification for such secrecy, which contrasts unfavourable even with the UN Security Council.[51] This perception of secrecy was one of the cross-cutting issues which served to unite protesters against the WTO Ministerial Meeting in Seattle in November 1999.

The WTO has taken some steps to enhance NGO involvement; in July 1996 'Guidelines for the Arrangements on Relationships with Non-Governmental Organisations' were adopted as part of a general commitment to greater transparency.[52] Dunoff points also to the range of official but *ad hoc* activities

[48] *Ibid.*

[49] See in particular the WTO website: http://www.wto.org.

[50] Meetings of the General Council and of its Committees are closed and no minutes are published: see Annex C: Procedures for the Circulation and Derestriction of WTO Documents of the 1996 Guidelines for Relations with NGOs, *WTO Doc. WT/L/160.REV1* and the detailed discussion of the issue by G. Marceau and P. N. Pedersen in 'Is the WTO Open and Transparent? A Discussion of the Relationship of the WTO with Non-governmental Organisations and Civil Society's Claims for More Transparency and Public Participation' *33(1) JWT* (1999) 5. Annex C effectively gives any Member of the WTO body under the auspices of which the document was circulated a veto over its derestriction, although this has to be exercised positively: cf. Annex C, para. 3.

[51] Security Council Decisions and Resolutions are systematically published, as are Minutes of their meetings. While there is of course a 'shadow' process of debate and negotiation which precedes this public part of the Security Council's proceedings, there is at least an acknowledgement of the symbolic importance of openness and transparency.

[52] WTO *General Council Decision on Transparency* 18 July 1996, WTO *Doc. WT/L/162*. See also the further measures announced by WTO Director-General Ruggiero in 17 July 1998, *WTO Press Release 107 of 17 July 1998.*

involving NGOs,[53] though he admits that these contacts do not necessarily lead to inclusion of NGO views in the formal institutionalised proceedings of the organisation.[54]

As regards dispute resolution, the General Council decided at an early stage that all Panel Reports would be published as soon as they were adopted. Given the changeover from a positive assent to a negative assent procedure for the adoption of Panel Reports under the DSU,[55] this effectively means that all reports are published, whereas proceedings prior to the adoption of a report remain confidential. This position is probably justified; there is a clear tension between the need for confidentiality, critical to the success of negotiation, mediation and, at times, arbitration, and openness, critical to the legitimacy of adjudicative proceedings. As the DSU embraces all of these modes of dispute resolution,[56] it is clearly difficult to argue the case for greater openness in proceedings. On the other hand, it is to be hoped that the DSB itself will recognise the important role its proceedings play in the clarification and development of WTO law, as well as the wider environmental and social impacts of many of its decisions, and utilise fully the power confirmed in the *Shrimp/Turtle Case* to accept and consider, or even solicit, *amicus curiae* briefs.

The third role outlined by Esty for NGOs is in legitimising WTO decision-making in a field vulnerable to criticism as presenting a democratic deficit.[57] NGOs can operate both as a conduit for the dissemination of information and as a source of popular and/or informed perspectives on WTO activity. Doubts have been cast on this argument by opponents of NGO participation, who argue that NGOs themselves lack democratic legitimacy and that enhancing NGO participation would lead merely to special interest capture, as a small group of well-funded NGOs, lacking proper representativeness or accountability, pursued their own narrowly formulated agendas at the expanse of wider participation. This argument is supplemented by the observation that many of the NGOs seeking access to policy debates oppose trade liberalisation. Esty admits that such fears 'have some basis in fact; a number of environmental groups and many labour unions are fundamentally

[53] Examples include a Joint WTO/UNCTAD NGO Symposium on Trade-Related Issues Affecting Least-Developed Countries in September 1997 and a WTO Symposium of Non-Governmental Organisations on Trade, Environment and Sustainable Development in March 1998.

[54] J. L. Dunoff 'The Misguided Debate Over NGO Participation at the WTO' *1 JIEL* (1998) 433.

[55] DSU, Art. 16(4)

[56] DSU, Arts 3, 4 and 5.

[57] Esty 'Non-Governmental Organisations', *supra* note 40 at p. 128; see also S. Picciotto 'Networks in International Economic Integration: Fragmented States and the Dilemmas of Neo-Liberalism' *17 Northwestern Journal of International Law and Business* (1996–97) 1014.

opposed to free trade. Almost by definition, the groups that historically have not had entrée to the WTO and now want access are not trade-oriented'.[58] Esty counters this argument with the observation that many special interests already 'inhabit' the WTO, seeking protectionist ends, and that the inclusion of more NGO perspectives could only serve to reduce, not increase, the risk of special interest capture. Moreover, it is precisely because of a perceived need to ensure that an alternative to the orthodoxy of GATT is heard that groups such as environmental NGOs seek access. Petersmann has observed that environmentalists place emphasis on the WTO dispute resolution processes because more environmental disputes between states have been heard there than under any other international dispute settlement mechanism.[59]

The fourth role identified by Esty is in improving the effectiveness of WTO policy-making. This involves a recognition of the limitations of the organisation itself: 'the WTO has limited resources for oversight and auditing of its own performance or for forcing the compliance of national governments with internationally agreed goals'.[60] NGOs, it is argued, are well placed to contribute to the fulfilment of these functions, being possessed with a local presence and local knowledge on the one hand, and being able to bring that practical experience to bear on WTO policy-making on the other. Here the example of human rights NGOs can be cited as a valuable source of unofficial perspectives on the performance of states in relation to their human rights commitments. Others might, of course, argue that this role can be performed, as it is in many other arenas, without the creation of any formal role for NGOs. The knowledge that they generate and the expertise that they bring to bear could be left simply as part of the information background against which the policy-makers must operate, without privileging the position of NGOs as generators of that information and expert opinion. In this way NGOs would operate alongside business interests as lobbyists seeking to influence policy-makers. But for Esty that would overlook the role that NGOs could play in offering 'intellectual competition' to governments as policy-makers.[61] Moreover, leaving NGOs to channel their lobbying efforts towards national governments as policy-makers would overlook the essentially transnational nature of some NGOs.[62]

If the argument is accepted that NGOs can fulfil a useful and desirable role in international economic law- and policy-making, then the question remains as to what structures and mechanisms should be developed to

[58] Esty 'Non-Governmental Organisations', *supra* note 40 at p. 139.

[59] E. U. Petersmann *International and European Trade and Environmental Law After the Uruguay Round* 1995 at p. 22.

[60] Esty 'Non-Governmental Organisations', *supra* note 40 at p. 128.

[61] *Ibid.*, pp. 135–6.

[62] *Ibid.*, pp. 140–1.

enable this to occur. This requires a careful analysis of the role(s) which civil society can perform in a wide range of different contexts within the scope of the WTOs activities, a task which has not yet been undertaken, as noted by Scholte *et al*:

> Although . . . the WTO leadership has become convinced in general terms of the importance of civil society in emergent global governance, the organisation has for the most part lacked clearly formulated objectives and carefully constructed channels of communication for its interchanges with civic groups. On the whole the WTOs engagement of civil society has occurred through improvisation.[63]

The issue of NGO involvement in WTO decision-making played a commanding role in the 'battle for Seattle'. In the light of heightened political sensibilities after that meeting, it seems inevitable that the role of NGOs will now receive thorough consideration, and that change will be forthcoming.

8.4 **Individuals in international trade law**

The WTO is a treaty arrangement between states and its dispute settlement provisions similarly provided for a State–State process in which one Member can bring a complaint or action against another, ultimately before an adjudicative panel, claiming restitution or an acceptable alternative remedy in relation to a breach of the said treaty obligations. The dispute settlement arrangements conform to an established pattern in public international law in that they make provision for the parties to attempt to reach a settlement by non-adjudicative means (and facilitate this) and to this end preserve the confidentiality of the negotiating positions of the parties and of any settlement reached prior to a panel reaching its conclusions. In conformity also to the traditional public international law model, the parties whose interests may have been injured by the alleged breach (in this case business parties) currently have no formal part to play in the dispute resolution process, though in certain areas such as subsidies and dumping they may be involved in the investigative phase.[64] As was noted in Chapter 6, one of the most significant structural developments which has occurred in the context of both the EU and NAFTA has been the creation or evolution of a more direct role for the 'injured party' in relation to breaches of obligation in the trade sphere. This development was most profound in the EU, where the enlistment of national courts in the direct enforcement of EU obligations gave individuals and traders an unprecedented capacity to challenge restrictions on trade in goods or services, in exercise of the right of establishment

[63] Scholte *et al.* 'The WTO', *supra* note 42 at p. 119.

[64] For further discussion see Marceau and Pederson 'Is the WTO Open?', *supra* note 50 at pp. 37–42.

or in relation to alleged breaches of many other provisions of the EC Treaty. In NAFTA, the creation of an Investor–State dispute resolution mechanism involving 'compulsory arbitration' was noted. These examples are pointed to in support of the view that the WTO should develop a mechanism whereby individual traders or investors alleging breaches of WTO rules should have some way in which to raise their claim before an international panel. Similarly, the Draft MAI took the establishment of dispute settlement mechanisms as one of its basic objectives and proposed a mechanism, modelled on NAFTA, whereby investors would be able to take action directly against states whom they alleged, had breached MAI obligations or any other specific obligation undertaken in respect of that investment.[65]

Advocates of such a development have presented the argument as a case for 'constitutionalisation' of international economic law, following from a modern 'citizen-oriented' view of international law: '[i]f the democratic function of international guarantees of freedoms (e.g. for the international movement of goods, services and related payments) is to protect and extend the "private sovereignty" of citizens, rather than the regulatory powers of their governments, precise and unconditional international rules should be "directly applicable" by the citizens concerned and should be protected by national and international courts'.[66]

From this 'citizen-oriented' or human rights-based view of international law, it then appears to follow that citizens (in this case multinationals) should enjoy directly effective rights under international economic law disciplines, in the same way that under some human rights systems, individuals have direct access to international tribunals to pursue their claims against states. It is more than a slight of pen to link international economic law to human rights in this way; advocates of this 'citizen-oriented' view argue that 'markets and liberal national and international economic law are of constitutional significance for democracies and individual citizens'.[67]

> As a decentralized spontaneous information mechanism (e.g. on the availability and valuation of goods, services and employment opportunities) and 'sanctioning mechanism' (e.g. if producers do not meet their responsibility to adjust to competition and to changing preferences), markets enable a continuous 'dialogue about individual preferences and values' and are indispensable complements of individual freedom (e.g. to buy, sell and work), private property

[65] See Section 7.5, *supra*.

[66] E. U. Petersmann 'From the Hobbesian International Law of Coexistence to Modern Integration Law: The WTO Dispute Settlement System' Editorial in *1 JIEL* (1998) 175 at p. 178; see also E. U. Petersmann 'National Constitutions and International Economic Law' in M. Hilf and E. U. Petersmann (eds) *National Constitutions and International Economic Law* 1993 at p. 3; F. L. Morrison and R. E. Hudec 'Judicial Protection of Individual Rights Under the Foreign Trade Laws of the United States' in Hilf and Petersmann (eds), *ibid.*, at p. 91.

[67] Petersmann, 'From the Hobbesian International Law', *ibid.*, at p. 181.

> rights . . . and a civil society (e.g. based on freedom of opinion leading to 'opinion markets', freedom of association and political elections leading to 'political markets').[68]

Petersmann makes a similar case in respect of the EU: 'The experience of European integration confirms the economic theory of property rights according to which the proper functioning not only of economic markets but also of "political markets" depends on the appropriate assignment of individual freedoms and property rights. For a number of reasons, objective legal guarantees of economic liberty can become more effective if they are recognised to constitute individual rights'.[69] The reasons include the increased legal security and economic value of transactions which individual freedom of trade can promote, the potential of such rights to address market failures and government failures and, more generally, the increased scope for judicial review of government action which such rights facilitate.[70] Above all, where freedom of foreign trade is cast as an individual right, traditional judicial deference in respect of the 'public interest' element of foreign relations can be dispelled, and that public interest element recast in terms of 'the individual rights and interests of the citizens'.[71]

This, then, is the case for a new 'constitutional architecture' in international economic law guaranteeing access to tribunals for traders and investors whose 'rights' have been infringed by protectionist, mercantilist states. As was noted in the preceding chapter in relation to the MAI, this appears to place trade or economic 'rights' on a par, morally, with civil and political rights as traditionally conceived and indeed with the rights of groups and communities as expressed through the political process. Moreover, such proposals do not necessarily countenance the extension of parallel rights to groups which cannot find expression through such processes, as seen above in relation to the role of NGOs. The dissatisfaction engendered by cases such as *Ethyl* and *Metalclad*[72] is a reminder of the difficulties in ensuring that such processes really do meet the needs of modern political communities. But while many international organisations have institutionalised means for engaging in an exchange of views with representatives of the NGO community, few have given NGOs any decision-making role.[73] It is entering

[68] *Ibid.*

[69] Petersmann, *National Constitutions, supra* note 66 at p. 26.

[70] *Ibid.*, at pp. 26–7.

[71] *Ibid.*, at p. 28.

[72] See further Section 6.3, *supra.*

[73] Dunoff notes the example *par excellence* of the tripartite International Labor Organisation: though Dunoff rightly views it as atypical from an international legal perspective it should be noted that the formal involvement of the 'social partners' (employer and employee representatives) in law- and policy-making is firmly embedded in the structures of the EU in the field of social policy: Dunoff 'The Misguided Debate', *supra* note 54 at p. 455.

the realms of speculation to ask whether the existing state-centred approach to international law-making can be maintained in the twenty-first century.

8.5 The issue of forum

It is clear that it is neither possible nor desirable to attempt in some way to address issues concerning the treatment and taxation of foreign investment without reference to international trade law in general. Moreover, it seems clear in the wake of the MAI negotiations and the Ministerial Conference in Seattle that the linkage between these issues and social and environmental concerns cannot be ignored or sidelined. States will of course continue to devise policies unilaterally or in the context of free trade areas which impinge on foreign investment directly or indirectly, for instance through the use of conditionality or sanctions in relation to social issues, human rights or environmental concerns,[74] and emergent foreign investment disciplines should recognise the legitimacy of such actions, albeit while seeking to ensure that they are not used as disguised protectionism. The GATT environment cases discussed above[75] demonstrate, however, that there are significant problems to be overcome if a satisfactory legal solution is to be found. Some of the problems illustrated there are directly related to institutional and cultural characteristics of the WTO and of WTO disciplines.

Yet the MAI negotiations raise in a direct and unavoidable manner the question of which of the existing international fora is the most suitable for future negotiations. As Ganesan has pointed out 'the forum, scope and content of an MAI are interrelated, and the implications of an MAI will depend heavily on the forum chosen for it'.[76]

8.6 A forum for a future multilateral agreement on investment

The OECD has long history of active involvement in the areas of foreign investment regulation and taxation of transnational business, and has a number of characteristics in its favour – its links with business representatives, the respect which it commands, and its ability to influence the behaviour of Member and non-Member states alike through voluntarism based on principles of mutual respect and reciprocity. The OECD has also developed a significant level of technical and specialist knowledge and expertise,

[74] See references at notes 1, 35–7, *supra.*

[75] *Supra*, at Section 8.1

[76] A. V. Ganesan 'Strategic Options Available to Developing Countries With Regard to a Multilateral Agreement on Investment' UNCTAD Discussion Paper No. 134/1998.

which has enabled it to serve as a relatively depoliticised forum for discussion and development of disciplines in areas such as taxation, viewed as having a high degree of technical content, and being perceived as partly amenable to technical solutions.

However, while the OECD's 'depoliticised' *modus operandi* may be a key to its success in the area of taxation,[77] it is also precisely why it is not a suitable forum for the negotiation of a new global regime for the treatment and/or regulation of foreign investment; the decision to locate the MAI negotiations here was misguided in a number of respects. First, the limited membership of the OECD means that its authoritativeness in such a role is severely questionable, particularly in respect of development concerns.[78] Second, though it is noted for its close relationship with business interests, it had little or no track record in engaging with civil society.[79] Finally, the fact that the OECD was not 'in the public eye' as a forum where contentious political issues such as this would be addressed meant that resort to the OECD in relation to the MAI was perceived as an attempt to shield the negotiations from public scrutiny and to present the wider international community with a *fait accompli.*[80]

Alongside the OECD's record should be placed the past failures of less authoritative fora such as UNCTAD and the UN General Assembly to secure widespread support for proposals relating to the protection and regulation of foreign investment. Though UNCTAD continues to play a valuable role in voicing the concerns of less-developed states and in conducting studies highlighting the impact of foreign investment in developing countries and the issues of concern,[81] it would be an unlikely venue for a MAI, lacking both the political weight and the institutional structure which such an agreement would seem to require.

Therefore, unsurprisingly perhaps, there would appear to be increasing support for the WTO as a forum for such a development. A number of reasons support this conclusion. First, as seen in the previous chapter, during the 1990s there has been a significant alignment in thinking about the substance of trade obligations and the foreign investment agenda; indeed GATS has already given effect at the global level to the liberalisation agenda which was driving the MAI negotiations, albeit in a rather tentative fashion

[77] Even here its success has been limited: see further Section 5.2.1, *supra.*

[78] Section 7.7, *supra.*

[79] See for example M. Sforza-Roderick, S. Nova and M. Weisbro 'Writing the Constitution of a Single Global Economy' Preamble Collaborative, 1998, available at: http://www.islandnet.com/~ncfs/maisite/analysis.htm.

[80] *Ibid.*

[81] See, for instance, UNCTAD *World Investment Report 1999, Foreign Direct Investment and the Challenge of Development* 1999 and the current work of UNCTAD's Division on Investment, Technology and Enterprise Development, reported at http://www.unctad.org/.

at present. Thus the WTO as an institution already has a high level of familiarity with and expertise in MAI-type disciplines and might seem from that perspective to be the natural 'home' for a putative foreign investment agreement. Second, the WTO has the capacity to initiate and organise future rounds of negotiations in relation to liberalisation of foreign investment regulation, as has already been seen in relation, for instance, to telecommunications under GATS. These 'rounds' might be sector-specific, as in that case, or 'across the board';[82] either way, it is clear that an MAI-type approach to liberalisation would anticipate and depend upon such an approach and the WTO would seem well placed to host and facilitate such negotiations. Following recent trends (the Uruguay and subsequent negotiations), the WTO can also exploit on a scale previously unknown the link between different trade and investment sectors.

The WTO also has near-universal Membership and the expected accession of China will further enhance its reputation in this regard. Thus in terms of its Membership it has as good a chance as any other international institution of addressing the concerns of all the major groups of states and in this respect has more credibility than the OECD, for example. However, it would be naive in the extreme not to contemplate also that its very dominance of the trade field also serves to undermine the strength of small countries in WTO-based negotiations. In particular, the link referred to above is likely to make it extremely difficult for any small state to resist future legal disciplines negotiated under the auspices of the WTO.[83] The history of the Uruguay Round negotiations demonstrates that although developing countries as a group were able to extract some concessions in the new disciplines, their influence overall was low and the shape of the final package made opting-out virtually impossible.

The WTO also offers authority to future negotiations on investment regulation, including in particular the growing authority of its dispute resolution processes. Here, however, the difference in approach to dispute resolution between existing WTO disciplines and the Draft MAI should be noted – the Draft MAI, modelled on NAFTA, provided for Investor–State arbitration as well as State–State arbitration, whereas the WTO offers a State–State adjudicative mechanism. Though it is not impossible that two separate and different solutions could co-exist, such a development would seem unlikely and undesirable. It would seem unlikely that WTO Members would wish to detract from the growing reputation and authoritativeness of its DSB which, despite a strong start, is still relatively young. It would

[82] Here State A might offer concessions in sector X in exchange for concessions from B in sector Y and from C in sector Z.

[83] See, for example, M. Rom 'Some Early Reflections on the Uruguay Round Agreement as Seen From the Viewpoint of a Developing Country' *28(6) JWT* (1994) 5.

seem undesirable because it would lead to unevenness of protection (e.g. between foreign investors falling under the scope of GATS and those covered by a future investment regulation agreement[84]) and would establish different approaches between, for instance, traders of goods and foreign investors, which might be difficult to justify. Nevertheless some major developed countries may be reluctant to abandon the Investor–State approach of the Draft MAI in future negotiations and the question of the role of individuals (i.e. traders and investors) in international trading regimes, discussed above, may be thrown into sharp focus in any future negotiations on foreign investment regulation.

There are, however, doubts concerning the WTO's suitability as a forum for future negotiations on foreign investment regulation. These concern the WTO's ability to address social and environmental concerns, its openness and transparency, its ability and willingness to engage with civil society and its ability to offer protection to developing and least developed states; in short, the issues which derailed the Ministerial Conference in Seattle.

Doubts must also be raised as to whether, at the normative level, the WTO is able and willing to ensure that proper weight is given to social and environmental concerns in any future discipline on foreign investment regulation. Experience in the trade field suggests that the international community has a great deal to learn in this regard, and that the normative framework for international trade established in GATT and GATS requires review. Following the 'Battle of Seattle', these are issues of general concern for the WTO; there can be no doubt that any attempt to open negotiations on an MAI within the WTO would founder unless these issues can be satisfactorily resolved.

The ability of developing countries to protect their interests in a WTO-centred negotiation on foreign investment regulation must also be considered. The issue of linkage has already been noted above. Alongside the formal linkage between the separate WTO disciplines established in the Marrakesh Agreement,[85] which seems likely to be replicated in future rounds, there should be no doubt that developing countries would come under pressure from other directions to accede to any future MAI. The possibility of cross-retaliation under the DSU is another aspect of this formal legal linkage which may be of particular concern to developing countries. If an agreement on foreign investment were added to the array of WTO commitments, developing countries could find that a dispute over access or treatment of foreign investment led ultimately to cross-retaliation in the

[84] This would depend on the specific commitments made by a particular state under each agreement at a particular point in time.

[85] Agreement establishing the World Trade Organisation, 1994 in GATT *The Results of the Uruguay Round of Multilateral Trade Negotiations: The Legal Texts* 1994, p. 5.

area of trade in goods, for instance.[86] On the other hand, the WTO offers some advantages from the developing country perspective. One lies in the steady judicialisation of dispute settlement under the DSU, which in promoting the rule of law also serves to protect the economically weaker parties to disputes.[87] Another concerns the substance of any future foreign investment agreement; besides ensuring that all WTO Member developing countries are participants in the negotiations from the beginning, locating negotiations within the WTO might help to ensure that WTO precedents useful to developing countries are incorporated into a future agreement *ab initio*. For instance, Ganesan notes the important difference in approach between the Draft MAI and GATS; the Draft MAI, as noted in Chapter 7, pursues a 'top–down' approach to market access whereby states would undertake to open their economies to foreign investors in all areas other than those excluded, whereas GATS pursues a bottom–up approach, whereby market access is guaranteed only to those areas specified in each participating country's own schedule. The top–down approach, as well as requiring a sophisticated, well-informed and politically astute approach to negotiations on the part of each participant to ensure that their particular national interests are well protected from the outset,[88] is also likely to disadvantage states who wish to accede to the agreement after its conclusion, since they are inevitably in a weak bargaining position. Other useful GATT/WTO precedents might include the differential time-limits for implementation of WTO disciplines, as seen, for example, in the Agreement on TRIMs,[89] and the TPRM.[90]

[86] Cross-retaliation is initially discouraged under the DSU but can be authorised in certain circumstances (Art. 22, DSU). Full implementation to bring a measure into conformity with the covered agreements is preferred (Art. 22(1)) and, failing this, mutually acceptable compensation (Art. 22(2)). The suspension of concessions, as a final resort, should, where possible, be in the same sector(s) as that in which the Appellate Body found a violation or nullification or impairment (Art. 22(3)(a)), or, where that is not practicable or effective, in other sectors under the same agreement (Art. 22(3)(b)). Only where that is not practicable or effective and the circumstances are 'serious enough' should authorisation be granted by the DSB for the suspension of concessions or other obligations under other covered agreements (Art. 22(3)(c)).

[87] For a discussion see J. Whalley 'Developing Countries and System Strengthening in the Uruguay Round' in W. Martin and L. A. Winters (eds) *The Uruguay Round and the Developing Economies* 1995.

[88] The resources available to negotiating teams of developed and developing states to identify areas of concern and formulate and negotiate appropriate country-specific exceptions can hardly be compared. This resource issue has arisen in relation to dispute settlement under the DSU: see further, for example K. O. Kufuor 'From the GATT to the WTO – the Developing Countries and the Reform of the Procedures for the Settlement of International Disputes' *31*(5) *JWT* (1997) 117.

[89] Section 7.3.1, *supra.*

[90] Section 7.3.3, *supra.*

8.7 Prospects for a future multilateral agreement on investment

The question of a foreign investment agreement has been considered in the wake of the MAI negotiation by UNCTAD, where development issues have been at the forefront of discussion.[91] During expert meetings convened under the auspices of the Commission on Investment, Technology and Related Financial Issues,[92] the UNCTAD Secretariat prepared a *Catalogue of Criteria for Determining the Development-friendliness of International Investment Agreements.*[93] This document, though entirely informal in standing, and not representing any consensus among the Expert Group or expressing any established preference or hierarchy of criteria, does indicate that the gulf between developed and developing states is still very wide. Though accepting that an investment-friendly environment is also a development-friendly environment, the experts suggested that an investment agreement needed to be seen in context with the wider range of policies pursued by countries to promote growth and development and should pursue and strike a balance between the twin objectives of enhancing the ability of developing countries to pursue growth and development (by retaining the 'flexibility and opportunity to pursue their development objectives in the context of their own national situations') and creating a stable, predictable and transparent framework for foreign investment. In addition, balancing the interests of all parties to such an agreement was seen as important where the agreement involved parties at different levels of development.

More specifically investment arrangements could be considered investment-friendly if:

- they contain substantive provisions addressing both the promotion of investment and the promotion of growth and development;
- they reserve the right of host countries to regulate admission of foreign investment;
- they ensure compliance by investors with the laws and regulations of host countries;
- they allow for certain exceptions to national treatment on development grounds;
- they encourage the integration of foreign investment into the domestic economy and contribute to local capacity-building;
- they grant fair and equitable treatment for foreign investors;

[91] See *Proceedings of the United Nations Conference on Trade and Development*, Ninth Session, Report and Annexes.

[92] *Report of the Expert Meeting on Existing Agreements on Investment and Their Development Dimensions* (Geneva, 28–30 May 1997) TD/B/COM.2/5; *Report of the Expert Meeting on Existing Regional and Multilateral Agreements on Investment and Their Development Dimensions* (Geneva, 1–3 April 1998) TD/B/COM.2/11.

[93] TD/B/Com.2/Criteria/1(97).

- they minimize the asymmetry between the treatment of the movement of capital and the movement of certain category of natural persons;
- they allow for certain performance requirements which can promote development without prejudicing the investment;
- they allow for training of local personnel, equity participation of nationals in investments, joint ventures, technology transfer and technology upgrading, and progressive indigenization;
- they establish disciplines to prevent or control major forms of anti-competitive practices;
- they are in harmony with existing WTO agreements;
- they help prevent corruption in international investment transactions;
- they contain a transfer-of-payments clause that takes into account balance-of payments difficulties;
- they protect against non-discriminatory expropriation;
- they establish effective dispute-settlement procedures;
- they allow for impartial international arbitration;
- they provide for the observance of contractual obligations;
- they address environmental, consumer and labour concerns in accordance with the applicable norms, and the social responsibility of investors;
- they provide for financial and technical assistance to developing countries to enable them to make the best use of the agreements' dispute-settlement procedures;
- they allow, where appropriate, exceptions, transitional periods, safeguards and derogations, either in relation to specific issues or as overall provisions;
- they encourage home countries to promote outward FDI to developing countries; and
- they promote political and economic stability.[94]

This 'catalogue' contains many references to issues which were not explicitly addressed in the course of the MAI negotiations. In particularly the UNCTAD document stresses the principle of state sovereignty, the right of a state to regulate the admission and operations of foreign investment, and the need to regulate the activities of foreign investors. More recently, the concept of 'flexibility' in international investment agreements has been stressed.[95] While developing countries may be prepared, and may be preparing, to engage in constructive discussion with developed states over the objectives and content of an MAI, there is little indication that growing liberalisation on the ground is matched by a growing consensus over the future role of international law. When the concerns of environmental and social campaigners are added to the equation, progress may seem unlikely.

[94] *Informal Catalogue of Criteria for Determining the Development-friendliness of International Investment Agreements*, *supra* note 92, pp. 2–3.

[95] See, for instance, the statement of K. P. Sauvant of UNCTAD to the meeting of the WTO Working Group on the Relationship Between Trade and Investment, 3–4 June, 1999.

There were strong echoes of the protests against the MAI at the Third WTO Ministerial Conference in Seattle, among both the participants and the non-participating groups who lobbied and protested outside the talks. Agreeing a mandate on foreign investment was one of the contested issues, and the same concerns about participation and transparency as had been heard in relation to the MAI were much in evidence.[96]

There does, however, seem to be a growing acceptance that the WTO is the natural home for such an agreement, though many states, particularly developing states, regard this issue as not yet 'ripe' for further legal commitments. The prospect for a future MAI appears to be intrinsically linked to the demands for reform of the WTO organisation and to the ability of the international community to address the concerns raised at Seattle and move forward.

[96] See, for example, the African Trade Ministers' Statement, the Caribbean Community Communique and the Latin American and Caribbean countries' joint communique to the meeting, reproduced at http://www.twnside.org.sg/title/deb5-cn.htm.

Bibliography

Abbott, F. M. 'The North American Free Trade Agreement and Its Implications for the European Union' *4 Transnat'l L. & Contemp. Probs.* (1994) 119

Abbott, R. 'GATT and the Trade Policy Review Mechanism: Further Reflections on Earlier Reflections' *27(3) JWT* (1993) 116

Addo, M. K. 'The Role of International Financial Institutions in Privatisation and the Need for Constitutional Reform' in McEldowney, J. (ed.) *National and International Perspectives on Law and Privatisation* (London, BIICL, 1999) at p. 145

Addo, M. K. 'A Critical Analysis of the Perennial International Economic Law Problems of the EEC–ACP Relationship' *33 GYIL* (1990) 37

Akehurst, M. 'Jurisdiction in International Law' *46 BYIL* (1972–73) 145

Akinsanya, A. A. *The Expropriation of Multinational Property in the Third World* (New York, Praeger, 1980)

Albrecht, A. R. 'The Taxation of Aliens in International Law' *29 BYIL* (1952) 145

Allen, L. *OPEC Oil* (Cambridge, MA, Oelgeschlager, Gunn & Hain, 1979)

American Law Institute *Restatement of the Foreign Relations Law of the United States* (St. Paul, American Law Institute Publishers, 3rd edn, 1987)

Anon, 'From Concession to Participation: Restructuring the Middle East Oil Industry' *48 NYUL Rev.* (1973) 774

Appleton, A. E. '*Shrimp/Turtle*: Untangling the Nets' *2(3) JIEL* (1999) 477

Arora, A. and Favre-Bulle, X. 'The Single European Market and the Banking Sector' in Howells, G. G. (ed.) *European Business Law* (Aldershot, Dartmouth, 1996) at p. 197

Asante, S. K. B. Remarks in Panel Discussion 'Should Investment in the Third World be Internationally Protected? What Role for the United Nations?' *ASIL Proceedings* (1985) 378

Asante, S. K. B. 'International Law and Foreign Investment: A Reappraisal' *37 ICLQ* (1988) 588

Asante, S. K. B. 'The Concept of the Good Corporate Citizen in International Business' *4 ICSID-Foreign Investment Law Journal* (1989) 1

Baade, H. W. 'Permanent Sovereignty Over Natural Wealth and Resources' in Miller, R. S. and Stanger, R. J. (eds) *Essays on Expropriation* (Columbus, Ohio State University, 1967) at p. 3

Baxter, R. R. 'Treaties and Custom' *129 Hague Recueil* (1970–71) 25

Bedjaoui, M. 'Some Unorthodox Reflections on the "Right to Development"' in Snyder, F. and Slinn, P. (eds) *International Law of Development: Comparative Perspectives* (Abingdon, Professional Books, 1987) at p. 87

Beveridge, F. C. 'Privatisation and Deregulation – Changing Agendas in the International Law of Private Investment' in McEldowney, J. (ed.) *National and International Perspectives on Law and Privatisation* (London, BIICL, 1999) at p. 168

Beveridge, F. C. 'Taking Control of Foreign Investment: A Case Study of Nigeria' *40 ICLQ* (1991) 302

Beveridge, F. C. and Riley, C. A. 'The Tax Goals of the EC' in Howells, G. G. (ed.) *European Business Law* (Aldershot, Dartmouth, 1996) at p. 137

Bierstecker, T. J. *Multinationals, the State, and Control of the Nigerian Economy* (Princeton, Princeton University Press, 1987)

Booton, D. L. 'The Introduction of an Agreement on Trade-Related Intellectual Property Rights in the GATT Framework: International Production of Patents and the Implications for Developing Countries' (unpublished LL.M thesis, University of Liverpool, 1994)

Bowett, D. W. 'Economic Coercion and Reprisals by States' *13 VaJIL* (1972) 4

Bowett, D. W. 'Jurisdiction: Changing Patterns of Authority Over Activities and Resources' *53 BYIL* (1982) 1

Bowett, D. W. 'State Contracts With Aliens: Contemporary Developments on Compensation for Termination or Breach' *59 BYIL* (1988) 49

Boyd, F. C. 'Expropriation of Alien Property in International Law: A Study of Recent State Practice Concerning British Nationals' (unpublished) M.Phil. thesis, University of Nottingham, 1988

Bradley, A. W. 'Legal Aspects of the Nationalisations in Tanzania' *3 East African Law Journal* (1967) 149

Brewer, T. L. and Young, S. *The Multilateral Investment System and Multinational Enterprises* (Oxford, Oxford University Press, 1998)

Brewer, T. L. and Young, S. 'European Union Policies and the Problems of Multinational Enterprises' *29(1) JWT* (1995) 33

Brewer, T. L. and Young, S. 'Investment Issues at the WTO: The Architecture of Rules and the Settlement of Disputes' *1 JIEL* (1998) 457

Bronkers, M. C. E. J. 'The Impact of TRIPs: Intellectual Property Protection in Developing Countries' *31 CMLR* (1994) 1245

Bronkers, M. C. E. J. and Larouche, P. 'Telecommunications Services and the World Trade Organization' *31(3) JWT* (1997) 5

Brookens, B. O. 'Diplomatic Protection of Foreign Economic Interests. The Changing Structure of International Law in the New International Economic Order' *20 Journal of Inter-American Studies and World Affairs* (1978) 37

Brownlie, I. *Principles of Public International Law* (Oxford, Oxford University Press, 5th edn, 1998)

Brownlie, I. 'Legal Aspects of Natural Resources in International Law (Some Aspects)' *162 Hague Recueil* (1979-I) 245

Burton, F. N. and Inoue, H. 'Expropriations of Foreign-Owned Firms in Developing Countries: A Cross-National Analysis' *18 JWTL* (1984) 396

Canadian Environmental Law Association 'The Multilateral Agreement on Investment and the Environment: Context and Concerns' prepared for the House of

Commons Sub-Committee on International Trade, Trade Disputes and Investment, 24 November 1997, available at www.web.net/cela/maibrief.htm

Canadian Labour Congress 'The Multilateral Agreement on Investment – A Preliminary, Critical Analysis' undated

Cattan, H. *The Evolution of Oil Concessions* (New York, Oceana Publications for the Parker School of Foreign and Comparative Law, 1967)

Chalmers, D. 'Free Movement of Goods within the European Community: An Unhealthy Addiction to Scotch Whiskey?' *42 ICLQ* (1993) 269

Chalmers, D. 'Repackaging the Internal Market – the Ramifications of the Keck Judgment' *19 EL Rev.* (1994) 385

Charnovitz, S. 'Participation of Non-governmental Organisations in the World Trade Organisation' *17 University of Pennsylvania Journal of International Economic Law* (1996) 331

Charnovitz, S. 'The Moral Exception in Trade Policy' *38 VaJIL* (1998) 689

Clagett, B. M. 'Title III of the Helms–Burton Act is Consistent With International Law' *90 AJIL* (1996) 434

Collins-Williams, T. and Salembier, G. 'International Disciplines on Subsidies. The GATT, the WTO and the Future Agenda' *30(1) JWT* (1996) 5

Compa, L. A. and Diamond, S. F. (eds) *Human Rights, Labor Rights and International Trade* (Philadelphia, University of Pennsylvania Press, 1996)

Cosgrove, C. and Laurent, P. H. 'The Unique Relationship: The European Community and the ACP' in Redmond J. (ed.) *The External Relations of the European Community: The International Response to 1992* (Houndsmill, Macmillan, 1992)

Cowrie, F. 'State Aids in the Eighties' *EL Rev.* (1986) 247

Craig, P. and de Burca, G. *EC Law: Text, Cases and Materials* (Oxford, Oxford University Press, 2nd edn, 1998)

Crawford, J. *The Creation of States in International Law* (Oxford, Oxford University Press, 1979)

Cremona, M. 'Community Relations With the Visegrad Group' *EL Rev.* (1993) 345

Cullen, H. 'The Limits of International Trade Mechanisms in Enforcing Human Rights: The Case of Child Labour' *7 Int'l J. of Children's Rights* (1999) 1

Curtin, D. 'The Constitutional Structure of the Union: A Europe of Bits and Pieces' *30 CMLR* (1993) 17

Daly, M. 'Investment Incentives and the Multilateral Agreement on Investment' *32(2) JWT* (1998) 5

Dearden, R. G. 'Arbitration of Expropriation Disputes Between an Investor and the State Under the North American Free Trade Agreement' *29(1) JWT* (1995) 113

Demaret, P. 'The Treaty Framework' in O'Keeffe, D. and Twomey, P. (eds) *Legal Issues of the Maastricht Treaty* (London, Chancery, 1994) at p. 3

Denza, E. and Brooks, S. 'Investment Protection Treaties: United Kingdom Experience' *36 ICLQ* (1987) 908

Dhanjee, R. and Boisson De Chazournes, R. L. 'Trade-Related Aspects of Intellectual Property Rights (TRIPs): Objectives, Approaches and Basic Principles of the GATT and of Intellectual Property Conventions' *24(5) JWT* (1990) 5

Dias, C. 'Tanzanian Nationalisations: 1967–70' *4 Cornell JIL* (1970) 59

Diller, J. M. and Levy, D. A. 'Child Labour, Trade and Investment: Towards the Harmonization of International Law' *91 AJIL* (1997) 663

Domke, M. 'Indonesian Nationalisation Measures Before Domestic Court' *54 AJIL* (1960) 305

Domke, M. 'Foreign Nationalisations: Some Aspects of Contemporary International Law' *55 AJIL* (1961) 585

Domke, M. and van Liempt, G. 'Minimum International Labour Standards and International Trade: Would a Social Clause Work?' *128 International Labour Review* (1998) 433

Dunoff, J. L. 'The Misguided Debate Over NGO Participation at the WTO' *1 JIEL* (1998) 433

Edward, D. 'Establishment and Services: An Analysis of the Insurance Cases' *12 EL Rev.* (1987) 231

El Kosheri, A. 'The Law Governing a New Generation of Petroleum Contracts' *1 ICSID Rev.* (1986) 259

Esty, D. C. *Greening the GATT: Trade, Environment and the Future* (Madison, WI, Institute for International Economics, 1984)

Esty, D. C. 'Non-Governmental Organisations at the World Trade Organisation: Co-operation, Competition or Exclusion' *1 JIEL* (1998) 123

European Commission, 'Submission by the European Community and Its Member States to the WTO Working Group on the Relationship Between Trade and Investment', European Commission (DG 1) Brussels, 30 May 1997, available at http://europa.eu.int/comm/dg01/invwgti4.htm

European Commission, Directorate General 1, Working Group on the Relationship Between Trade and Investment, 'Identification of Common Features and Differences of Existing International Investment Instruments From the Perspective of the European Community and Its Member States', 27 March 1998, at http://europa.eu.int/comm/dg01/invwgti1.htm

European Commission, 'Contribution of the European Commission on the Revision of the OECD Guidelines for Multinational Enterprises', European Commission (DG 1) Brussels, 3 February 1999, available at http://europa.eu.int/comm/dg01/invoecd1.htm

Evans, G. E. 'Intellectual Property as a Trade Issue. The Making of the Agreement on Trade-Related Aspects of Intellectual Property Rights' *18 World Competition* (1984) 137

Fagre, N. E. and Wells, L. T. Jnr. 'Bargaining Power of Multinational and Host Governments' *13 Journal of International Business Studies* (1982) 9

Farmer, P. and Lyal, R. *EC Tax Law* (Oxford, Oxford University Press, 1994)

Fischer-Zernin, J. 'GATT Versus Tax Treaties? The Basic Conflicts Between International Taxation Methods and the Rules and Concepts of GATT' *21(3) JWTL* (1987) 39

FitzGerald, E. V. K., Cubero-Brealey, R. and Lehmann, A. *The Development Implications of the Multilateral Agreement on Investment* (London, Department for International Development (DfID), UK, 1998)

Flory, M. 'A North–South Legal Dialogue: The International Law of Development' in Snyder, F. and Slinn, P. (eds) *International Law of Development: Comparative Perspectives* (Abingdon, Professional Books, 1987) at p. 11

Forsyth, D. J. C. and Solomon, R. F. 'Restrictions on Foreign Ownership of Manufacturing Industry in a Less Developed Country: The Case of Ghana' *12 Journal of Developing Areas* (1978) 281

Fowler, M. R. and Bunck, J. M. 'The Chunk and Basket Theories of Sovereignty' in Thompson, W. W. (ed.) *Community, Diversity, and a New World Order: Essays in Honor of Inis L. Claude, Jr.* (Lanham MD, University Press of America, 1994) at p. 137

Freestone, D. A. 'The Precautionary Principle, International Law and Global Climate Change' in Churchill, R. R. and Freestone, D. A. (eds) *International Law and Global Climate Change* (London, Graham and Trotman, 1991) at p. 21

Gallins, G. 'Bilateral Investment Protection Treaties' *2 Journal of Energy and Natural Resource Law* (1984) 77

Gal-Or, N. 'Private Party Direct Access: A Comparison of the NAFTA and the EU Disciplines' *XXI(1) Boston Coll. Int. and Comp. Law Rev.* (1998) 1

Ganesan, A. V. 'Strategic Options Available to Developing Countries With Regard to a Multilateral Agreement on Investment' *UNCTAD Discussion Paper No. 1341998*

Garcia-Amador, F. V., Sohn, L. B. and Baxter, R. R. *Recent Codification of the Law of State Responsibility for Injuries to Aliens* (Dobbs Ferry, New York, Oceana Publications, 1974)

Garcia-Amador, F. V. 'The Proposed New International Economic Order: A New Approach to the Law Governing Nationalisation and Compensation' *12 Lawyer of the Americas* (1980) 1

GATT *The Results of the Uruguay Round of Multilateral Trade Negotiations: The Legal Texts* (Geneva, GATT, 1994)

GATT *Analytical Index: Guide to GATT Law and Practice* (Geneva, GATT, 6th edn, 1994)

Gess, K. N. 'Permanent Sovereignty Over Natural Resources' *13 ICLQ* (1964) 398

Gormley, L. 'Reasoning Renounced? The Remarkable Judgment in Keck and Mithouard' *Euro Bus L Rev.* (1994) 63

Gray, C. *Judicial Remedies in International Law* (Oxford, Clarendon, 1987)

Greenaway, D. 'Trade Related Investment Measures and Development Strategies' *45 Kyklos* (1992) 139

Greenwood, C. 'State Contracts in International Law – The Libyan Oil Arbitrations' *53 BYIL* (1982) 27

Guha Roy 'Is the Law of State Responsibility Part of Customary International Law?' *55 AJIL* (1959) 863

Hall, S. 'The ECHR and Public Policy Exceptions to the Free Movement of Workers Under the EEC Treaty' *16 ELRev.* (1991) 466

Hammer, R. M. 'Will the Arm's Length Standard Stand the Test of Time? The Specter of Apportionment' in Alpert, H. H. and van Raad, K. (eds) *Essays on International Taxation* (Deventer, Boston, Kluwer Law and Taxation, 1993) at p. 201

Harden, I. (ed.) *State Aid: Community Law and Policy* (Cologne, Bundesanzeiger, 1993)

Harris, D. J., O'Boyle M. and Warbrick C. *Law of the European Convention on Human Rights* (London, Butterworths, 1995)

Hellerstein, W. 'Are Days of World-Wide Unitary Taxation by States Limited?' *72 Journal of Taxation* (1990) 172

Higgins, R. 'The Taking of Property by the State: Recent Developments in International Law' *176 Recueil des Cours* (1982–3) 259

Hilf, M., Jacobs, F. G. and Petersmann, E. U. (eds) *The European Community and GATT* (Deventer, Kluwer, 1986)

Hilf, M. and Petersmann, E. U. (eds) *National Constitutions and International Economic Law* (Deventer, Kluwer, 1993)

Horn, N. (ed.) *Legal Problems of Codes of Conduct for Multinational Enterprises* (Deventer, Kluwer, 1980)

Hossain, K. (ed.) *Legal Aspects of a New International Economic Order* (London, Pinter, 1980)

Hudec, R. E. *Developing Countries in the GATT Legal System* (Aldershot, Gower, 1987)

ICSID *Bilateral Investment Treaties (1959–76)* (Washington D.C., ICSID, 1997)

IMF *Officially Supported Export Credits – Development and Prospects, World Economic and Financial Surveys* (Washington, IMF, 1995)

Irish, C. 'International Double Taxation Agreements and Income Taxation at Source' *23 ICLQ* (1974) 292

Jackson, J. H. *The World Trading System: Law and Policy of International Economic Relations* (Cambridge, MA, MIT Press, 2nd edn, 1997)

Jackson, J. H., Davey, W. J. and Sykes, A. O., Jr. *Legal Problems of International Economic Relations: Cases, Materials and Text* (St. Paul, West Publishing Co., 3rd edn, 1995)

Jain, S. *Nationalization of Foreign Property: A Study of North–South Dialogue* (New Dehli, Deep and Deep Publications, 1983)

Jennings, R. Y. and Watts, A. D. (eds) *Oppenheim's International Law Vol. 1* (Harlow, Longmans, 9th edn, 1992)

Jiménez de Aréchaga 'General Course in Public International Law' *159 Recueil des Cours (1978–I)* 1

de Jonquieres, G. 'Network Guerillas' *Financial Times* (London, 30 April 1998)

Knaw, E. M. A. '"Trade Related Investment Measures" in the Uruguay Round: Towards a GATT for Investment?' *16 NCJ Int'l L. and Com. Reg.* (1990) 309

Knechtle, A. A. *Basic Problems in International Fiscal Law* (Deventer, Kluwer, English edn, 1979)

Kobrin, S. J. 'Enterprise and Forced Divestment in LDCs' *International Organisation* (1980) 65

Kohona, P. J. B. 'Dispute Resolutions Under the World Trade Organisation: An Overview' *28(2) JWT* (1994) 5

Kufuor, K. O. 'From the GATT to the WTO – the Developing Countries and the Reform of the Procedures for the Settlement of International Disputes' *31(5) JWT* (1997) 117

Kuilwijk, K. J. 'Castro's Cuba and the US Helms–Burton Act' *31(3) JWT* (1997) 49

Langille, B. A. 'Eight Ways to Think About International Labour Standards' *31(4) JWT* (1997) 27

Lasok, D. 'State Aids and Remedies Under the EEC Treaty' *ECLR* (1986) 53

Lillich, R. B. (ed.) *International Law of State Responsibility for Injuries to Aliens* (Charlottesville, University Press of Virginia, 1983)

Lillich, R. B. 'The Rigidity of Barcelona' Editorial Comment *65 AJIL* (1971) 522

Lipson, C. *Standing Guard: Protecting Foreign Capital in the Nineteenth and Twentieth Centuries* (Berkeley, University of California Press, 1985)

Lipstein, K. 'The Place of the Calvo Clause in International Law' *22 BYIL* (1945) 130

Low, P. and Subramanian, A. 'TRIMs in the Uruguay Round: An Unfinished Business?' in Martin, W. and Winters, L. A. (eds) *The Uruguay Round and the*

Developing Economies, World Bank Discussion Papers 307 (Washington, World Bank, 1995) at p. 413

Lowe, A. V. 'Blocking Extraterritorial Jurisdiction: The British Protection of Trading Interests Act, 1980' *75 AJIL* (1981) 257

Lowe, A. V. 'Public International Law and the Conflict of Laws: The European Response to the United States Export Administration Regulations' *33 ICLQ* (1984) 515

Lowe, A. V. 'US Extraterritorial Jurisdiction: The Helms–Burton and D'Amato Acts' *46 ICLQ* (1997) 378

Lowenfeld, A. F. 'Jurisdiction Issues Before National Courts: The *Insurance Antitrust* Case in Meessen, K. M. (ed.) *Extraterritorial Jurisdiction in Theory and Practice* (London, Kluwer Law International, 1996) at p. 1

McCrudden, C. 'International Economic Law and the Pursuit of Human Rights: A Framework for Discussion of the Legality of "Selective Purchasing" Laws Under the WTO Government Procurement Agreement' *2 JIEL* (1998) 3

MacDonald, G. 'Recent Legislation in Nigeria and Ghana Affecting Foreign Private Direct Investment' *6 Int. Lawyer* (1972) 548

MacDougall, D. and Cameron, P. 'Trade in Energy and Natural Resources' *28(3) JWT* (1994) 171

McDaniel, P. R. 'NAFTA and Formulary Apportionment: An Exploration of the Issues' in Alpert, H. H. and van Raad, K. (eds) *Essays on International Taxation* (Deventer, Boston, Kluwer Law and Taxation, 1993) at p. 293

McDougal, M. S., Lasswell, H. D. and Chen, L. *Human Rights and World Public Order* (New Haven, Yale University Press, 1980)

McGee, A. (ed.) *The Single Market in Insurance: Breaking Down the Barriers* (Aldershot, Ashgate, 1998)

McGoldrick, D. 'From the New International Economic Order to the Agenda for Development' in McEldowney, J. F. (ed.) *National and International Perspectives on Law and Privatisation* (London, BIICL, 1999) at p. 190

McKean, W. *Equality and Non-discrimination Under International Law* (Oxford, Clarendon, 1983)

McNiel, D. E. 'The First Case Under the WTO's Sanitary and Phytosanitary Agreement: The European Union's Hormone Ban' *39 Va.JIL* (1998) 89

Mann, F. A. 'The Doctrine of Jurisdiction in International Law' *III Recueil des Cours* (1964–I) i

Mann, F. A. 'Note on British Treaties for the Promotion and Protection of Investments' *52 BYIL* (1981) 241

Marceau, G. C. 'NAFTA and WTO Dispute Settlement Rules' *31(2) JWT* (1997) 25

Marceau, G. C. and Pedersen, P. N. 'Is the WTO Open and Transparent? A Discussion of the Relationship of the WTO With Non-governmental Organisations and Civil Society's Claims for More Transparency and Public Participation' *33(1) JWT* (1999) 5

Maresceau, M. (ed.) *The Political and Legal Framework of Trade Relations Between the European Community and Eastern Europe* (Dordrecht, Boston, Martinus Nijhoff, 1989)

Maresceau, M. and Montaguti, E. 'The Relations Between the European Union and Central and Eastern Europe: A Legal Appraisal' *32 CMLR* (1995) 1327

Martha, R. S. J. *The Jurisdiction to Tax in International Law: Theory and Practice of Legislative Fiscal Jurisdiction* (Dordrecht, Kluwer Academic, 1989)

Mattoo, A. 'National Treatment in the GATS – Corner-stone or Pandora's Box?' *31(1) JWT* (1997) 107

Merkin, R. and Rodger, A. *EC Insurance Law* (London, Longman, 1997)

Metzgar, S. D. 'Nationality of Corporate Investment under Investment Guaranty Schemes – The Relevance of Barcelona Traction' *65 AJIL* (1971) 532

Moran, T. H. and Pearson, C. S. 'Do TRIMs Trip Up Foreign Investment? An International Business Diplomacy Perspective' in Wallace C. D. (ed.) *Foreign Direct Investment in the 1990s: A New Climate in the Third World* (Dordrecht, Martinus Nijhoff, 1990) at p. 28

Morrison, F. L. and Hudec, R. E. 'Judicial Protection of Individual Rights Under the Foreign Trade Laws of the United States' in Hilf, M. and Petersmann, E. U. (eds) *National Constitutions and International Economic Law* (Deventer, Kluwer, 1993) at p. 91

Morrison, J. 'Margin of Appreciation in European Human Rights Law' *6 Human Rights Journal* (1973) 263

Morrissey, O. and Rai, Y. 'The GATT Agreement on Trade Related Investment Measures: Implications for Developing Countries and Their Relationship with Transnational Corporations' *31 Journal of Development Studies* (1995) 702

Mosley, P. and Toye, J. 'The Design of Structural Adjustment Programmes' *6 Development Policy Review* (1988) 395

Muchlinski, P. T. *Multinational Enterprises and the Law* (Oxford, Blackwell, 1995)

Mukherjee, N. 'GATS and the Millennium Round of Multilateral Negotiations – Selected Issues from the Perspective of the Developing Countries' *33(4) JWT* (1999) 87

Murray, R. 'The Internationalization of Capital and the Nation-State' *67 New Left Review* (1971) 84

OECD Development Centre *The Relation of Expropriatory Action By Developing Countries to Foreign Private Investment Flows* (Paris, OECD, 1972)

OECD Committee on Fiscal Affairs, *International Tax Avoidance and Evasion. Four Related Studies* (Paris, OECD, 1987)

OECD *The Export Credit Financing System in OECD Member and Non-Member Countries* (Paris, OECD, 1995)

OECD *Tax Sparing: A Reconsideration* (Paris, OECD, 1998)

OECD *Harmful Tax Competition: An Emerging Global Issue, Synthesis and Summary of Recommendations* http://www.oecd.org/daf/fa/tax_comp/taxcomp.htm

O'Donnell, T. 'The Margin of Appreciation Doctrine: Standards in the Jurisprudence of the ECHR' *4(4) HRQ* (1982) 474

O'Keeffe, D. and Twomey, P. (eds) *Legal Issues of the Maastricht Treaty* (London, Chancery, 1994)

O'Keeffe, D. and Twomey, P. (eds) *Legal Issues of the Amsterdam Treaty* (Oxford, Hart Publishing, 2000)

O'Keeffe, D. 'Practical Difficulties in the Application of Article 48 of the EEC Treaty' *19 CMLR* (1982) 35

Osunbor, O. A. 'Nigeria's Investment Laws and the State's Control of Multinationals' *3 ICSID-FILJ* (1988) 38

Oxfam UK and Ireland Briefing Paper 'The OECD Multilateral Agreement on Investment (MAI)' October 1997

Paasivirta, E. 'Internationalisation and Stabilisation of Contracts *Versus* State Sovereignty' *60 BYIL* (1989) 315

Petersmann, E. U. *International and European Trade and Environmental Law After the Uruguay Round* (London, Kluwer, 1995)

Petersmann, E. U. *The GATT/WTO Dispute Settlement System: International Law, International Organisation and Dispute Settlement* (London, Kluwer, 1997)

Petersmann, E. U. 'National Constitutions and International Economic Law' in Hilf, M. and Petersmann, E. U. (eds) *National Constitutions and International Economic Law* (Deventer, Kluwer, 1993) at p. 3

Petersmann, E. U. 'International Trade Law and International Environmental Law' *27(1) JWT* (1993) 43

Petersmann, E. U. 'From the Hobbesian International Law of Coexistence to Modern Integration Law: The WTO Dispute Settlement System' Editorial in *1 JIEL* (1998) 175

Picciotto, S. *International Business Taxation* (London, Weidenfeld and Nicolson, 1992)

Picciotto, S. 'Jurisdictional Conflicts, International Law and the International State System' (1983) *11 International Journal of the Sociology of Law* 11

Picciotto, S. 'Networks in International Economic Integration: Fragmented States and the Dilemmas of Neo-Liberalism' *17 Northwestern Journal of International Law and Business* (1996–97) 1014

Pogany, I. 'The Regulation of Foreign Investment in Hungary' *4 ICSID-FILJ* (1989) 39

Pogany, I. 'Recent Developments in the Law Relating to Foreign Investment in Hungary' *6 ICSID-FILJ* (1991) 114

Pogany, I. 'Privatisation and Regulatory Change in Hungary' in Moran, M. and Prosser, T. (eds) *Privatisation and Regulatory Change in Europe* (Buckingham, Open University Press, 1994) at p. 111

Quick, R. and Bluthner, A. 'Has the Appellate Body Erred? An Appraisal and Criticism of the Ruling in the WTO *Hormones Case*' *2(4) JIEL* (1999) 641

Qureshi, A. H. *The World Trade Organisation: Implementing International Trade Norms* (Manchester, Manchester University Press, 1996)

Qureshi, A. H. *International Economic Law* (London, Sweet and Maxwell, 1999)

Qureshi, A. H. 'The Freedom of a State to Legislate in Fiscal Matters under General International Law' *Bulletin for International Fiscal Documentation* (1987) 14

Qureshi, A. H. 'Some Lessons from Developing Countries' Trade Policy Reviews in the GATT Framework: An Enforcement Perspective' *18 World Economy* (1995) 489

Qureshi, A. H. 'Trade-Related Aspects of International Taxation. A New WTO Code of Conduct?' *30(2) JWT* (1996) 161

Reinbothe, J. and Howard, A. 'The State of Play in the Negotiations on TRIPs (GATT/Uruguay Round)' *5 EIPR* [1991] 157

Robertson, A. and Demetriou, M. 'But That was Another Country . . .': The Extra-territorial Application of US Antitrust Laws in the US Supreme Court' *43 ICLQ* (1994) 417

Roin, J. A. 'The Grand Illusion: A Neutral Tax System for the Taxation of International Transactions' *75 Virginia Law Review* (1989) 919

Rom, M. 'Some Early Reflections: The Uruguay Round Agreement as Seen From the Viewpoint of a Developing Country' *28(6) JWT* (1994) 5

Rose, V. (ed.) *Bellamy and Child's Common Market Law of Competition* (London, Sweet and Maxwell, 4th edn, 1993)

Rouhani, F. *A History of OPEC* (New York, Praeger, 1971)

Salacuse, J. W. 'BIT by BIT' *Int. Lawyer* (1996) 655

Sanda, A. O. *The Challenge of Nigeria's Indigenisation* (Ibadan, Nigerian Institute of Social and Economic Research, 1982)

Sapir, A. 'The GATS From 1994 to the Year 2000' *33(1) JWT* (1999) 51

Sauvé, P. 'A First Look at Investment in the Final Act of the Uruguay Round' *28(5) JWT* (1994) 5

Sauvé, P. 'Assessing the GATS – Half Full or Half Empty?' *29(4) JWT* (1995) 125

Schina, D. *State Aids Under the EEC Treaty* (Oxford, ESC, 1987)

Schoenbaum, T. J. 'International Trade and the Protection of the Environment: The Continuing Search for Reconciliation' *91 AJIL* (1997) 268

Scholte, J. A., O'Brien, R. and Williams, M. 'The WTO and Civil Society' *33(1) JWT* (1999) 107

Schrijver, N. *Sovereignty Over Natural Resources: Balancing Rights Over Duties* (Cambridge, Cambridge University Press, 1997)

Sen, B. *A Diplomat's Handbook of International Law and Practice* (The Hague, Nijhoff, 1965)

Sforza-Roderick, M., Nova, S. and Weisbro, M. 'Writing the Constitution of a Single Global Economy' Preamble Collaborative, 1998, available at: http://www.islandnet.com/~ncfs/maisite/analysis.htm

Shea, D. *The Calvo Clause: A Problem of Inter-American and International Law and Diplomacy* (Minneapolis, University of Minnesota Press, 1955)

Shenkin, T. S. '"Trade-Related Investment Measures" in Bilateral Investment Treaties and the GATT. Moving Toward a Multilateral Investment Treaty' *55 U. Pitt. L. Rev.* (1994) 541

Shihata, I. 'Destination Embargo of Arab Oil: Its Legality Under International Law' *68 AJIL* (1974) 591

Shuman, M. H. 'GATTzilla v. Communities' *27 Cornell ILJ* (1994) 527

Shwadran, B. *Middle East Oil Crises Since 1973* (Boulder, Colorado, Westview Press, 1986)

Simmonds, K. R. 'The Fourth Lome Convention' *28 CMLR* (1991) 521

Smis, S. and van der Borght, K. 'The EU–US Compromise on the Helms Burton and D'Amato Acts' *93 AJIL* (1999) 227

Snyder, F. and Slinn, P. (eds) *International Law of Development: Comparative Perspectives* (Abingdon, Professional Books, 1987)

Snyder, J. L. and Agostini, S. 'New US Legislation to Deter Investment in Cuba. A First Glance' *30(3) JWT* (1996) 37

Sohn, L. B. and Baxter, R. R. 'The Harvard Draft Convention On the International Responsibility Of States For Injuries To Aliens' *55 AJIL* (1961) 545

Sornarajah, M. *The Pursuit of Nationalised Property* (Dordrecht, Nijhoff, 1986)

Sornarajah, M. *The International Law on Foreign Investment* (Cambridge, Cambridge University Press, 1994)

Staker, C. 'Public International Law and the *Lex Situs* Rule in Property Conflicts and Foreign Expropriations' *58 BYIL* (1987) 151

Steger, P. and Hainsworth, S. M. 'World Trade Organisation Dispute Settlement: The First Three Years' *1 JIEL* (1998) 199

Steinberg, R. H. 'Trade-Environment Negotiations in the EU, NAFTA, and WTO: Regional Trajectories of Rule Development' *91 AJIL* (1997) 231

Steiner, J. 'Drawing the Line: Uses and Abuses of Article 30 EEC' *29 CMLR* (1992) 749

Stern, B. 'Can the US Set Rules for the World?' *31(4) JWT* (1997) 5

Stewart, T. P. (ed.) *The GATT Uruguay Round: A Negotiating History (1986–1992) Volume II: Commentary* (Deventer, Boston, Kluwer Law and Taxation Publishers, 1993)

Stilwell, R. 'Encouraging Investment in LDC's: The US Investment Guaranty Programme' *8 Brooklyn Journal of International Law* (1982) 365

Stocking, G. W. *Middle East Oil: A Study in Political and Economic Controversy* (London, Lane, 1970, 1971 edn)

Strange, S. '*Cave! Hic Dragones*: A Critique of Regime Analysis' in Diehl, P. F. (ed.) *The Politics of Global Governance: International Organisations in an Interdependent World* (Boulder, Colorado, Lynne Rienner Publishers, 1997) at p. 41

Surrey, S. S. 'The UN Group of Experts and the Guidelines for Tax Treaties Between Developed and Developing Countries' *19 Harvard ILJ* (1978) 1

Swaak-Goldman, O. Q. 'Who Defines Members' Security Interests in the WTO?' *9 Leiden JIL* (1996) 361

Terra, B. J. M. and Wattel, P. J. *European Tax Law* (Deventer, Kluwer Law and Taxation, 1993)

Todaro, M. P. *Economic Development in the Third World* (Harlow, Addison Wesley, 7th edn, 2000)

Toope, S. J. *International Mixed Arbitration* (Cambridge, Grotius, 1990)

Truitt, J. F. *Expropriation of Private Foreign Investment* (Bloomington, Indiana University, Graduate School of Business, 1974)

Tschanz, P. 'The Contributions of the Aminoil Award to the Law of State Contracts' *18 International Lawyer* (1984) 245

UN Centre on Transnational Corporations *Bilateral Investment Treaties in the Mid-1990s* 1998 UNCTAD/ITE/IIT/7 1998

UN Centre on Transnational Corporations *International Income Taxation and Developing Countries* 1988 UN Doc. ST/CTC/56 1988

UNCTAD *The Impact of Trade Related Investment Measures on Trade and Development* UN Doc. ST/CTC/120 1991

UNCTAD *Catalogue of Criteria for Determining the Development-Friendliness of International Investment Agreements*, TD/B/COM.2/Criteria/1 (97)

UNCTAD *Report of the Expert Meeting on Existing Agreements on Investment and Their Development Dimensions* (Geneva, 28–30 May 1997) TD/B/COM.2/5

UNCTAD *Report of the Expert Meeting on Existing Regional and Multilateral Agreements on Investment and Their Development Dimensions* (Geneva, 1–3 April 1998) TD/B/COM.2/11

UNCTAD *World Investment Report 1999: Foreign Direct Investment and the Challenge of Development* (United Nations, Geneva, 1999)

UN Commission on Transnational Corporations *Multinational Corporations in World Development* 1973 UN Doc. E/C. 10/38, 1973

UN Commission on Transnational Corporations *Transnational Corporations in World Development: A Re-examination* 1978, UN Doc. E/C. 10/38, 1978

UN Commission on Transnational Corporations *Transnational Corporations in World Development. Third Survey* 1983, UN Doc. ST/CTC/46, 1983
UN Commission on Transnational Corporations *International Income Tax and Developing Countries* 1988, UN Doc. ST/CTC/56 (New York, United Nations, 1988)
UN Secretary-General *Development and International Economic Co-operation – An Agenda for Development* Report of the Secretary-General, *UN Doc. A/48/935*, 1994
US Department of State, Bureau of Intelligence and Research *Nationalisation, Expropriation and Other Takings of Foreign Property Since 1960* November 1971
US Department of State, Bureau of Intelligence and Research *Disputes Involving US Foreign Direct Investment: July 1, 1971 through July 31, 1973* February 1974
US Department of State, Bureau of Intelligence and Research *Disputes Involving US Foreign Direct Investment: Aug 1, 1973–Jan 31, 1975* March 1975
US Department of State, Bureau of Intelligence and Research *Disputes Involving US Foreign Direct Investment: Feb 1, 1975–Feb 28, 1977* September 1977
US Department of State, Bureau of Intelligence and Research *Disputes Involving US Foreign Direct Investment: Mar 1, 1977–Feb 29, 1980* August 1980
US Department of State, Bureau of Intelligence and Research *Disputes Involving US Foreign Direct Investment: Mar 1, 1980–Sept 30, 1982* February 1983
Usher, J. A. *EC Institutions and Legislation* Longman European Law Series (Harlow, Addison Wesley Longman, 1998)
Vagts, D. F. 'Foreign Investment Risk Reconsidered: The View From the 1980s' *2 ICSID Rev.–FILJ* (1987) 1
van Liempt, G. 'Minimum International Labour Standards and International Trade: Would a Social Clause Work?' 128 *International Labour Review* (1998) 433
Vandevelde, K. J. 'Reassessing the Hickenlooper Amendment' *29 VaJIL* (1988) 115
Vandevelde, K. J. 'The BIT Programme – A Fifteen Year Appraisal' *ASIL Proceedings* (1992) 532
Vandevelde, K. J. 'The Political Economy of A Bilateral Investment Treaty' *92 AJIL* (1998) 627
Vanistandael, F. 'The Limits to the New Community Tax Order' *31 CMLR* (1994) 293
Vanistandael, F. 'The Consequences of Schumacker and Wielockx: Two Steps Forward in the Tax Progression of Echternach' *33 CMLR* (1996) 255
Vann, R. J. 'A Model Tax Treaty for the Asian-Pacific Region?' *Bulletin for International Fiscal Documentation* (1991) 99–111; 151–63
Vattel, E. *Le Droit des gens* Book 11 (Washington, Carnegie Institute of Washington, 1916)
Verway, W. D. and Schrijver, N. J. 'The Taking of Foreign Property Under International Law: A New Legal Perspective?' *15 NYIL* (1984) 3
Villiger, M. E. *Customary International Law and Treaties* (Hague, Kluwer Law International, 2nd edn, 1997)
Vogel, K. 'Worldwide v's Source Taxation of Income – A Review and Reevaluation of Arguments' in McLure, C. E., Sinn, H. W., Musgrave, P. B. *et al.* '*Influence of Tax Differentials on International Competitiveness*' (Deventer, Kluwer, 1990) at p. 115
Voss, J. 'The Protection and Promotion of European Private Investment in Developing Countries' *31 ICLQ* (1982) 686

Waer, P. 'Social Clauses in International Trade: The Debate in the European Union' *30(4) JWT* (1996) 25

Waelde, T. W. 'International Investment Under the 1994 Energy Charter Treaty' *29(5) JWT* (1995) 5

Wang, Y. 'Most Favoured Nation Treatment Under the GATS – And Its Application in Financial Services' *30(1) JWT* (1996) 91

Ward, H. 'Common But Differentiated Debates: Environment, Labour and the World Trade Organisation' *45 ICLQ* (1986) 592

Wattel, P. J. 'The EC Court's Attempts to Reconcile the Treaty Freedoms With International Tax Law' *33 CMLR* (1996) 223

Weatherill, S. and Beaumont, P. *EC Law* (London, Penguin, 3rd edn, 1999)

Weatherill, S. 'After *Keck:* Some Thoughts on How to Clarify the Clarification' *33 CMLR* (1996) 885

Weiss, F. 'The General Agreement on Trade in Services' *32 CMLR* (1993) 1197

Weston, B. H. 'The Charter of Economic Rights and Duties of States and the Deprivation of Foreign-Owned Wealth' *75 AJIL* (1981) 437

Whalley, J. 'Developing Countries and System Strengthening in the Uruguay Round' in Martin, W. and Winters, L. A. (eds) *The Uruguay Round and the Developing Economies*, World Bank Discussion Papers 307 (Washington, World Bank, 1995) at p. 305

Williams, D. W. *EC Tax Law* (London, Longman, 1998)

Williams, D. W. '*Asscher*: The European Court and the Power to Destroy' *6 EC Tax Review* (1997) 4

Williams, M. *International Economic Organisations and the Third World* (New York, Harvester Wheatsheaf, 1994)

Woolcock, S. 'The European *acquis* and the Multilateral Trade Rules: Are They Compatible?' *31 Journal of Common Market Studies* (1993) 539

World Development Movement 'A Dangerous Leap in the Dark' 1997, available at http://www.gn.apc.org/negreens/mai-leap.htm

Wouters, J. 'Fiscal Barriers to Companies' Cross-Border Establishment in the Case-Law of the EC Court of Justice' *14 YEL* (1994) 73

Index

Note: 'n' after a page reference indicates a note number on that page.